NOVELL'S

NetWare® 5 Basics

NOVELL'S

NetWare® 5 Basics

KELLEY J. P. LINDBERG

KEVIN SHAFER

Novell. PRESS

Novell Press, San Jose

Novell's NetWare® 5 Basics
Published by
Novell Press
2211 North First Street
San Jose, CA 95131

Copyright © 1999 Novell, Inc. All rights reserved. No part of this book, including interior design, cover design, and icons, may be reproduced or transmitted in any form, by any means (electronic, photocopying, recording, or otherwise) without the prior written permission of the publisher.

ISBN: 0-7645-4563-9

Printed in the United States of America

10 9 8 7 6 5 4 3 2 1

1P/SV/QY/ZZ/FC

Distributed in the United States by IDG Books Worldwide, Inc.

Distributed by CDG Books Canada Inc. for Canada; by Transworld Publishers Limited in the United Kingdom; by IDG Norge Books for Norway; by IDG Sweden Books for Sweden; by IDG Books Australia Publishing Corporation Pty. Ltd. for Australia and New Zealand; by TransQuest Publishers Pte Ltd. for Singapore, Malaysia, Thailand, Indonesia, and Hong Kong; by Gotop Information Inc. for Taiwan; by ICG Muse, Inc. for Japan; by Norma Comunicaciones S.A. for Colombia; by Intersoft for South Africa; by Le Monde en Tique for France; by International Thomson Publishing for Germany, Austria and Switzerland; by Distribuidora Cuspide for Argentina; by LR International for Brazil; by Galileo Libros for Chile; by Ediciones ZETA S.C.R. Ltda. for Peru; by WS Computer Publishing Corporation, Inc., for the Philippines; by Contemporanea de Ediciones for Venezuela; by Express Computer Distributors for the Caribbean and West Indies; by Micronesia Media Distributor, Inc. for Micronesia; by Editorial Norma S.A. for Guatemala; by Chips Computadoras S.A. de C.V. for Mexico; by Editorial Norma de Panama S.A. for Panama; by American Bookshops for Finland. Authorized Sales Agent: Anthony Rudkin Associates for the Middle East and North Africa.

For general information on IDG Books Worldwide's books in the U.S., please call our Consumer Customer Service department at 800-762-2974. For reseller information, including discounts and premium sales, please call our Reseller Customer Service department at 800-434-3422.

For information on where to purchase IDG Books Worldwide's books outside the U.S., please contact our International Sales department at 317-596-5530 or fax 317-596-5692.

For consumer information on foreign language translations, please contact our Customer Service department at 800-434-3422, fax 317-596-5692, or e-mail rights@idgbooks.com.

For information on licensing foreign or domestic rights, please phone +1-650-655-3109.

For sales inquiries and special prices for bulk quantities, please contact our Sales department at 650-655-3200 or write to IDG Books Worldwide, 919 E. Hillsdale Blvd., Suite 400, Foster City, CA 94404.

For information on using IDG Books Worldwide's books in the classroom or for ordering examination copies, please contact our Educational Sales department at 800-434-2086 or fax 317-596-5499.

For press review copies, author interviews, or other publicity information, please contact our Public Relations department at 650-655-3000 or fax 650-655-3299.

For authorization to photocopy items for corporate, personal, or educational use, please contact Novell, Inc., Copyright Permission, 1555 North Technology Way, Mail Stop ORM-C-311, Orem, UT 84097-2395; or fax 801-228-7077.

For general information on Novell Press books in the U.S., including information on discounts and premiums, contact IDG Books Worldwide at 800-434-3422 or 650-655-3200. For information on where to purchase Novell Press books outside the U.S., contact IDG Books International at 650-655-3021 or fax 650-655-3295.

Library of Congress Cataloging-in-Publication Data

Lindberg, Kelley J.P.

Novell's NetWare 5 Basics / Kelley J.P. Lindberg, Kevin Shafer.
    p.   cm.
    ISBN 0-7645-4563-9 (alk. paper)1
    1. NetWare (Computer file) 2. Local are networks (Computer networks) I. Shafer, Kevin. II. Title.
    TK5105.8.N65L5652 1999
    005.7'1369—dc21   99-31810
                                      CIP

John Kilcullen, *CEO, IDG Books Worldwide, Inc.*
Steven Berkowitz, *President, IDG Books Worldwide, Inc.*
Richard Swadley, *Senior Vice President & Publisher, Technology*

The IDG Books Worldwide logo is a registered trademark or trademark under exclusive license to IDG Books Worldwide, Inc. from International Data Group, Inc. in the United States and/or other countries.

Marcy Shanti, *Publisher, Novell Press, Novell, Inc.*

Novell Press and the Novell Press logo are trademarks of Novell, Inc.

Welcome to Novell Press

Novell Press, the world's leading provider of networking books, is the premier source for the most timely and useful information in the networking industry. Novell Press books cover fundamental networking issues as they emerge — from today's Novell and third-party products to the concepts and strategies that will guide the industry's future. The result is a broad spectrum of titles for the benefit of those involved in networking at any level: end user, department administrator, developer, systems manager, or network architect.

Novell Press books are written by experts with the full participation of Novell's technical, managerial, and marketing staff. The books are exhaustively reviewed by Novell's own technicians and are published only on the basis of final released software, never on prereleased versions.

Novell Press at IDG Books Worldwide is an exciting partnership between two companies at the forefront of the knowledge and communications revolution. The Press is implementing an ambitious publishing program to develop new networking titles centered on the current versions of NetWare, GroupWise, BorderManager, ManageWise, and networking integration products.

Novell Press books are translated into several languages and sold throughout the world.

Marcy Shanti
Publisher
Novell Press, Novell, Inc.

Novell Press

Publisher
Marcy Shanti

IDG Books Worldwide

Acquisitions Editor
Jim Sumser

Copy Editor
Larisa North

Development Editor
Kurt Stephan

Production
Publication Services, Inc.

Technical Editor
Mark Parratt

Proofreading and Indexing
Publication Services, Inc.

About the Authors

Kelley J. P. Lindberg, a CNE and award-winning author, worked for Novell for nearly 12 years before becoming a full-time writer. At Novell, she was the project manager for intraNetWare, as well as several previous versions of NetWare. She has written many other books about Novell products, most of them available from Novell Press. She currently lives in Utah.

Kevin Shafer has worked as a contract development editor and copy editor for IDG Books Worldwide, a technical editor for Silicon Valley electronics companies, a managing editor and technical editor for Osborne/McGraw-Hill, and is currently an editorial manager at IDG Books Worldwide. He is also the author of *Novell's Encyclopedia of Networking*, *Novell's Dictionary of Networking*, and *Novell's Guide to Networking Hardware*.

For Orion, the brightest star in my sky.

—Kelley J. P. Lindberg

For Dori, the center of my universe.

—Kevin Shafer

Preface

Networking has become a ubiquitous way of life in today's business world. Few businesses, large or small, are able to work without a net (so to speak). People everywhere need to communicate and collaborate with coworkers, colleagues, clients, suppliers, acquaintances, consultants, experts, and customers — and they need to do it faster and faster every week. Networks are simply the infrastructure that lets that communication and collaboration happen.

Ray Noorda, former CEO of Novell, was fond of saying, "NetWare should be like underwear. The only time you should really notice it is when it's missing." While this quote had many interpretations (some of which got pretty funny late at night in the engineering labs at Novell), the primary meaning was that a network should just *work*. Once it's up and running, a network should be a silent partner in communication. Users shouldn't need to worry about the network; instead, they should be able to focus completely on their work at hand.

Like any good performer, your networking system should make everything look easy. However, if you're a performer (or a network administrator, for that matter), you know that the key to looking graceful is careful preparation ahead of time.

This book will help you prepare, providing you with a solid foundation in the basics of installing and managing a NetWare 5 network.

Why Start with the Basics?

NetWare 5 is an incredibly powerful, complex network operating system. It is designed to accommodate any size network, from a handful of computers in a dentist's office to a global conglomeration of thousands of workstations scattered across hundreds of locations. To provide for such a broad range of networking needs, NetWare 5 has been built with a flexible, modular design that allows you to start simply, and then add, tweak, or turn on additional capabilities that you need or grow into.

If you're new to NetWare 5, or to networking in general, "starting simply" probably sounds like a good idea. You may be surprised, however, to learn that "starting simply" is also a good idea for even experienced network administrators, because basic, straight-out-of-the-box NetWare 5 is preset and optimized for most average networks. In other words, it's designed to run extremely well on most small-to-medium networks, without all of that tweaking.

After the network administrator has learned more about the advanced capabilities of NetWare 5, or when network needs begin to expand or change, it's very easy to add to or enhance the network. This can be done by taking advantage of NetWare 5's built-in, advanced features, or by adding Novell or third-party products designed to fit smoothly into a NetWare network.

You've probably heard about the old 80-20 rule: 80 percent of the people use 20 percent of the features in any high-tech product. Chances are good that you're in the 80 percent when it comes to running a NetWare 5 network— and you're in good company. And this book is for you.

Novell's NetWare 5 Basics introduces you to the fundamental concepts and management procedures you need to install and run your NetWare 5 network. In this book, you'll find:

- ▶ Explanations of the basic concepts you need to know about networking, intranets, and the Internet.

- ▶ Step-by-step instructions showing the easiest (and often the most efficient) ways to install servers, workstations, and printers.

- ▶ Clear descriptions of how to get your users working (and how to keep them working) on the network, while making sure they don't compromise your network's security.

- ▶ Troubleshooting hints and suggestions.

- ▶ A "Beyond the Basics" section at the end of each chapter, showing where you can go for more information when you're ready to learn about advanced features of NetWare 5.

What You Need to Know

Novell's NetWare 5 Basics is designed to provide you with the fundamental concepts and procedures you need to understand, install, and manage a basic NetWare 5 network.

This book assumes that you are familiar with the operating systems that run on the workstations you'll be maintaining, such as DOS, Windows 95, Windows 98, and Windows NT. Advanced features and concepts of NetWare 5 networks are mentioned only briefly, with references to places you can go for more information about them.

TIP

You should have access to the online documentation that came with your NetWare 5 operating system, in case you need more detailed instructions or explanations of the advanced concepts and procedures that aren't covered in this book.

Another resource for learning more about NetWare 5's advanced features is the book *Novell's NetWare 5 Administrator's Handbook*, from Novell Press. It is a quick-reference handbook that concisely covers the features of NetWare 5, including the advanced ones, without delving too deeply into conceptual information.

What This Book Contains

The basic components of NetWare 5 are explained throughout the chapters of this book.

▶ Chapter 1 describes the components that make up a network — network hardware, network software, network topologies, protocols, and network cabling architectures — and the NetWare 5 features, such as Novell Directory Services and security features, that make the components work together.

▶ Chapter 2 explains how to install a NetWare 5 server, how to upgrade a server from a previous version of NetWare, and how to manage the server after it's installed.

▶ Chapter 3 describes how to install network workstations.

▶ Chapter 4 provides an overview of Novell Directory Services (NDS) and explains how to plan your NDS tree and the objects in the tree. It also describes how to set up the NetWare Administrator utility on your workstation.

▶ Chapter 5 includes instructions for creating and managing users and groups on the network. It also explains how to set up login scripts to automatically set up your users' access to network directories and applications.

▶ Chapter 6 covers the various security tools provided in NetWare 5, which you can use to make sure your network is as secure as you need it to be.

▶ Chapter 7 discusses file management, including tips on how to plan the directory structure, how to work with files and directories, how to salvage deleted files, and how to back up and restore files.

▶ Chapter 8 explains how to set up print services on your network. It describes both the queue-based print service (used in previous versions of NetWare) and the NDPS print service (a new printing service available in NetWare 5).

▶ Chapter 9 describes how to set up and use the Netscape FastTrack Server for NetWare — a high-performance Web server included in NetWare 5.

▶ Chapter 10 explains how to install and use the online documentation that came with your NetWare 5 network operating system.

► Chapter 11 provides tips on how to plan ahead so you can restore your network quickly after a disaster (such as a fire or even a crashed server). It also describes a variety of additional resources you can turn to for more help or information (such as user groups, Novell's Internet site, Novell publications, and so on).

This book also includes a glossary and, of course, a detailed index to help you get to the information you need quickly.

Acknowledgments

A book like this is a joy to write when you are surrounded by a team of great people. Now is my opportunity to thank those terrific folks for all their hard work.

First, I want to thank my coauthor, Kevin Shafer, for being willing to step in and help get this book finished so I could take some time off to welcome my son into the world. I also want to thank the Novell Press people at IDG Books Worldwide, Inc. They are some of the nicest, most talented folks I've ever worked with. I especially want to thank Jim Sumser — he's tops on my list. His confidence in me is an anchor; his friendship is a bonus.

Of course, Kevin and I couldn't have finished this book without great editors — many thanks go to development editor Kurt Stephan and copy editor Larisa North for keeping the book on an even keel. And Mark Parratt gets a big round of applause for doing the technical review to ensure we didn't lead any readers astray. I'm also very grateful for all the other people working behind the scenes — the production coordinator, illustrators, desktop publishers, indexer, and everyone else who makes a Novell Press book happen.

I want to thank the employees of Novell, Inc., for creating the best networking software in the world. The technology invented inside those buildings has changed the world, and leads the competition by light-years. The engineers, writers, testers, project managers, and other miracle workers there are the finest you could ever hope to meet.

As usual, my friends and family were extremely supportive and encouraging, and always ready to preserve my sanity by knowing just when to invite me to lunch. I don't know what I'd do without all of you.

And finally, I want to thank my husband, Andy, and my son, Orion, for filling my life with adventure, love, and an interesting assortment of squeaky toys.

— Kelley J. P. Lindberg

Contents at a Glance

Contents

Chapter 7 Managing Network Files 201

Chapter 8 Setting Up Printers 233

Starting a NetWare 5 Network

A network consists of hardware components (such as computers, cables, network boards, printers, and so on) plus software components (such as the network operating system, drivers, client software, and protocols). Network communication depends on characteristics such as the network architecture and the network topology. NetWare 5 incorporates a variety of features to both control and enhance the performance of the network.

If you do business in today's world, you're probably using a network. There's no escaping the need to be in constant communication with coworkers, clients, and competition — and networks help us stay connected.

All computer networks perform the same basic function: they connect computers, printers, plotters, modems, the Internet, and any other resources we may be using. The difference in various networks is how those components are connected, how well they work once connected, and how easy they are to use.

In this chapter, we'll look at the components that make up a NetWare 5 network.

Network Building Blocks

Like all networks, a NetWare 5 network consists of hardware and software working together. One of the characteristics of Novell networks is that you have a tremendous choice of hardware and software to use.

Early on, Novell established itself as the "freedom of choice" networking company. While most other manufacturers in the fledgling networking industry were making products that connected only one type of computer (such as an all-PC network, or an all-Macintosh network), Novell was connecting everything to everything else. PCs, Macintoshes, minis, and mainframes all became part of the Novell networking universe. The operating system (OS) you use on those computers is also up to you. DOS, Windows and all its flavors (3.1, 95, 98, NT, and so on), UNIX, OS/2, Mac OS — Novell's NetWare products support them all.

Despite the wide variety of options available to you, it is still easy to talk about the basic building blocks that make up a NetWare 5 network. This section explores the three building blocks of any network:

- The *network's hardware*, including the server, workstations, printers, storage devices, cabling, network boards, and the network architectures those hardware elements create

- The *network's software*, including the software that must run on the server and the workstations to enable those machines to communicate, as well as the software that provides the network services that users need to use (such as printing services, mail services, file services, and so on)

▸ The *communication protocols* that regulate how all of the network's components communicate with each other

Network Hardware

First, take a look at the types of hardware that typically make up a network, as illustrated in Figure 1.1. A network generally consists of a server, workstations, printers, storage devices, various other peripherals, and lots of cabling.

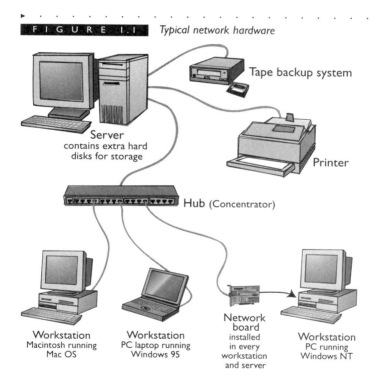

FIGURE 1.1 *Typical network hardware*

Tape backup system

Server
contains extra hard
disks for storage

Printer

Hub (Concentrator)

Workstation
Macintosh running
Mac OS

Workstation
PC laptop running
Windows 95

Network
board
installed
in every
workstation
and server

Workstation
PC running
Windows NT

The Server

The "brains" of the NetWare 5 network are contained within the server. The server is just a computer with NetWare 5's network operating system running on it.

The computer you use as a server must be a PC (it can't be a Macintosh), but it doesn't have to be a special type of PC. It can be any PC-based computer, as long as it has enough memory and storage space to do the job properly.

Imagine that you have a small network (say, a half-dozen workstations), and you expect your users to store their files and primary applications on their own workstations. You also expect your users to use the server to access the occasional application and the office printer. In this situation, you may not need the top-of-the-line machine. You might get away with a lower-end or older computer, such as a Pentium 166MHz machine with one or two giga-bytes of disk space and 64MB of RAM.

If, however, you intend for your users to store all their work files on the server and run all their applications from the server, you will probably dis-cover that a lower-end machine won't be able to keep up with your needs. Instead, you'll want to choose a more powerful machine with lots of expand-able storage capacity and RAM.

NOTE

The server on a NetWare 5 network is a single-minded machine. It can't be used as a workstation if you're using it as a server (unlike some of the lower-end networking products you might have used before).

In the past, Novell created and marketed versions of NetWare where the server performed double duty as both a server and workstation. The demand for this type of product from Novell was low, however. While this feature is adequate for very small networks (five or so workstations), it doesn't expand well to support larger networks. The dedicated server proved more reliable and useful for customers needing larger networks, more power, greater capacity, and more features.

Workstations

Workstations on a NetWare 5 network come in all shapes and sizes, includ-ing desktops, laptops, and notebook computers (as shown in Figure 1.2). A workstation is nothing more than the computer on which a user does his or her work. You can select a variety of operating systems to run on your work-stations. The following types of workstations can be used on a NetWare 5 net-work:

- DOS workstations
- Windows 3.1 workstations
- Windows 95

- ▶ Windows 98
- ▶ Windows NT
- ▶ Macintosh
- ▶ OS/2
- ▶ UNIX

FIGURE 1.2 *Typical workstations*

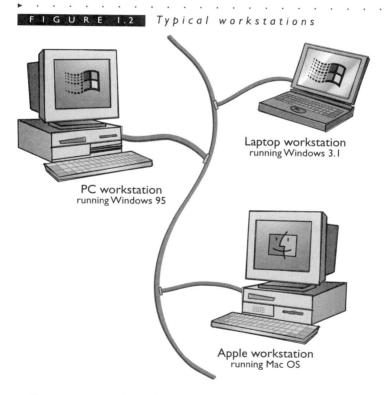

Laptop workstation
running Windows 3.1

PC workstation
running Windows 95

Apple workstation
running Mac OS

You use a network workstation the same way you would use a standalone workstation. You use the same OS you're used to (such as Windows 95 or Windows 98), and you work with files in the same manner. For the average network user, a network is just an extension of the workstation — more storage space and printers, faster access time, easier backups (because someone else can do them!), and so on.

Printers, Plotters, and Other Fun Things

Just about every network has at least one printer attached to it; however, many networks don't stop there. You can install a variety of printers, plotters, scanners, modems, and other types of equipment on a network, as long as those machines have suitable drivers that enable them to talk to the network. (*Drivers* are software programs that let hardware communicate with other parts of a computer or network.) These types of equipment are often referred to as *peripherals*. Figure 1.3 shows some of the typical peripherals on a network.

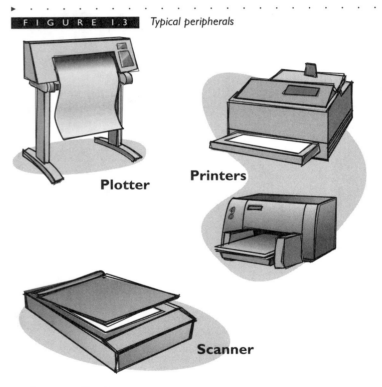

FIGURE 1.3 *Typical peripherals*

Plotter   **Printers**

Scanner

Storage Devices

Just as every house seems to need more closet space, every network seems to need more storage space. Fortunately, manufacturers are happy to oblige.

When your server begins to run short of storage space, there are several types of products you can use to extend your network's capacity. Your solution can be as simple as adding a larger hard disk, multiple disks, a CD-ROM drive, or an optical CD storage system to your server. It can also involve installing tape drives. (Some examples of storage devices are shown in Figure 1.4.)

FIGURE 1.4 *Typical storage devices*

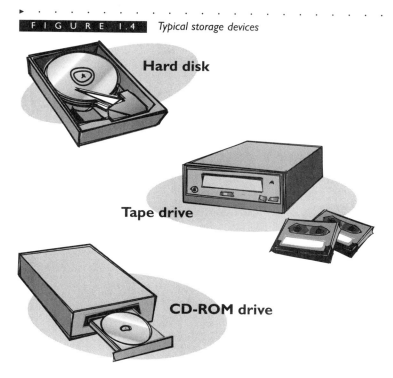

Hard disk

Tape drive

CD-ROM drive

Each hard disk or other type of storage device installed in your server has its own *controller board*. The controller board is a circuit board on the storage device that plugs into the computer. Through this board, the computer and the disk communicate. Sometimes this board comes preinstalled and you never see it. Other times, you may have to install it yourself.

Many of these products can be used in conjunction with your server and your NetWare 5 network. Check with the manufacturers to be sure they'll work for you.

Some type of backup system is an essential element of your network. Whether you use a tape backup system or a system that uses CD-ROMs or other optical media, you can't afford to skimp on this piece of equipment. Backups are essential to make sure you minimize the amount of work you lose if something happens to your original files.

Cabling and Network Boards

When you thought of network hardware, did you think about cabling? Maybe not, since this type of hardware is often invisible and forgotten when it works, but a royal pain when it doesn't.

Network cabling is used to connect all of the network's hardware components (such as workstations, servers, and printers) together. It comes in many forms, from coaxial cable (like your TV cable), to twisted pair and shielded twisted pair, to fiber optic cable. Some devices use more exotic forms of connections (such as infrared wireless connections), but currently, most networks still use physical cables. Figure 1.5 shows some typical examples of the different types of cabling used by networks.

FIGURE 1.5   *Types of cables*

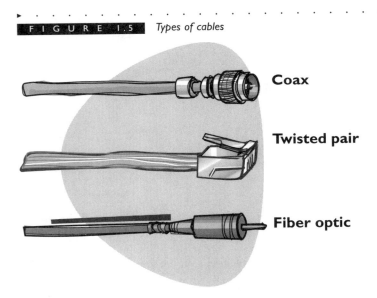

Coax

Twisted pair

Fiber optic

The type of network cabling you choose will also dictate another type of hardware you need — connection hardware (such as connectors, terminators, and hubs). Your connection hardware must match your network cabling. Figure 1.6 shows some examples of the different types of connection hardware.

FIGURE 1.6 Examples of connection hardware used with network cabling

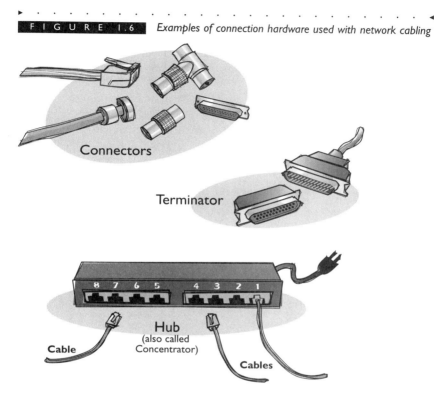

The three types of connection hardware shown in Figure 1.6 are as follows:

▸ *Connectors* join cables together or connect them to other pieces of hardware. Connectors come in a wide variety of shapes and sizes, depending on the type of cable and equipment with which they're designed to work.

▸ *Terminators* may be required by your cabling system. Terminators are attached to the open ends of any cables. They keep electrical signals from reflecting back across the network, corrupting information or communications.

▸ *Hubs*, which are used with some cabling systems, are a piece of equipment into which all workstation cables must feed before being connected to the main network cable. Passive hubs simply gather the signals and relay them. Active hubs (sometimes called *concentrators*) boost the signals before sending them on their way.

Now that you have cables to connect your computers, you may be wondering where to plug them into the computer. The cables plug into a *port* (connector) on the computer's network interface board.

Each device (computer, printer, and so on) on a network must contain a network interface board (also called *network board*). A network board is a special type of circuit board that allows the machine to connect to the network. With computers, you often need to purchase these network boards separately. However, some computers and devices, such as printers, may have these boards (or their equivalents) built in during manufacturing.

The type of network board you use depends on your cable type. Figure 1.7 shows a common type of network board. Figure 1.8 shows where the cable connects to the network board when the board is installed in a computer.

► ◄

FIGURE 1.7 *Typical network board*

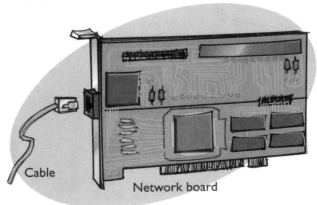

Cable

Network board

NOTE

Network interface boards may also be referred to as *network cards*, *network interface cards* (NICs), and *network adapters*. If they're built into the machine (rather than purchased and installed separately), they may be called *built-in adapters*.

FIGURE 1.8 *Network board installed in a computer*

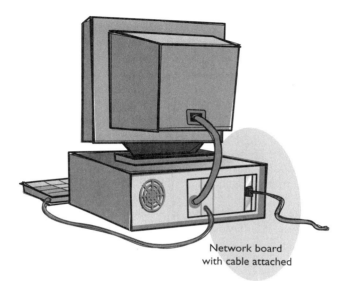

Network board
with cable attached

Network Architectures and Topologies

All of the cabling, connectors, and boards used in a network must work together. The cabling scheme that allows these components to interoperate is called the *network architecture*. The following network architectures are the most common ones used today:

- *Ethernet* — This is the most common network architecture. It provides good performance at a reasonable cost, and is relatively easy to install.

- *Token Ring* — Token Ring works well in situations that involve heavy data traffic because it is reliable. It is also fairly easy to install, but more expensive than Ethernet networks.

- *AppleTalk networks* — AppleTalk is a networking protocol suite built into every Macintosh. It runs on several different network architectures (including LocalTalk, EtherTalk, and TokenTalk), and provides peer-to-peer networking — serverless networking — between all Macintoshes and Apple hardware.

- *High-speed architectures* — The newer high-speed architectures, such as Fiber Distributed Data Interface (FDDI) and Fast Ethernet, are becoming more prevalent. They are capable of supporting speeds up to 100Mbps. Gigabit Ethernet provides a bandwidth of 1,000Mbps, or 1 gigabit per second (Gbps). This new technology is 100 times faster than the original Ethernet. Most of these architectures use fiber-optic cabling.

Because each of these network architectures handles data in a different way, each requires a unique type of network hardware. Before installing any network hardware, be sure to refer to the hardware manufacturer's documentation. The manufacturer's documentation should indicate specific restrictions or suggestions for their hardware, such as length limits for cables.

Although all devices on a given network must use the same network architecture, you can easily connect two networks that use different architectures. You use a *bridge* to join the two architectures so communication can flow between the two networks. Users don't know they're using two different physical networks. The bridge appears seamless, making the two networks look like one continuous network.

The network architecture determines the type of hardware used in a network. The way the hardware is laid out, however, is called the *network topology*. Three basic topologies can be used with most architectures:

▶ *Bus* — In this topology, all the network components are laid out sequentially along the main network cable (see Figure 1.9).

▶ *Star* — All of the network components in this topology radiate out from a central location (usually a hub or concentrator), as shown in Figure 1.10.

▶ *Ring* — In this topology all of the network components form a ring. Any network communication goes one direction around the loop until it finds the desired component. Figure 1.11 shows a ring topology.

Variations or combinations of these topologies are commonly used. The network architectures mentioned previously can support the following basic topologies:

▶ *Ethernet* — Ethernet can support either bus or star topologies.

▶ *Token Ring* — Token Ring is cabled like a star topology, but actually acts like a ring. Data flows from workstation to workstation around the ring. Each device in the ring examines the data to determine the destination of the data.

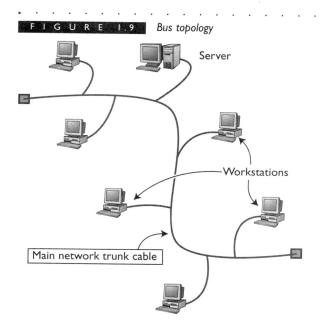

FIGURE 1.9   *Bus topology*

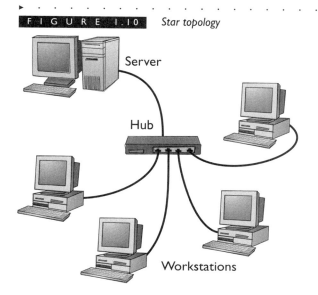

FIGURE 1.10   *Star topology*

FIGURE 1.11
Ring topology

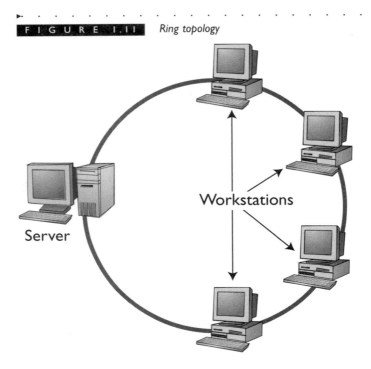

Workstations

Server

- *AppleTalk* — AppleTalk has an Ethernet variation (called *EtherTalk*) that runs on bus or star topologies. It also has a Token Ring variation (called *TokenTalk*) that runs on a ring topology.

Network Software

Now, consider the software components that enable all of the network hardware to work. You need the network operating system, client software, print servers (and other types of servers), and drivers. Although not required, routers and gateways are also common components of a network.

The Network Operating System (the Server)

First, go back to the brains of the network. The NetWare 5 server is a computer with the NetWare 5 network operating system installed on it. The *network operating system* (sometimes called the NOS) replaces the computer's regular operating system (such as DOS or Windows 95). The network operating system controls traffic between the clients and the server.

On an ordinary computer, the OS (such as Windows 95) controls how data is transferred and how files are stored within the computer. It also dictates how attached pieces of hardware (such as disk drives or printers) communicate with the computer.

When NetWare 5 takes over the computer, it does the same tasks but on a larger (network-wide) scale. It controls data transfer over the network, the way users' files are stored on the server, and all communication between the network and attached hardware (such as network printers). In addition, NetWare 5 manages network security (providing access to authorized users only), handles communication between multiple networks, and regulates other network activities.

Normally, a computer running an operating system such as Windows will have a single hard disk, and that hard disk will have a single *partition*. A disk partition is just a portion of the hard disk that is formatted in such a way that it can store and handle files. (In most cases, the entire disk belongs to the partition, but it is possible to create more than one partition on a single hard disk.)

You have probably formatted floppy disks before. When you format a floppy disk, you prepare the disk's magnetic surface in a particular structure that will be recognized by the operating system you're using. If you've ever tried to use a Macintosh-formatted floppy disk in a PC, you know that different operating systems expect entirely different disk formats.

Hard disks are formatted for operating systems in the same manner as floppy disks. One difference between hard disks and floppies, however, is that you can divide a hard disk into more than one partition. That way, you can format one partition to meet one operating system's structure, and another partition to meet a second operating system's structure. Few people ever do this on standalone computers because there are few reasons why this is necessary — most people only use a single OS on their standalone computers. For a NetWare 5 server, however, this feature is very valuable.

When you install NetWare 5 on your server computer, you divide the server's hard disk into two partitions. One partition — a very small one — will be formatted with DOS so the computer can boot up normally and run any DOS programs that the server needs. The other partition — which is the bulk of the hard disk — will be formatted with the NetWare 5 operating system. While this is a different format from DOS, it performs many of the same functions. It enables all network files and directories (or folders) to be created and stored on the server's hard disk, just as they would be stored on a DOS disk. The main difference is simply that NetWare 5 requires some specific formatting characteristics to handle all of its security and management features.

NOTE

Disk partitions are not physical sections of the disk — you can't see the partitions by opening up the computer and looking at the hard disk. Partitions are simply portions of the hard disk's storage area that are programmed to handle different operating systems. You create the partitions by using the DOS commands FDISK and FORMAT, as described in Chapter 2.

Client Software (the Workstations)

To allow workstations to communicate with the network, you must install some special NetWare 5 software on each one. This workstation software is called *client software*, because it acts like a client, requesting services from the network server.

In simple terms, NetWare 5's client software on the workstation forms a connection with the network. This enables users to log in, transfer data across the network, and find and use network resources (such as printers).

Novell's NetWare 5 client software doesn't replace the workstation's regular OS, such as Windows 95/98. Instead, the client software allows the workstation's own OS to handle normal processing tasks, and then steps in whenever a task requests a network service. When a network request comes along, the client software manages the request and data transfer across the network.

When you install the NetWare 5 client software, you also get some additional utilities to help you use the network more efficiently. These utilities are explained in Chapter 5.

The Print Server

The print server is a software program that runs on the NetWare 5 server. It manages the method in which print jobs are handled by the network and its printers.

With a print server on the network, users can easily send their print jobs to network printers. Print servers control print traffic, manage the order and priority of print jobs, and verify that users are permitted to use the printers they select.

What Does the Term *Client/Server* Really Mean?

Think of the server as the software that services clients. When a client (such as a workstation, application, or peripheral) needs to access a network resource or service, the server manages that access.

The term *client/server*, which has been a common buzzword for several years, is used to describe this relationship. Applications, such as database programs, are client/server applications if the processing is distributed so that some of the work is done by multiple clients, and other parts of the work are done by the main (server) portion of the program.

Novell has moved away from the term *client/server*, and now uses the term *client/network*. This is because NetWare 5 no longer views a single server computer as the center of the network. Instead, NetWare 5 weaves multiple servers, and all of the network resources and services, into a seamless web of a network. That way, clients who access network services may access them from any number of servers or locations. Servicing clients then becomes more of a network role than a single server role.

TIP

Other companies — most notably Microsoft — also produce client software that can be used with networks. If you're using NetWare 5, you should replace Microsoft's client with the NetWare 5 client, because the NetWare 5 client is optimized to run with NetWare 5.

Other Types of Servers (Web, Mail, and Fax)

You may have additional types of servers, such as fax servers or mail servers, installed on your NetWare 5 network. These servers are similar to print servers — they are software programs that manage the communication traffic associated with that type of product (for example, faxes or e-mail). A Web server is basically software that is used to post and control information on the World Wide Web (WWW).

Some of these specialty servers may be programs installed and running on the NetWare 5 server. Other specialty servers may be running on separate computers connected to the network. For example, if you have a smaller network, you could have a mail server running within your NetWare 5 server. On a larger network, you may decide to dedicate a separate machine for the mail server.

NOTE

The term *server* is often used to describe any software program that provides a service to network clients. Technically, the term *server* seldom refers to a physical computer. When users refer to the mail server, they really mean the primary servicing portion of the e-mail software program.

In common usage, however, people often use the word *server* when referring to both the program and the machine it's running on (such as the NetWare 5 server). This is especially true when a single computer houses a single server program for the sake of efficiency.

Drivers

Drivers are small software programs associated with a piece of hardware. A driver enables the hardware device to communicate with the computer in which it's installed. You are probably familiar with some of the drivers involved with a standalone computer, such as a mouse driver (which controls how your mouse works with your computer) and drivers for devices such as monitors and sound cards.

On a network, you also encounter LAN drivers, which enable a network board to communicate with the computer in which it's installed. When you buy a network board, the package usually includes a diskette with the board's associated LAN driver on it. Most network boards require their own matched brand of driver.

Disk drivers are another important type of driver. They make it possible for the computer to communicate with its hard disk (actually, with the hard disk's controller board). CD-ROM drives and tape drives also have their own corresponding drivers. The term *device drivers* is sometimes used as a generic name for all the hardware-related drivers your computer may require. When you install NetWare 5, the installation program looks at your hardware and attempts to find a matching LAN driver and disk driver. It then attempts to install them automatically from the set of drivers shipped on the NetWare 5 CD-ROM. If it can't find a driver it needs, the installation program will ask you to insert a diskette with the necessary driver on it.

TIP

Novell's NetWare 5 includes a large selection of the most common types of LAN drivers. However, board manufacturers frequently update their drivers, so if you're installing a network board, check with the manufacturer for an updated driver. (Web sites are a good place to check for updated drivers.)

Routers and Gateways

Routers are software programs that enable network communication to travel across mixed networks. Routers take packets of data from one network, and reformat them (if necessary) to conform to the next network's requirements. The routers then send the packets along to their destination.

Many people think of routers as hardware components, too, because router programs are sometimes housed in their own hardware devices. The actual routing of packets from one network to the other is controlled by the software. The router's hardware forms the necessary physical connection by linking the cabling systems together.

Routing software is built into the server in NetWare 5. The server machine itself forms the physical connection between two networks — for example, the server may have both an Ethernet network board and a Token Ring network board installed in it. The router software then manages the flow of data packets between the two networks via their respective network boards. Figure 1.12 illustrates two networks joined by routing software in a server.

FIGURE 1.12 *Router running in a server*

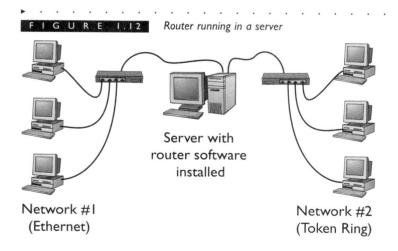

Server with router software installed

Network #1
(Ethernet)

Network #2
(Token Ring)

Other companies also create extremely good routers that can work with NetWare 5. These third-party routers are usually contained within their own specialized hardware to make routing work more efficiently with their routing software.

Routers can track routes between servers or networks. They keep track of which servers are up and running, which route between two servers is shortest, and so on. This ensures that network communication isn't interrupted or slowed down unnecessarily.

Routers can also connect two networks that are using different protocols — they take data packets from one protocol and reformat them to work on the next protocol down the line.

Gateways are another product that can translate one protocol's format into another, and back again. The difference between routers and gateways is a little confusing, and with advancements in technology, the line between them is getting somewhat blurred.

One way to look at the difference — though it's not necessarily a precise definition — is that a router links multiple networks so they appear to be one seamless network. If your company has hundreds of servers scattered all over the globe, you're using a large number of routers every time you communicate with someone. The routers work together to scatter information across a spider web of connections to get the data to its destination. A piece of data, when traveling across the network, may go through a variety of paths. If one router is down, the data can travel through another router on a different path, but still wind up at the same destination.

A gateway generally connects your network to a completely different type of network or computer system, through a single point. If, for example, you're using a workstation on a network and you want to connect to a mainframe computer, your communications can go through a gateway installed somewhere on the network. The gateway takes your data and transfers it to the mainframe, reversing the process when the mainframe replies to you. If the gateway is down, you won't be able to communicate with the mainframe. There usually isn't another gateway that is set up to automatically retrieve your data and send it on an alternate route to the mainframe.

Network Protocols

Network is a fairly generic term for linking several computers and related equipment. A network can be small (a few workstations in a dentist's office, for example) or it can be huge (thousands of workstations across a global organization, all linked together). There are no real restrictions on what a network can comprise.

A *protocol* is a set of defined rules that controls how processes or machines communicate. For example, a protocol regulates how two computers establish a connection so they can communicate, and how they terminate the connection when finished. In addition, protocols control how data is transferred over a network. When data is sent across the network, it (the data) is packaged in small units, called *packets*. Think of these packets like the packages you mail at the post office. Each packet includes a small amount of data, plus addressing information to ensure the data gets to the right destination. The packets may also include information that informs the receiving station of the data's safe arrival, and other helpful tidbits. A protocol dictates exactly how these packets should be formed, so that every device on the network can understand the packets it receives.

Several different types of protocols have been developed by various organizations to control how information is exchanged across a network. Many of these protocols are supported by NetWare 5. Each protocol forms packets in a unique way.

Discussions about protocols can be very confusing because there are so many different types of protocols, as well as protocols that layer on top of each other. Protocols are associated with several types of characteristics, such as:

▸ The network architecture they support

▸ The way they transmit data

▸ How they determine where data should go

▸ The types of communication they're facilitating

For a workstation to communicate on the network, it must use the same protocol that is used on the network. Fortunately, NetWare 5 networks can be configured to use different protocols, or even multiple protocols at the same time.

When you configure your NetWare network, you will configure primarily two types of protocols:

▸ *Data link protocols (Ethernet, Token Ring, AppleTalk, or FDDI)*. These protocols create, transmit, and receive data packets in a form that is appropriate for the particular network architecture you're using.

▸ *Network protocols (IPX, IP, or AppleTalk)*. These protocols are responsible for tracking hardware and network addresses. Once those addresses are determined, these protocols find and establish routes between sources and destinations, so that data can be safely transferred. Network protocols allow applications to communicate over different network links, regardless of differences in data link protocols, packet formats, or hardware specifications.

You decide on the data link protocol you want to use when you select your network architecture. Configuring these protocols essentially means that you load a LAN driver for a network board and specify a few parameters for that board. This is accomplished during the server installation.

Choosing a network protocol may be a little more complicated. Fortunately, NetWare 5 supports both of the major network protocols: IPX, which is Novell's own protocol, and IP, which is used by the Internet.

NOTE

NetWare 5 also supports the AppleTalk protocol. If you want your network to support AppleTalk, you can add the AppleTalk protocol to the server so that the network supports both IPX or IP and AppleTalk. See the NetWare documentation for more information about using AppleTalk on your NetWare network.

The Internet and Intranets

The *Internet* is a specific, giant network. Originally, it was started as a way to link various research, defense, and education systems together. Since then, it has grown by leaps and bounds as thousands of other networks have connected to it. Universities, corporations, individual users, small businesses, nonprofit organizations, and anyone else wanting to join the party have connected to the Internet, stretching its borders around the globe.

The allure of the Internet is that it expands your network of communication far, far beyond your own organization. Entering the Internet is like entering the largest library in the world. Avenues for information are seemingly endless. You can find the equivalent of "study groups" or round-table discussions on nearly any topic. You can also be as passive or as interactive as you care to be with the information you find.

These aspects of the Internet (libraries of archived information, active discussion groups, and so on) quickly proved useful to the corporations and organizations that accessed them. Before too long, some of those organizations realized that the same type of forum would be extremely useful to disseminate internal information to employees. They wanted to put a Web server on their internal network and make it so no one outside the company could see it. Novell was one of the first companies — if not *the* first — to call this type of network an intranet.

Just as the whole world seemed to get the hang of the Internet, a new buzzword was invented, and the computing industry began another one of its typical feeding frenzies. That new buzzword was *intranet*. Intranets are really just a merging of the Internet idea with the networking idea.

With an intranet, employees can access the company's Web server, and the information on it, through the same browsers they use to surf the Internet. The only difference between an intranet and the Internet is that the intranet can only be accessed by people on the company's own network — outsiders can't access it.

On an intranet (more specifically, on the company's private Web site), employees can post information that internal employees may need, without posting it to the entire world on the Internet. For example, a company's internal Web site might include forums for:

- ▶ Project information (such as schedules, status reports, and product specs)

- ▶ Information about employee benefits (such as online employee handbooks, holiday schedules, and phone numbers for health plan doctors)

- ▶ Databases of technical information for use by customer service employees

- ▶ Product descriptions

- ▶ Even fun and after-hours topics, such as employee "for sale" bulletin boards, the cafeteria lunch menu, employee newsletters, or information about upcoming company parties

NOTE

NetWare 5 includes a Web server and browser. These components enable companies to turn their networks into intranets for their employees. With NetWare 5's security features, a company can go beyond restricting the outside world from its intranet; it also lets the organization restrict how (and which) internal employees can access the information. Novell also added features that enable companies to connect their intranet to the Internet, without compromising security. That way, employees can surf out, without intruders surfing in.

NetWare 5 and the Internet

Although the Internet has been around for many years, its popularity with the general population and businesses didn't really begin to explode until the last few years. Before that time, businesses concentrated primarily on their own internal networks. For the large majority of businesses, that meant NetWare.

During NetWare's development, Novell created a protocol suite, called IPX/SPX, to handle network communication. IPX/SPX was designed to be incredibly reliable and easy to manage, in contrast to some of the other protocols available. Thousands of network applications have been developed using this protocol suite.

Meanwhile, the Internet was growing, based on another protocol suite called TCP/IP. The TCP/IP protocol suite was more cumbersome to manage, with its IP addresses and domains, but the Internet had enough appeal that network administrators were willing to learn the intricacies of IP addressing if they had to.

As the need for communicating with the IP-based Internet grew, Novell began supporting the TCP/IP protocols within NetWare. For years, Novell has offered TCP/IP solutions that allowed TCP/IP packets to be encapsulated within an IPX packet (called *tunneling*), which enabled TCP/IP support while still taking advantage of IPX/SPX speed, reliability, and ease of management.

As the Internet continues to grow, and as new applications are being developed that use the IP protocol, many network administrators are now asking for a single protocol that they can use on their entire network, so that they no longer need to worry about two protocols. In addition, Novell has begun aggressively pursuing a goal of supporting "open standards" (as opposed to proprietary ones) so application developers can more readily create applications for use in any networked environment.

In response to these growing needs, NetWare 5 is the first version of NetWare to provide pure (non-tunneled) support of IP on the network. In fact, NetWare 5 has been changed to use the IP protocol as its default protocol instead of IPX.

Just because NetWare 5 has IP as its default protocol doesn't mean, however, that you must use IP if you don't want to. In fact, as is typical with NetWare throughout its history, the choice is up to the network administrator. You can choose to set up your network to use pure IP, both IP and IPX, or pure IPX.

Choosing a Network Protocol

You can choose to run your network in a pure IP environment, with no IPX packets anywhere on the network. This requires that all your applications use only IP and not IPX/SPX.

In reality, chances are good that you have IPX dependencies right now in your network. IPX/SPX uses a protocol called SAP (Service Advertising Protocol) to locate resources on the network. Many network applications, including most current virus detectors and backup programs, use SAP or other parts of SPX to operate on the network.

A NetWare 5 network can run pure IP, but still support IPX-based applications through the IP Compatibility Mode feature. Compatibility Mode enables you to gradually phase IPX traffic out of your network while you transition to a pure IP environment.

Compatibility Mode is automatically installed as part of NetWare 5; you don't need to do anything to turn it on — it automatically works. In addition, Compatibility Mode doesn't take any overhead if there are no IPX packets to deal with. Therefore, running Compatibility Mode is the best way to transition your network to pure IP.

Instead of running pure IP, you can choose to load both the IP protocol and the IPX protocol on your server. This is called a *dual stack* environment. (A protocol suite is sometimes referred to as a protocol *stack* when it is loaded on the server.) If you select a dual stack network, you won't have the Compatibility Mode. The two protocols will work independently of each other.

Of course, if you are currently running pure IPX and don't anticipate needing to support IP in the future, you can continue to run an all-IPX network. If you choose, you can connect an IPX-based network to the Internet by using a product such as Novell's BorderManager, which includes an IPX/IP Gateway that workstations can use. Workstations can also connect to the Internet directly through modems.

How NetWare 5 Ties the Blocks Together

Now you have a bunch of hardware and a bunch of software all hooked up together. You need a powerful system to connect everything and ensure that the whole network runs smoothly, users can gain access, security is controlled, and nothing falls through the cracks. The tool for this job is NetWare 5.

NetWare 5 has several new features not found in previous versions of NetWare, including the following:

▶ *NetWare 5 Installation* — The installation and upgrade procedures for NetWare 5 now include a graphical user interface (GUI) install, an Upgrade Wizard, improved licensing, and improved driver support. Chapter 2 discusses the installation of the NetWare 5 server, and Chapter 3 discusses the installation of NetWare 5 workstations.

▶ *Novell Directory Services (NDS)* — NetWare 5 replaces the bindery found in NetWare 3.1x and 2.x with NDS. All the NetWare 4 or NetWare 5 servers in a network tree now share a single, distributed database. By creating a user or other object once in the network tree, each server will recognize that same user or object. Chapter 4 discusses the management of NDS.

▶ *Z.E.N.works* — Introduced in NetWare 5, this new tool uses NDS to simplify the management of Windows-based workstations. By delivering workstation management tasks directly to the user desktop, Z.E.N.works reduces the cost and complexity of maintaining network computers. Chapter 5 discusses some of the key features of Z.E.N.works.

▶ *Security* — Earlier security features for NetWare have been improved in NetWare 5 by utilizing security measures to filter out unauthorized network users. These features include login security, NDS security, file system security, and file system access rights. Chapter 6 discusses the management of network security.

▶ *File System* — In addition to NDS, NetWare 5 now includes Novell Storage Services (NSS), which is a new high-performance file storage and access technology that operates independently of the default NetWare file system. Chapter 7 discusses managing network files.

▶ *Novell Distributed Print Services (NDPS)* — The queue-based printing system found in earlier versions of NetWare has been replaced in NetWare 5 with NDPS, which improves overall network performance, reduces network printing problems, and provides better administration of network printing. Chapter 8 discusses the setting up of printers for the network.

▶ *FastTrack Server* — The Netscape FastTrack Server for NetWare is a new high-performance Web server included in NetWare 5. The FastTrack server supports many leading Internet application development languages, and enables NetWare 5 to be a powerful Web development platform. The FastTrack Server has many features that were not available with the Novell Web Server found in earlier versions of NetWare. Chapter 9 discusses the Netscape FastTrack Server for NetWare.

The first key to managing a complex system is to impose a structure on it that will organize and simplify all of the components. Novell Directory Services (NDS) is NetWare 5's foundation for organizing the network.

To understand how NetWare 5 ties together the network building blocks, let's first look at the fundamentals of NDS. Next, we'll look at how NetWare 5 regulates security. Finally, we'll see how NetWare 5 pulls it all together so the network administrator can manage the network.

Novell Directory Services (NDS)

NDS is simply a database that contains information about every object in the network. Using this database, NetWare 5 can identify each object and know where it's supposed to be in the network, who's permitted to use it, and to what it's supposed to be connected.

Every physical component on the network, such as a server, printer, or workstation, has its own unique NDS object defined in the NDS database. Software entities, such as print servers, print queues (directories that contain pending print jobs), and volumes, also have their own NDS objects. In fact, all users and organizations (departments, companies, or even project teams if you like) have their own objects defined in the NDS database. If a user, server, or other type of entity doesn't have an NDS object defined for it in the database, that user or device can't access network services.

If your network is small and contains only one server, the NDS database is stored on that server. If you have more than one server on your network, all of them share a single, distributed NDS database. That way, any object defined anywhere in the network will be recognized by all of the servers in that network.

Having a distributed database makes the database itself more flexible and easier for the network administrator to use. For example, instead of being limited to a single server, an administrator can make changes to the database from any number of servers, and all of those servers will receive the same updates.

In addition, a distributed database means that a single server can't make the whole network fail. If one server goes down, the whole database still exists on other servers, so users can still log in, most services will still be available, and so on. In most cases, the only problem a downed server may cause is to prevent a user from accessing files and services stored on that particular server. If, however, the user stored files on his or her workstation, the user can still print those files on network printers, send e-mail to other users, and the like.

NOTE One of the beauties of NDS is that all servers on the network share a single NDS database. Before NDS, if you wanted to work on three different servers, you had to get the administrator to define you three different times — once on each server. Now, however, all servers share the same information, so once you're defined, any server on the network will recognize you.

Likewise, you no longer need to know which server contains the service you need, such as a particular printer. Because all servers recognize the printer, you can get straight to the printer without having to locate a specific server first.

The NDS database is structured in a hierarchical format, which means that objects in the database can be at different levels or grouped into subordinate divisions. By using this format, NDS objects can be organized into groups and subgroups, so it's easier to manage all of them. If, for example, you group all your marketing users under a single Organization object, it is easy to change the user accounts of every marketing user simultaneously by just manipulating the Organization object under which they're grouped.

The structure of NDS objects, and the way they are grouped together, is called the *Directory tree* (or, sometimes, the *NDS tree*). The discussion throughout this book talks about the Directory tree, and where objects — and you — are located in it.

The Directory tree is called a tree because a diagram of the NDS objects in your network's NDS database will look like an upside-down tree, with a root at the top and branches and subbranches fanning out beneath it, as shown in Figure 1.13.

► · ◄

FIGURE 1.13 *NDS Directory tree*

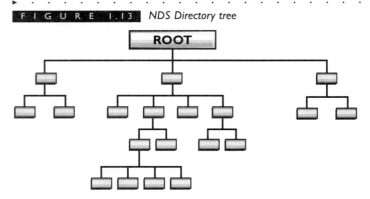

Most small- or average-sized NetWare 5 networks have a single NDS tree (and a single NDS database) that defines the entire network. Larger networks may have multiple trees, though this isn't always necessary. For example, a large company that consists of three different subsidiaries who seldom communicate with each other might have a separate tree for each subsidiary.

NDS makes it easy for network administrators to keep track of their networks and update new information as users or network devices come and go. By defining objects once for an entire network, administrators cut out a lot of the repetitive work they once had to do with earlier versions of NetWare and other network products. Chapter 4 goes into more explanation about NDS objects and trees.

Security

An object defined on the network can be recognized and accessed by any server on the entire network. Some people are concerned the first time they hear this, worrying that it means anyone can have free access to every object on the network. Rest assured, the network doesn't have to be a free-for-all.

By using a distributed, shared database, NDS ensures that an object on the network can be recognized by any other object on the network. However, that doesn't mean that every other object will be *allowed* to access the object. A powerful array of security features is included with NetWare 5. These security features control exactly what an object is allowed to do once it's on the network.

The three primary types of security features contained within NetWare 5 are:

▶ *Login security* — This controls whether or not users can log in to the network. (You can also specify such restrictions as when they can log in and what kind of password they use.)

▶ *NDS security* — NDS regulates how objects can use other objects. (For example, you can specify whether or not User A can change User B's permissible login times, or whether User C can delete or change a print server.)

▶ *File system security* — This specifies whether individual users or groups can open, change, delete, or create new files and directories.

These three types of security offer enough flexibility and protection to secure networks from nearly any type of intrusion, or unintended or accidental access. The network administrator controls this security, allowing as much (or as little) access as necessary. The administrator can also share security duties with other users, so different people control access to different parts of the network. Chapter 6 explains NetWare 5 security in greater detail.

Network Management

NetWare 5 provides a host of tools that network administrators can use to manage the entire network. Its utilities enable the administrator to create and change NDS objects, modify security features, detect trouble on the network, back-up (archive) and restore files safely, regulate printing, and so on.

Depending on the size and complexity of the network, the amount of time an administrator spends managing it can be minimal or a full-time job. In a simple, small network, the administrator's tasks usually involve setting things up (such as installing a new workstation for an employee), upgrading applications every once in a while, creating a new user object when a new hire arrives, backing up files, and the like.

In a large, complex network for a company that's changing rapidly, the administrator may carry out those same tasks, but at a much faster pace and in greater numbers. In addition, larger networks tend to have more complexity of hardware, protocols, and applications that keep a network administrator hopping to keep up.

Regardless of the size of the network, NetWare 5 management tools help the administrator keep the network running smoothly.

Beyond the Basics

This chapter introduced you to the fundamental basics of an NetWare 5 network. Later chapters in this book will go into detail on some of these features.

You'll find the following topics addressed later in this book:

- ▶ For more on the installation of servers, see Chapter 2.
- ▶ For more on the installation of workstations, see Chapter 3.
- ▶ For more on NDS objects and Directory trees, see Chapter 4.
- ▶ For more on FastTrack Server, see Chapter 9.

The NetWare 5 management tools you're most likely to need are discussed throughout this book, for example:

- ▶ To manage users, see Chapter 5.
- ▶ To manage security, see Chapter 6.
- ▶ To manage files and applications on the network, see Chapter 7.
- ▶ To manage print services, see Chapter 8.

Some features or aspects of a NetWare 5 network that were touched on in this chapter are more advanced than the scope of this book — specifically, network architectures and protocols. You can find more detailed information about those features in Novell's online documentation (which came with your NetWare 5 package) and in *Novell's NetWare 5 Administrator's Handbook* (from Novell Press), which can be used as an advanced companion to this book. For more information about connecting to the Internet, you may also want to see *Novell's Guide to Internet Access Solutions* from Novell Press.

Installing and Managing NetWare 5 Servers

The first step in getting a NetWare 5 network up and running is to install the server. After the server is installed, you can use it to manage network activity.

In a nutshell, when you install the server, you:

▶ Set up the network's data storage on the server's hard disk.

▶ Create the NDS Directory tree structure, if this is the first server in the network, or add the server into an existing tree if one already exists.

▶ Create the first user in the network (user Admin, who has complete security access to the network after installation).

▶ Specify the type of network architecture the network will be using (such as Ethernet).

▶ Install all of the NetWare 5 utilities that both the network administrator and the users need when working on the network.

Because this book discusses the basics of NetWare 5, in this chapter we'll look at the easiest way to install a new NetWare 5 server.

In many cases, you may be upgrading an existing NetWare 3 or NetWare 4 server to NetWare 5. Therefore, this chapter will also look at the easiest way to upgrade an existing server (which, coincidentally, uses the same utility as a brand new installation).

Finally, the chapter will end with a look at some of the basic management activities you can do with the server after it is set up.

NOTE

In some cases, you may want to upgrade a server that is running NetWare 3.1x. However, instead of upgrading the existing server, you decide you want to replace the old server with a completely new machine (usually because the older server machine doesn't meet the new hardware requirements for a NetWare 5 server). In this case, you won't use the regular upgrade procedure described in this chapter.

Instead, you will use a utility called the Novell Upgrade Wizard to transfer the network data from the old server machine, across the network, onto the new machine. Once the new machine is functioning as a server, you can take down the old machine and get rid of it (or turn it into a workstation). The Novell Upgrade Wizard is not explained in this book. For more information about this utility, refer to the Novell online documentation.

Preparing to Install or Upgrade a Server

Before you install or upgrade your server, you need to make sure you're prepared. Follow these three steps to prepare for the installation:

▸ Make sure the server itself is ready, with the necessary amount of memory installed, a smaller DOS partition created, network boards installed, and so on.

▸ Ensure the server is going to be protected.

▸ Arm yourself with all of the necessary information you'll need to answer questions during the installation procedure.

Getting the Server Ready

Before running the installation program, you need to make sure the server hardware is ready. The server should have enough processor speed, memory, and hard disk space to suit your needs. The larger your network, the more powerful your server will need to be. The following are the *minimum* hardware requirements for a NetWare 5 server:

▸ An IBM-compatible PC with a Pentium processor (300MHz Pentium II recommended)

▸ VGA or higher-resolution monitor (SVGA recommended)

▸ 64MB of RAM (128MB recommended if running Java programs)

▸ 50MB DOS partition (256MB recommended)

▸ 500MB free hard disk space for the SYS: volume (1GB of volume space recommended for additional Novell products)

▸ One or more network boards (such as an Ethernet or Token Ring board) to connect to the rest of the network

▸ Appropriate network cabling (Ethernet, Token Ring, and so on) and related hardware components (hubs, backup units, and so on)

▸ A CD-ROM drive

NetWare 5 requires a minimum of 550MB of hard disk space (50MB on the DOS partition and 500MB for the NetWare SYS: volume). However, this doesn't allow for additional files (such as applications, work files, and so on) to be stored on the server, and allows no room for growth. You will probably want to have much more disk space available. In fact, you may decide you want multiple hard disks installed in the server.

Planning the Server Memory

One of the most important characteristics of your server — more important in many cases than processor speed — is memory. You need to make sure that your server has enough memory to keep things humming along smoothly.

Officially, a NetWare 5 server should have a minimum of 64MB of RAM. Depending on the size of the network (the number of servers, number of users on the server, total disk space on the server, and so on), you will probably want more memory than that.

Novell recommends that you multiply the amount of your server's disk space by 0.008, and then add that amount to the base 64MB of RAM. For example, assume you have a 2GB disk (approximately 2,000MB). Thus, 2,000 times 0.008 equals an additional 16MB of RAM.

Then add another 1MB to 4MB for additional cache buffer RAM, to increase performance. The more memory you add here (up to 4MB), the better the performance will be.

Therefore, if you decide to add 4MB of cache buffer RAM to the example 2GB hard disk, you end up with a minimum of 84MB of RAM:

$$64 + (2,000 \times 0.008) + 4 = 84MB$$

If you are planning to run Java programs with NetWare 5, Novell recommends a minimum of 128MB of RAM. Because RAM is relatively inexpensive for the benefit you receive from it, don't skimp on it unnecessarily.

Installing the Network Boards

If you install and configure the network board(s) in the server before installation, the installation program will be capable of analyzing the hardware and (in most cases) will automatically load the necessary LAN driver. Refer to the network board manufacturer's documentation for configuration instructions.

If this is not the first server in the network, connect the server to the rest of the network by installing the network board in the server, and then connecting a network cable from the network board to a hub or other network connection. By connecting the server's cable to the network before the server is even installed, you allow the installation program to automatically identify the existing Directory tree and other important network information.

Installing Additional Hard Disks

If you need to add extra hard disks to the server — now is the time to do it. Install all hard disks according to the manufacturer's instructions. Then the installation program will automatically recognize the disks and treat them accordingly.

Creating a Small DOS Partition

Before you run the installation program to install a brand new server, you will want to reformat the server's hard disk to create a smaller DOS partition than usual.

NOTE If you're upgrading an existing server, you may not need to reformat this disk. An existing server will most likely have a DOS partition and a NetWare partition on it already. Just make sure the DOS partition is large enough for NetWare 5 (at least 50MB).

Normally, when you purchase a new computer, the hard disk is preformatted to support the workstation's operating system (DOS, Windows 95, Windows 98, and so on).

When you want to turn a computer into a server, you need to reformat the hard disk so it can contain two separate partitions, each formatted in a different way.

The first disk partition you will create is a DOS partition. The DOS partition is the portion of the hard disk that is reserved for DOS system files and other DOS files that you want to store on the server. The files needed to boot the machine and let it communicate with its fundamental hardware are located in the DOS partition. In addition, some NetWare 5 files will exist on the DOS partition. The DOS partition does not need to be as large as the NetWare partition.

The rest of the disk will contain at least one NetWare partition, which stores the majority of the NetWare 5 files and all of the network data. This partition will contain a volume named SYS. The SYS volume is very important, because it contains all the required NetWare files. You can create additional volumes to store other types of network files if you wish, or you can make SYS large enough to store everything on your network.

Plan for at least a 50MB DOS partition, but a rule of thumb is to add 1MB to the DOS partition for every megabyte of server RAM installed. A safe plan is to create a DOS partition that is about twice as big as your server RAM (for example, 128MB to 256MB) to ensure you have enough room for any files you want to load.

The first hard disk in the server must have a DOS partition. If the server contains additional hard disks, those additional hard disks don't need DOS partitions—they can be fully devoted to NetWare partitions. Figure 2.1 shows a simple way to set up a server, where the first disk has the DOS partition and a single NetWare partition (set up as a single NetWare volume named SYS. The additional hard disks in the server have been set up to contain a single NetWare partition each, with corresponding volumes named VOL1 and VOL2.

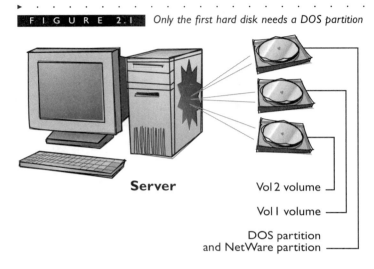

FIGURE 2.1 *Only the first hard disk needs a DOS partition*

Server

Vol 2 volume ⌐

Vol I volume ———

DOS partition
and NetWare partition ———

NOTE

If the computer you are turning into a server is currently running Windows 95 or 98, you'll need to reformat the computer's hard disk to support DOS instead. NetWare 5 doesn't need to have Windows 95 or 98 on the hard disk, so there's no need to retain Windows 95 or 98 on this machine.

To eliminate Windows 95 or 98 and format the DOS partition, boot the computer from the NetWare 5 License diskette. (To do this, put the diskette in drive A and turn on the computer.) This diskette contains the DOS utilities called FDISK and FORMAT. By running these utilities, as explained in the following procedure, you'll reformat the disk to support DOS. (Do not use the version of DOS that comes on Windows 95, 98, or NT computers to format the disk. That version of DOS may create problems.)

You should create the DOS disk partition before running the installation program. (The installation process will create the partition for you if you want, but it's generally easier to do it yourself so you can avoid having to reinstall the CD-ROM drive's drivers and other configuration information after the installation program runs.) Here are the basic steps to format the DOS partition (refer to your computer manufacturer's documentation for more specific instructions):

I. First, save the computer's disk drivers (including the CD-ROM driver), AUTOEXEC.BAT, and CONFIG.SYS onto a diskette so you can copy them back onto the disk after you've reformatted it. You may also have other files that are loaded by the AUTOEXEC.BAT file (or other boot files) that you want to retain. Copy those files to the diskette, too.

2. Use DOS's FDISK command to create a DOS partition. Use the formula described earlier to determine the size you need. (If the computer you're using doesn't have DOS installed, you can boot from the license diskette that came with NetWare 5. The necessary DOS commands to reformat the server's hard disk are contained on that diskette.) To run FDISK, make sure you're at the DOS prompt, and then type **FDISK**. Follow the instructions on the screen to delete the current DOS partition and then create a new primary partition.

3. Use DOS's FORMAT command to format the partition. To use this utility, type the following command at the DOS prompt. The "/S" option copies the DOS COMMAND.COM file to the disk.

```
FORMAT drive letter /S
```

4. Leave the rest of the disk space alone for now — that space will be converted into NetWare volumes during the installation program.

Installing the CD-ROM Drive

If the CD-ROM drive isn't already installed in the server, install it (as a DOS device) according to the manufacturer's documentation. Most CD-ROM drives have an automatic installation program that you run after you've connected the drive to modify the AUTOEXEC.BAT and CONFIG.SYS files. This way, the CD-ROM's drivers can load and work properly.

Verifying the Date and Time

Use the DOS DATE and TIME commands to verify that the server's time and date are set correctly, and change them if necessary.

To use the DATE command, go to the DOS prompt and type **DATE**. The computer will display what it thinks is the current date, and then it will ask you to enter a new date. If the date is wrong, type in the new date in a *mm-dd-yy* format. If the date is already correct, just press Enter and the date will remain unchanged. The TIME command is used the same way.

Protecting the Server

Protecting the server is a very important safeguard that cannot be over-looked. Damage to the server can affect the entire network.

Preventing Physical Damage

If the server is in an exposed public area where anyone can have access to it, accidents may happen. For example, someone might trip over the power cord, or turn off the server thinking it was a regular computer that had been left on accidentally. After-hours janitorial people are notorious for unplugging computers to plug in vacuum cleaners.

Of more concern than accidents, however, is the possibility of deliberate tampering. Computer specialists will tell you over and over again that the best security software in the world (such as NetWare 5's security features) can't protect your server if an unauthorized person can gain physical access to the server. If an intruder can get to your server physically, he or she can remove hard disks, reboot the server, load virus programs from diskette, and so on.

In other words, if you really want to protect your server and the data on it, lock the server in a secure room and hide the key. In fact, you may also want to remove its keyboard and monitor, and access it only with the Remote Console feature when necessary. (Remote Console is explained later in this chapter.)

Bracing Against Earthquakes

If you work in an earthquake-prone area, you should also secure the server to a desk or counter. A good-sized shake, such as the one that hit San Francisco a few years ago, can send computers flying across the room. A moderate one can tip over the racks on which the computers are sitting. Don't risk losing your network simply because the server fell off the table.

Minimizing Electricity-Related Problems

The electrical power coming from the power company into your office is not always consistent. Because of this, you need to make sure your server will not be damaged and files won't be corrupted if a brownout, spike, surge, or blackout occurs.

The best protection for your server is to use an uninterruptible power supply (UPS). A UPS provides the server with a backup battery that takes over in case of a power outage. This backup battery allows enough time for the UPS to shut down the server cleanly, leaving no open files exposed to corruption. A good UPS also protects against spikes, surges, brownouts, and line noise (interference on the wire).

If possible, attach each workstation to a UPS, too. If a UPS isn't feasible, at least use surge suppressors on the workstations and peripherals (such as printers) to prevent electrical surges and spikes from damaging the equipment. Figure 2.2 shows a typical UPS and surge suppressor.

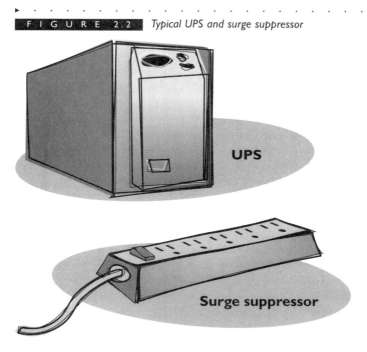

FIGURE 2.2 *Typical UPS and surge suppressor*

NOTE

Uninterruptible power supplies and surge suppressors can be found at many computer equipment stores (and even some of those big warehouse stores that sell computer and office supplies). Depending on your needs, these protection devices can be fairly inexpensive. Before purchasing one, check recent reviews in the trade press for top-ranking products, or at least verify what type of equipment the device is designed to protect.

For example, surge suppressors come in a variety of "strengths" — meaning that some can withstand higher voltage spikes and surges than others. Make sure you get devices that will adequately protect the equipment you have. If you're unsure, don't hesitate to call the manufacturer (or look up their Web site) for recommendations. One of the top UPS and surge suppressor manufacturers, American Power Conversion (APC), has a Web site at www.apcc.com. Its Web site contains useful information about power and APC's products.

When Power Corrupts

A *brownout* (also called a *sag*) occurs when power in the area is diminished, but doesn't go out completely. Generally, lights grow dimmer and appliances run slower, sporadically, or not at all. These can be caused by too many machines trying to start up at the same time or by a single heavy-load machine. Power companies may deliberately cause brownouts when electrical demand exceeds supply (such as on hot summer days when all the air conditioners are running), thereby allowing customers to avoid a total blackout. Brownouts can put undue stress on your computer's components, causing damage.

A *spike*, which is often caused by lightening strikes, occurs when the electrical voltage suddenly and drastically increases, usually doubling (or more) the normal peak voltage. This is the type of power problem than can fry your electrical appliances if they're plugged in, and the reason why experts say you shouldn't talk on the telephone during thunderstorms. Spikes can also occur when power is turned back on after an outage.

A *surge* is a brief increase in power, but not as great an increase as a spike. Surges may occur when a heavy-load machine is turned off and power surges to other devices that were on the same circuit. While a surge may not destroy your computer, it can stress delicate parts and cause premature failure.

A *blackout* is a complete power outage. Obvious problems with this are that you will lose any unsaved data instantly. But this kind of instant outage can also corrupt open files, including files that keep track of where everything is on your hard disk. More damage can be caused by the spike that might occur when the power comes back on.

Information You'll Need Before Installing the Server

Regardless of whether you are upgrading or installing a new server, there are several decisions you have to make about your server. You'll need to provide the answers to some of these questions during the installation, so make sure you know what you want before you begin.

The following sections describe the information you will need to have handy during the installation.

NDS Information

If your organization does not have any NetWare 4 or NetWare 5 servers already installed, you will create a basic Novell Directory Services (NDS) Directory tree during the installation of the first server. This Directory tree will contain and organize all the objects (such as printers, users, servers, and volumes) on your network.

If an NDS Directory tree already exists in your organization, you will add the new NetWare 5 server that you are installing to the existing Directory tree.

In most cases, the NDS Directory tree will have only one Organization object, usually named with the name of your organization. An Organization object is sometimes referred to as a *container object*, because it contains other objects.

In a smaller networking environment, the Organization object may be the only container object you have. All other network objects will reside under this Organization object (often abbreviated as an "O" object). If you set up your NDS tree this way during the server installation, the server you're installing, its hard disk volumes, and a user named Admin will all be created as NDS objects underneath this Organization object.

However, in larger situations, you may need to use objects called Organizational Unit objects. These are also container objects, and they can be placed under the Organization object to subdivide your network entities into smaller, more manageable groups. For example, you may want to create Organizational Unit objects for each division in your company, or even for individual departments or project teams. You can select multiple levels of Organizational Unit objects, if you desire. You can install a server into an Organizational Unit object (also called an "OU" object), and that server and its volumes will become objects inside that OU.

If you are installing a server into an existing Directory tree, the installation program will ask you to select the existing tree into which you want to install this server. In this case, this server's object (and its volumes) will be created underneath the Organization or Organizational Unit object you specify.

TIP

To make sure you set up your network's Directory tree logically for your situation, you may want to refer to Chapter 4 to learn more about NDS objects and trees before you go through the installation program.

Server Hardware and Volume Information

In addition to planning your Directory tree, you should have the following information about the server, its hardware, and its volumes before starting the installation or upgrade:

- ► *The server's name* — You can choose any name between 2 and 47 characters long, using letters, numbers, hyphens, or underscores.

- ► *The server's time zone* — You'll need to know the acronym for the server's time zone and whether that time zone supports Daylight Saving Time. (This information will probably be filled in automatically during the installation, but you'll want to verify it.)

- ► *The name of your organization (for instance, your company name)* — This Organization object name will become the Directory tree's name, as well. (If you're installing a server into a pre-existing tree, you'll need to know the name of the existing tree.)

- ► *The server's location (name context) in the Directory tree* — Before you install the server, be sure you are familiar with Novell Directory Services and how you want your network to be laid out in the Directory tree. You'll need to specify to which Organization object and Organizational Unit objects this server belongs. For more information about NDS, see Chapter 4.

- ► *The types of network boards you will install in the server* — You'll need to know the type of network board inside the server and the name of its corresponding LAN driver. In many cases, NetWare 5 will automatically detect the board and load the correct driver. However, if NetWare 5 doesn't recognize the necessary LAN driver, you'll need to supply the driver on a separate diskette (usually available from the manufacturer) along with the driver's settings. Check the manufacturer's documentation for information on the correct settings to use. (Settings may include the interrupt that the board uses, the slot it's installed in, or the like.)

- ► *The server's storage devices and their corresponding adapters* — Know the types of storage devices (CD-ROM drives, hard disks, tape drives, and so on) that are installed in your server. Also know the name of the storage adapter (board) that each device is attached to in the server. Some storage devices come with their own adapters. Other devices may share a single adapter. Again, NetWare 5 will recognize most common storage devices and adapters and automatically load the correct drivers for them, but you'll need to have the drivers on hand in case the installation program can't recognize them.

▶ *The size of volume SYS* — A volume named SYS is mandatory; it contains NetWare system and utility files. The server must have a minimum of 500MB of hard disk space for volume SYS. However, you may want to plan for a larger SYS volume, such as 1000MB, so you can install additional products into volume SYS.

▶ *The size and names of any additional NetWare volumes* — It's often a good idea to reserve volume SYS for NetWare files and applications only, and to create additional volumes to hold the regular applications and files that users create and use on the network.

▶ *Whether you want any volumes to support Mac OS or UNIX files* — By default, the server supports DOS files, which only use short (11-character) filenames and the long filenames allowed by OS/2, Windows 95, Windows 98, and Windows NT. This default does not support Mac OS or UNIX files, because those files require completely different file formats.

To support the different file formats used by other operating systems, you will have to load a special program, called a *name space module*, for those files after installation. Then you will assign that name space to the volume where you want to store those files. The steps for this will be explained at the end of the installation procedure.

The following name space modules support the different file formats and filename restrictions, as shown in Table 2.1.

T A B L E 2 . I	*Name Space Modules*
NAME SPACE MODULE	**FILES SUPPORTED**
LONG.NAM	Windows 95, Windows 98, Windows NT, OS/2
MAC.NAM	Mac OS
NFS.NAM	UNIX

Protocol Information

Another aspect of your network that you must plan before installing your server is the protocol you want to use for network communications. As discussed in Chapter 1, NetWare 5 supports both IP and IPX protocols. You have four choices when installing your server:

- ▶ You can install IPX only.
- ▶ You can install IP with Compatibility Mode turned on.
- ▶ You can install IP with Compatibility Mode turned off.
- ▶ You can install both IP and IPX.

If you have no need for the IP protocol on your network, using IPX alone is probably the simplest option, because you don't need to understand or plan for things like IP addresses, subnet masks, and so on. The only specific IPX information you will need to plan is the server's internal IPX network number. A number will be generated randomly for you, or you can specify your own. Each IPX server on the network must have a unique internal IPX network number.

If you want to use the IP protocol, you will most likely choose to install IP with Compatibility Mode turned on. This will allow all existing IPX-based applications and services to continue to work on your IP-based network. If you are sure you have a pure IP environment, with no dependencies on IPX anywhere in any of your applications or services, you can install IP and then turn off the IPX Compatibility Mode option. However, since the Compatibility Mode option is dormant and requires no overhead if there are no IPX packets to deal with, leaving it turned on is generally a safer option.

Choosing to install both IP and IPX protocols on the same network means you must manage both types of protocols. You will need to install a Migration agent on the server to make sure that both halves of the network (the IP segment and the IPX segment) can communicate with each other.

If you decide to install IP on your server, you will need to have the following information available during the installation:

- ▶ *The server's IP address* — Each IP server must have a unique IP address. If you plan to connect your network to the Internet, you will have to register with the Internet Network Information Center (InterNIC) and obtain a unique IP address from them. For more information about getting a registered IP address, contact InterNIC at hostmaster@internic.net, or call your Internet service provider (ISP).

▸ *The server's subnet mask* — The subnet mask is a number designating a portion of the network. Subnet masks allow you to divide a large network into smaller, more manageable units.

▸ *The router/gateway address* — You can either specify a router (or gateway) address, or you can allow the server to locate the nearest one automatically. If you do not want to specify a particular address, you will leave that option blank in the installation procedure.

▸ *Whether you want to install a Migration Agent on this server* — A Migration Agent can be enabled as part of the IPX Compatibility Mode. A Migration Agent acts as a gateway between an IP segment of the network and an IPX segment. The Migration Agent takes packets from each side of the network and repackages them in the other protocol's format for transmission across the network to other destinations.

▸ *DNS information* — If you want to use Domain Name Services on your network, you will need to know your network's domain name, as well as the address of name servers you want to use. For more information about DNS and name servers, see the Novell online documentation. (Search for the DNS/DHCP Administrator's Guide, which is included in the online documentation.)

Printing Information

NDPS is the new printing service for NetWare 5. While you can still use the older queue-based printing service that was used in previous versions of NetWare, NDPS support is recommended because of its new features and capabilities. See Chapter 9 for more information about both NDPS and queue-based printing in NetWare 5, and then decide whether or not to install NDPS on this server.

Installing a New NetWare 5 Server

To install a new NetWare 5 server, complete the steps in the following sections.

Beginning the Installation

To begin the installation, perform the following steps:

1. Set up the server hardware, as described in the previous sections.

   a. Install and configure any new memory, network boards, and hard disks in the server.

   b. Using the DOS FDISK and FORMAT commands, create a DOS disk partition. Leave the rest of the disk space free.

   c. If necessary, install the CD-ROM drive as a DOS device on the server, and then reboot the server to make sure the drive is recognized by the computer and that its settings take effect.

   d. Using the DOS DATE and TIME commands, verify that the computer's time and date are set correctly, and change them if necessary.

   e. Edit the CONFIG.SYS file to make sure the FILES and BUFFERS commands are set to at least the following values. (You will have to reboot the computer to make these settings take effect.)

   ```
   FILES=40

   BUFFERS=30
   ```

2. Insert the *NetWare 5 Operating System* CD-ROM into the computer's CD-ROM drive.

3. From the DOS command prompt on the server, change to the CD-ROM drive's letter (often D), and enter the following command:

   ```
   INSTALL
   ```

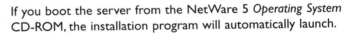

If you boot the server from the NetWare 5 *Operating System* CD-ROM, the installation program will automatically launch.

NOTE

4. If prompted, choose the language you want to use.

5. A screen called "Novell Terms and Conditions" will appear. This describes the legal terms and conditions you must agree to in order to install NetWare 5. Press any key to page through the document. When you have finished reading the terms and conditions, press F10 (or select Accept the Agreement) to accept the agreement.

6. From the screen that appears, choose the New Server type of installation (see Figure 2.3), and then select a startup directory. The

default startup directory (where the server's startup files will be located) is C:\NWSERVER.

FIGURE 2.3   *Selecting New Server installation of NetWare 5*

```
NetWare Installation

Welcome to the NetWare server installation.

    Select the type of installation and specify the directory
    where the server startup files will be installed.

    A new installation will destroy data on existing NetWare partitions.

    Use the Tab or arrow keys to move between windows.
    To learn more about the installation, press F1.

    ┌─────────────────────────────────────────────────────────┐
    │ Is this a new server or an upgrade? New server          │
    │                                                          │
    │ Startup directory                     C:\NWSERVER        │
    └─────────────────────────────────────────────────────────┘

                      ┌─────────────┐
                      │  Options    │
                      ├─────────────┤
                      │ │Continue   │
                      │ │Modify     │
                      └─────────────┘

Alt+F10=Exit   F2=Advanced settings   F3=Response file   Esc=Back   F1=Help
```

7. (Optional) From the same screen, press F2 to specify advanced settings. From the Advanced Settings screen, you can make the following changes:

   a. If necessary, choose whether you want the installation program to access the CD-ROM drive through a NetWare driver or a DOS device. If possible, choose NetWare. However, if a NetWare driver doesn't exist for your CD-ROM drive, you can choose DOS.

   b. If necessary, specify a server ID number (only necessary if you don't want to use the one that will be assigned automatically). This number is similar to an IPX internal network number.

   c. If necessary, specify that you do not want the AUTOEXEC.BAT file to automatically load the server (SERVER.EXE). If you do not allow AUTOEXEC.BAT to automatically load the server, you will have to load the server by typing **SERVER** at the DOS prompt any time the server is rebooted.

   d. If necessary, specify any particular SET parameters that may be required by your device drivers.

Now the installation program will begin; continue with the instructions in the next section to specify the server's information.

Specifying the Server's Information

To specify the server's information, perform the following steps:

1. Specify the country code, code page, and keyboard mapping for your server (see Figure 2.4). Different countries have slightly different versions of DOS developed to support varying languages, and some countries or languages have their own unique types of keyboards. If you need to change these settings, choose Modify, and then press Enter on the field you want to change and choose the correct selections from the lists that appear.)

FIGURE 2.4 Selecting country code, code page, and keyboard mapping

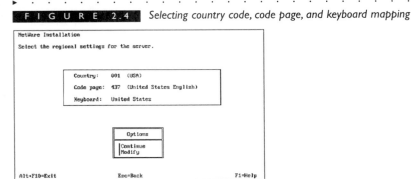

2. Select the Mouse and Video type for the server, as shown in Figure 2.5. At this point, the installation program copies files, including device drivers, to the DOS partition.

FIGURE 2.5 Selecting mouse and video type

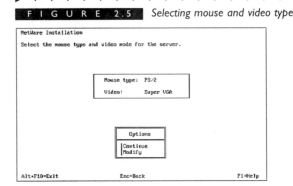

3. Select your computer's device drivers. At this point, you can select
    Platform Support Modules (if your computer supports more than one
    processor), Hot Plug Support Modules (if your computer supports
    PCI Hot Plug technology), and Storage Adapters. If the installation
    program detects any of these drivers or a storage adapter (board), it
    will display them for you. (See Figure 2.6.) If the information is
    correct, choose Continue. If not, choose Modify and specify the
    drivers you need. You can also configure the drivers at this point. (If
    the installation program does not detect any PSM or Hot Plug
    drivers, your computer probably does not support these
    technologies.)

FIGURE 2.6 *Selecting device drivers and storage drivers*

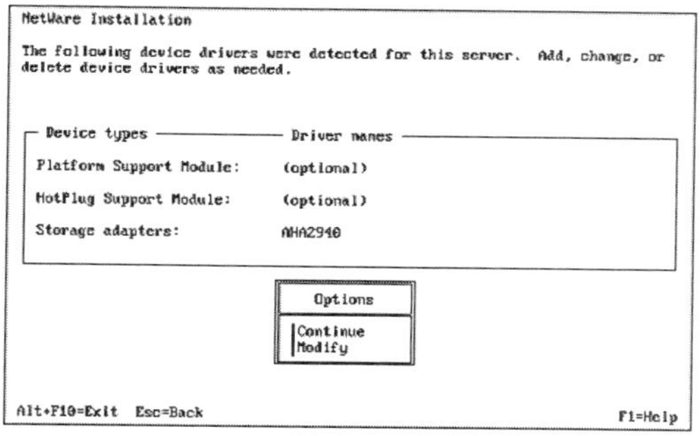

4. Select your computer's storage devices (which are controlled by the
    adapters you chose in Step 3) and network boards. If the installation
    program detects any of these devices or network boards, it will display
    them for you, as shown in Figure 2.7. If the information is correct,
    choose Continue. If not, choose Modify and specify the drivers you
    need. You can also configure the drivers at this point. (This screen
    also lets you specify any optional NLMs that are required for the
    installation program to continue. For example, you can load
    ROUTE.NLM if you are installing the server into a Token Ring
    network.)

FIGURE 2.7 *Verifying that the correct drivers have been selected*

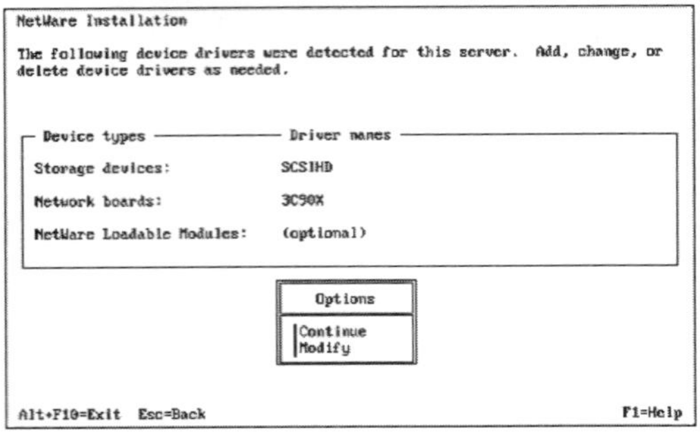

```
NetWare Installation

The following device drivers were detected for this server. Add, change, or
delete device drivers as needed.


  ┌─ Device types ─────────── Driver names ─────────
  
    Storage devices:        SCSIHD
    
    Network boards:         3C90X
    
    NetWare Loadable Modules:  (optional)
  └──────────────────────────────────────────────────

                        ┌──────────────┐
                        │   Options     │
                        ├──────────────┤
                        │Continue       │
                        │Modify         │
                        └──────────────┘

Alt+F10=Exit  Esc=Back                          F1=Help
```

5. (Optional) If you are installing NetWare 5 on a computer that was previously used as a server, the installation program will detect existing NetWare partitions and the SYS volume. Choose either "Replace volume SYS and its NetWare Partition" or "Remove all NetWare volumes and NetWare/NSS Partitions." The first option will erase volume SYS only, leaving any other volumes intact. You will then see a screen displaying Available Free Spaces, from which you can select the free space you want to use for SYS. The second option will remove all volumes, allowing you to create new volumes from scratch.

6. A screen appears, showing the proposed size for the NetWare partition that will contain the SYS volume, as shown in Figure 2.8. You can change the size of this partition (and therefore, of volume SYS) by choosing Modify. Highlight the NetWare Partition Size field, and enter the size you want to use. Remember that volume SYS should be a minimum of 500MB. If you want to include the online Novell documentation on SYS, choose a minimum size of 1,000MB. When you specify a size for the partition, the SYS size will change automatically to match it. The Hot Fix size will be determined by default. Accept the default Hot Fix size. Any disk space left over after you've specified the NetWare partition and volume SYS can be used later to specify additional traditional or NSS volumes.

7. Press F10 to save the information for volume SYS.

At this point, the installation program mounts volume SYS and begins copying files to it. Then the installation program launches the NetWare 5

Installation Wizard, a graphical program that will take you through the rest of the server installation, as explained in the following section.

Setting Up the Server's Environment

Continue with the following steps to set up the server's environment:

I. First, you will be asked to name the new server, as shown in Figure 2.8. Enter a name for this server, then click Next.

FIGURE 2.8 *Entering a name for the server*

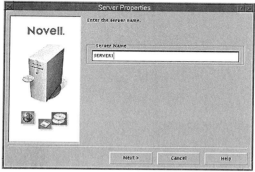

2. (Optional) If you left disk space for additional volumes, you can configure new volumes now. If you used all the available disk space for volume SYS, skip to Step 3. If you do not want to create new volumes now, click Next and skip to Step 3. If you do want to create new volumes, complete the following steps:

a. Click the Free Space in the list of volumes, and then click Create.

b. Enter a volume name.

c. Select whether you want the volume to be a Traditional volume or an NSS volume. (See Chapter 8 for more information about the difference.)

d. Enter the size of the volume in the Space to Use field, then click Apply to Volume.

e. Click OK to return to the list of volumes, and then click Next to continue.

3. Specify whether you want to mount volumes now or when the server reboots after the installation is complete. If you want to install some Novell products during this installation procedure to volumes other than SYS, choose to mount the volumes now. Otherwise, if you intend only to install products into SYS, you can choose to mount the volumes later.

4. When the Protocols screen appears, click the server in the diagram to display the network boards installed in it.

5. Click a network board, and choose the protocol you want to use for that board. You can choose IP, IPX, or both. If you choose IP, you must also specify the server's IP address and subnet mask, as shown in Figure 2.9. You can also specify a router address if you need to (or leave that field blank to allow the network to find the nearest router automatically). Choosing IP alone will automatically install the IPX Compatibility Mode.

F I G U R E   2 . 9   *Selecting the protocols for this server*

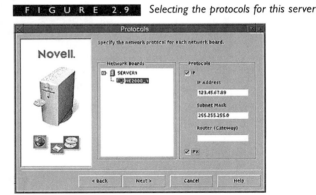

6. Select the time zone in which this server will exist (see Figure 2.10). If your location uses Daylight Saving Time, make sure the box is checked to allow for that adjustment.

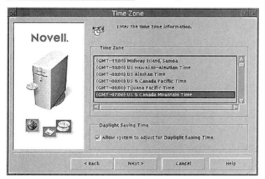

FIGURE 2.10 *Selecting the time zone for this server*

7. Choose whether you want to create a new NDS tree or install this server into an existing NDS tree, as shown in Figure 2.11. Then click Next.

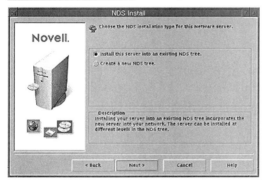

FIGURE 2.11 *Selecting the NDS installation type for this server*

8. If you are installing this server into an existing NetWare Directory tree, select the correct tree. If this is a new tree, give the tree a name.

9. Create a context for the server. By entering the name of the organization (such as your company) and the names of descending levels of Organizational Units (such as a division and a department), you actually create the branch of the NDS tree that will contain this server if the branch doesn't already exist. If a branch already exists, click the Browse button and select the Organizational Unit objects you want.

10. Enter a name, context, and password for the Admin user, as shown in Figure 2.12. If this is the first server in the tree, enter any password you want. If this server is being installed into an existing tree, type in the Admin name and password that has already been assigned, or enter the name and password of another User object already in the NDS tree. This User object must have enough NDS trustee rights to add the server to the context specified. See Chapter 7 for more information about NDS trustee rights.

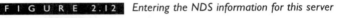

FIGURE 2.12 *Entering the NDS information for this server*

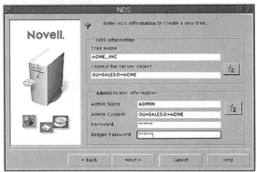

11. Next, you'll see a summary screen that indicates the name you gave your Directory tree (the same name as the organization), the *Directory Context* (or location in the tree) where your server has been installed, and the Administrator user's full name. Record this information for future reference, and then click Next to continue.

NOTE

When an object is created, it has a name, such as "BlueSky" or "Fred" or "Printer1." It also has a longer name, called a full name (or *full distinguished name*), that indicates its position in the tree. Basically, an object's full name consists of the object's name, followed by the names of the objects above it. Each name is separated by a period. For example, if a user named Fred is located under an Organization object called BlueSky, the user's full name will be Fred.BlueSky.

Sometimes, the type of object is also indicated in a full name. If an object is an Organization, the indicator "O=" will be added to the beginning of that object's name. If the object is an

Organizational Unit, "OU=" is used. All other noncontainer objects, such as users, servers, printers, and the like, are designated with "CN=". This abbreviation stands for "Common Name." (These object types are designated by official naming standards set in the industry, and are described more fully in Chapter 4.) Therefore, Fred's full name would be CN=Fred.O=BlueSky.

12. When prompted, insert the license diskette and specify the location of the license file (usually A:\LICENSE\). Then click Next to continue.

13. After the remaining files are copied to the server, the Additional Products and Services screen appears, as shown in Figure 2.13. Choose any additional products you want to install, such as NDPS, NDS Catalog Services, or Novell PKI Services. It is strongly recommended that you choose NDPS, as well as any others that are checked by default. You can click each service to see a description of that service at the bottom of the screen. When finished selecting the products you want, click Next to continue.

FIGURE 2.13 *Selecting other products to install*

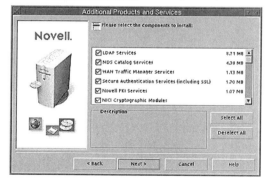

14. Depending on the products you selected, you may receive additional screens to specify information for those products. Follow the prompts on the screen.

15. When the Summary screen appears, review the list of products to be installed, as shown in Figure 2.14. At this point, you can either click Finish to complete the installation, or you can customize the

properties of some of the products you've selected, as explained in the following step. To finish the installation, skip to Step 17. To customize products you've selected, continue with Step 16.

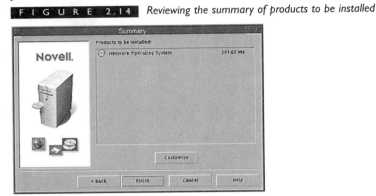

FIGURE 2.14 *Reviewing the summary of products to be installed*

16. To customize any of the choices you've made, click the Customize button. Then select the product, click the Properties button, then open any configuration tabs and specify the information you want to change. When finished, click OK to return to the Product Customization screen. When you've finished customizing products, click Close from the Product Customization screen.

17. From the Summary screen, click Finish. The installation program will finish installing all the products you've selected.

18. When asked if you want to reboot the server, click Yes. (You can also choose to view the readme file before rebooting the server.) Remove the installation CD before you reboot the server.

When the computer reboots, it will automatically load the server. When the server is running, you will see the server desktop — a graphical screen that can display utilities. To bring up the ConsoleOne utility, click the Novell button at the bottom of the screen and select ConsoleOne. To toggle the screen to a text-based server screen (the more familiar server prompt for users who have worked with previous versions of NetWare), press Alt+Esc.

NOTE

If you specified during the installation program that you did not want the SERVER.EXE file executed from within AUTOEXEC.BAT, the server will not automatically load when the computer is rebooted. You will have to load the server manually from DOS. To do this, type **CD NWSERVER** to change to the correct directory, then type **SERVER.**

The server installation is now complete. If you want to store Macintosh or UNIX files on your server, however, there is one additional task you must complete, as described in the following section. If you do not need to add support for Macintosh or UNIX files to your server, skip to the section "After the Installation — Managing Your Server" later in this chapter.

Adding the Macintosh and UNIX Name Spaces

If you want the server to be able to store Mac OS files or UNIX files on your server, you must load the appropriate name space on the server. Then you must add the name space to one or more volumes. (Support for the longer file-names that Windows 95, Windows 98, Windows NT, and OS/2 need to operate are loaded by default every time volumes are created.) Complete the following steps to load name spaces on your server:

1. To allow the server to store non-DOS files, enter the following command at the server console. Replace *name* with MAC for Mac OS files, or NFS for UNIX files:

   LOAD name

   For example, to make the server support Mac OS files, type the following:

   LOAD MAC

2. Then specify a particular volume that will store these files by using the ADD NAME SPACE command. Type this command in the following format (replace *name* with MAC, or NFS, and replace *volumename* with the name of the volume, such as SYS or VOL1):

   ADD NAME SPACE name TO volumename

   For example, to add the MAC name space to volume SYS, type the following:

   ADD NAME SPACE MAC TO SYS

The server can now support the file formats and naming conventions for the operating system you've specified. To see what you can do with the server now, skip to the section titled "After the Installation — Managing the Server" later in this chapter.

Upgrading from Previous Versions of NetWare

To upgrade an existing NetWare 3.1x, 4.01, 4.02, 4.1x, or intraNetWare server to NetWare 5, use the INSTALL program and choose the Upgrade From NetWare 3.1x or 4.x option. This is the simplest way to upgrade a server.

NOTE

Make sure the server you are upgrading meets the minimum hardware requirements for a NetWare 5 server, as explained earlier in this chapter. If the computer's DOS partition is too small, you will need to reformat the disk to create a larger DOS partition. Therefore, you will need to install the server using the New Server procedure instead of the Upgrade procedure.

For NetWare 4.x servers, INSTALL will copy new NetWare 5 files and the new NetWare 5 operating system onto the existing server. It will also upgrade Novell Directory Services (NDS).

When upgrading a NetWare 3.11 or 3.12 server, the server's existing network data (stored in a database called a *bindery*) is upgraded into an NDS database. All of the server's bindery objects become NDS objects, and they are all placed in the same location (name context) in the Directory tree as the server.

TIP

In most cases, it's best to upgrade all NetWare 4.x servers to NetWare 5 as soon as possible, to avoid maintaining a network with multiple versions of NDS on it. NetWare 5 fixed several problems with the older versions of NDS, and it is easier to maintain NDS if all servers are operating at the same level.

Because NetWare 3.1x did not use NDS, it is not necessary to upgrade all NetWare 3.1x servers quickly. There is no conflict between NetWare 3.1x servers and the NetWare 5 NDS.

NetWare 3.x binderies were a simpler form of network database than the NDS database. Binderies were flat instead of hierarchical, meaning all objects were at the same level, and couldn't be grouped into containers. In addition, binderies were specific to particular servers. This means that if you wanted user John to access three different NetWare 3.1x servers, you had to create John as a separate user on all three servers.

NDS is a great improvement over a bindery because it is much more flexible, letting a network administrator have more control over how the network is organized is managed. With NDS, a single NDS database is common to all servers in the network. Therefore, you only need to create John once, and then just give him trustee rights to files on those three servers. See Chapter 6 for more information on trustee rights.

Keep this in mind if you are upgrading several NetWare 3.1x servers into a NetWare 5 Directory tree. If you have three instances of user John on three different NetWare 3.1x servers, and you install all three servers into the same location (underneath the same Organization), the installation program will ask you if you want to delete, rename, or merge the user with the one that already exists. If one of the NetWare 3.1x users named John is actually a different person than the other two Johns, you should rename one of them before starting the upgrade to ensure that they don't merge.

TIP

To upgrade a NetWare 4.x server to NetWare 5, the NetWare 4.x server must be currently running a compatible version of NDS. The main NDS program is called DS.NLM, and this program must be at least version 5.99 or higher. The patch to update the DS.NLM utility is on the NetWare 5 Operating System CD-ROM under the \PRODUCTS\411_UPG directory. The patch should be applied to all servers running NetWare 4.x or higher.

To see the DS.NLM version, go to the server's keyboard and type **MODULES**. This command will display the version of all NLM programs (NetWare Loadable Module programs) currently running on this server. Watch for the version number of DS.NLM. If the version number is not 5.99 or above, you must update the existing DS.NLM before you can upgrade the server to NetWare 5. Do this by following the instructions in the README file on the NetWare 5 CD-ROM. If you are running NetWare 4.x, see the 411_UPG.TXT file in the PRODUCTS\411_UPG directory.

Use the instructions in the following sections to upgrade your existing NetWare 3.1x or 4.x server to NetWare 5.

Setting Up the Server Hardware and Volume SYS

The installation program has two parts. The first half, which takes you through the hardware setup and creates volume SYS, is text-based and runs in DOS on the server. Throughout the text-based installation program, you usually have to choose between "Modify" and "Continue" at each screen. Choose Modify to make changes to the default values that the installation program offers. Choose Continue to accept the values and continue with the installation. In some screens, when you make changes to the values, you will have to press F10 to save your changes and continue.

The second half of the installation program, which sets up the server's environment, switches to a graphical format, called the NetWare 5 Installation Wizard. During that portion of the installation (which is running in Java), you can use a mouse. To begin the upgrade, follow these steps:

NOTE Because deleted files in NetWare 3.1x and 4.1x remain on the server in a salvageable state, you may want to see whether there are any deleted files you want to salvage before you upgrade the server. The upgrade process will purge any deleted files still on the server.

1. Make two backups of all network files.

2. While the server is still running the older version of NetWare, locate the server's LAN drivers and a file called AUTOEXEC.NCF in the SYS: volume. Copy the LAN drivers and AUTOEXEC.NCF file onto a diskette, so you have backups of these files if necessary. (AUTOEXEC.NCF is a server configuration file that NetWare 5 uses to configure the server every time it boots. This file loads programs the server needs.)

3. Bring down the existing server by typing the following command at the server's keyboard:

DOWN

Now the computer is just running DOS. The NetWare 5 operating system has been halted.

4. From the server's boot directory, copy the server's boot files (.BAT files, .NAM files, disk drivers, INSTALL.NLM, SERVER.EXE, STARTUP.NCF, VREPAIR.NLM, and V_*namespace*.NLM files) to the same diskette you used in Step 2. (These are files that boot up the server and that allow you to fix problems that may occur. You'll learn more about them in later chapters.)

5. If you are upgrading from NetWare 3.1*x*, locate the SERVER.31*x* directory, and rename it to NWSERVER. (In many versions of DOS, you can use the DOS RENDIR command to change the directory's name, by typing **RENDIR SERVER.31x NWSERVER.**)

6. If necessary, set up the server hardware.

   a. Install and configure network boards in the server. Refer to the network board manufacturer's documentation for configuration instructions.

   b. Install the CD-ROM drive as a DOS device on the server, following the manufacturer's instructions.

   c. Using the DOS DATE and TIME commands, verify that the computer's time and date are set correctly, and change them if necessary.

   d. Edit the CONFIG.SYS file to make sure the FILES and BUFFERS commands are set to the following minimum values. (You will have to reboot the computer to make these commands take effect.)

   ```
   FILES=40
   BUFFERS=30
   ```

7. Insert the *NetWare 5 Operating System* CD-ROM into the computer's CD-ROM drive. Change to the CD-ROM drive's letter (usually D), and type the following:

   ```
   INSTALL
   ```

8. If prompted, choose the language you want to use.

9. Read the Terms and Conditions that outline the license agreement for using NetWare 5, and then press F10 (or select Accept the Agreement) to accept the agreement.

10. From the screen that appears, choose Upgrade From 3.1*x* To 4.1*x*, and then select a startup directory. The default startup directory (where the server's startup files will be located) is C:\NWSERVER.

11. (Optional) From the same screen, press F2 to specify advanced settings. From the Advanced Settings screen, you can make the following changes:

   a. If necessary, choose whether you want the installation program to access the CD-ROM drive through a NetWare driver or a DOS device. If possible, choose NetWare. However, if a NetWare driver doesn't exist for your CD-ROM drive, you can choose DOS.

b. If necessary, specify that you do not want the AUTOEXEC.BAT file to automatically load the server (SERVER.EXE). If you do not allow AUTOEXEC.BAT to automatically load the server, you will have to load the server by typing **SERVER** at the DOS prompt anytime the server is rebooted.

c. If necessary, specify any particular SET parameters that may be required by your device drivers.

12. Select your computer's mouse type and video type.

At this point, the installation program copies files, including device drivers, to the DOS partition.

13. Select your computer's device drivers. At this point, you can select Platform Support Modules (if your computer supports more than one processor), Hot Plug Support Modules (if your computer supports PCI Hot Plug technology), and Storage Adapters. If the installation program detects any of these drivers or a storage adapter (board), it will display them for you. If the information is correct, choose Continue. If not, choose Modify and specify the drivers you need. You can also configure the drivers at this point. (If the installation program does not detect any PSM or Hot Plug drivers, your computer probably does not support these technologies.)

14. Select your computer's storage devices (which are controlled by the adapters you chose in Step 13) and network boards. If the installation program detects any of these devices or network boards, it will display them for you. If the information is correct, choose Continue. If not, choose Modify and specify the drivers you need. You can also configure the drivers at this point. (This screen also lets you specify any optional NLMs that are required for the installation program to continue. For example, you can load ROUTE.NLM if you are installing the server into a Token Ring network.)

At this point, the installation program mounts volume SYS and begins copying files to it. Then the installation program launches the NetWare 5 Upgrade Wizard, a graphical program that takes you through the rest of the server installation, as explained in the following sections.

Setting Up the Server's Environment

Continue with the following steps to set up the server's environment.

1. (Optional) If your server has available disk space that has not been converted into a volume yet, you can configure new volumes now. If all the available disk space has already been taken up by volumes, skip to Step 2. If you are prompted to create new volumes, but you do not want to create new volumes now, click Next and skip to Step 2. If you do want to create new volumes, complete the following steps:

   a. Click the Free Space in the list of volumes, and then click Create.

   b. Enter a volume name.

   c. Select whether you want the volume to be a Traditional volume or an NSS volume. (See Chapter 8 for more information about the difference.)

   d. Enter the size of the volume in the Space to Use field, then click Apply to Volume.

   e. Click OK to return to the list of volumes, and then click Next to continue.

2. Specify whether you want to mount volumes now or when the server reboots after the installation is complete. If you want to install some Novell products during this installation procedure to volumes other than SYS, choose to mount the volumes now. Otherwise, if you intend only to install products into SYS, you can choose to mount the volumes later.

3. When the Protocols screen appears, click the server in the diagram to display the network boards installed in it. Because previous versions of NetWare used the IPX protocol, this server already has IPX installed. You cannot remove IPX during an upgrade. However, you can add IP to the server, or you can specify that you want to retain only IPX.

4. Click a network board, and choose the protocol you want to use for that board. You can click IP to add it, or you can leave only IPX checked. If you choose IP, you must also specify the server's IP address and subnet mask. You can also specify a router address if you need to (or leave that field blank to allow the network to find the nearest router automatically).

5. If you are upgrading from NetWare 3.1x, select the time zone in which this server will exist. (NetWare 4.1x servers already have this information stored.) If your location uses Daylight Saving Time, make sure the box is checked to allow for that adjustment.

6. Choose whether you want to create a new NDS tree or install this server into an existing NDS tree. Then click Next.

7. If you are upgrading a NetWare 4.1x server that already has NDS installed, enter the Admin user's name and password. Then skip to Step 9.

8. If you are upgrading a server that does not have NDS already installed (such as a bindery-based NetWare 3.1x server), you have to set up NDS information now.

   a. If you are upgrading this server into an existing tree, enter the tree name. If you are upgrading this server and creating a new tree, enter a name for the new tree.

   b. Create a context for the server. By entering the name of the organization (such as your company) and the names of descending levels of Organizational Units (such as a division and a department), you actually create the branch of the NDS tree that will contain this server if the branch doesn't already exist. If a branch already exists, click the Browse button and select the Organizational Unit objects you want. See Chapter 4 for more information about NDS tree structures.

   c. Enter a name, context, and password for the Admin user. If this is the first server in the tree, enter any password you want. If this server is being installed into an existing tree, type in the Admin name and password that has already been assigned, or enter the name and password of another User object already in the NDS tree. This User object must have enough NDS trustee rights to add the server to the context specified. See Chapter 6 for more information about NDS trustee rights.

9. At the summary screen that appears, review the information that indicates the name you gave your Directory tree (the same name as the organization), the *Directory Context* (or location in the tree) where your server has been installed, and the Administrator user's full name. Record the Admin's name and context for future reference. Then click Next to continue.

10. When prompted, insert the license diskette and specify the location of the license file (usually A:\LICENSE\). Then click Next to continue.

11. After the remaining files are copied to the server, the Additional Products and Services screen appears. Choose any additional products you want to install, such as NDPS, NDS Catalog Services, or Novell PKI Services. It is strongly recommended that you choose NDPS, as well as any others that are checked by default. You can click each service to see a description of that service at the bottom of the screen. When finished selecting the products you want, click Next to continue.

12. Depending on the products you selected, you may receive additional screens to specify information for those products. Follow the prompts on the screen.

13. When the Summary screen appears, review the list of products to be installed. At this point, you can either click Finish to complete the installation, or you can customize the properties of some of the products you've selected, as explained in the following step. To finish the installation, skip to Step 15. To customize products you've selected, continue with Step 14.

14. To customize any of the choices you've made, click the Customize button. (See Figure 2.15.) Then select the product, click the Properties button, then open any configuration tabs and specify the information you want to change. When finished, click OK to return to the Product Customization screen. When you've finished customizing products, click Close from the Product Customization screen.

F I G U R E 2.15   *Selecting a component to customize*

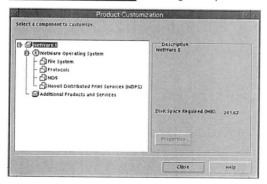

NOTE

For more information on how to customize products, see *Novell's NetWare 5 Administrator's Handbook.*

15. From the Summary screen, click Finish. The installation program will finish installing all the products you've selected.

16. When asked if you want to reboot the server, click Yes. (You can also choose to view the README file before rebooting the server.) Remove the installation CD before you reboot the server.

17. (NetWare 3.1x upgrades only) If you have upgraded a NetWare 3.1x server, you should run DSREPAIR.NLM on the server to verify the integrity of all new NDS information. After the server reboots and brings up the graphical server desktop, press Alt+Esc to go to the server's text-based screen and its prompt. At the prompt, type **DSREPAIR**. Then select Unattended Full Repair.

When the computer reboots, it will automatically load the server. When the server is running, you will see the server desktop — a graphical screen that can display utilities. To bring up the ConsoleOne utility, click the Novell button at the bottom of the screen and select ConsoleOne. To toggle the screen to a text-based server screen (the more familiar server prompt for users who have worked with previous versions of NetWare), press Alt+Esc.

NOTE

If you specified during the installation program that you did not want the SERVER.EXE file executed from within AUTOEXEC.BAT, the server will not automatically load when the computer is rebooted. You will have to load the server manually from DOS. To do this, type **CD NWSERVER** to change to the correct directory, and then type **SERVER**.

The server upgrade is now complete. If you want to store Macintosh or UNIX files on your server, however, you must complete one additional task, as described in the following section. If you do not need to add support for Macintosh or UNIX files to your server, skip to the section "After the Installation — Managing Your Server" later in this chapter.

Adding the Macintosh and UNIX Name Spaces

If you want the server to be able to store Mac OS files or UNIX files on your server, you must load the appropriate name space on the server. Then you must add the name space to one or more volumes. (Support for the longer file-

names that Windows 95, Windows 98, Windows NT, and OS/2 need to operate are loaded by default every time volumes are created.) Complete the following steps to load name spaces on your server:

1. To allow the server to store non-DOS files, enter the following
   command at the server console. Replace *name* with MAC for Mac OS
   files, or NFS for UNIX files:

   LOAD name

   For example, to make the server support Mac OS files, type the
   following:

   LOAD MAC

2. Then specify a particular volume that will store these files by using
   the ADD NAME SPACE command. Type this command in the
   following format (replace *name* with MAC, or NFS, and replace
   volumename with the name of the volume, such as SYS or VOL1):

   ADD NAME SPACE name TO volumename

   For example, to add the MAC name space to volume SYS, type the
   following:

   ADD NAME SPACE MAC TO SYS

The server can now support the file formats and naming conventions for
the operating system you've specified. The following section shows what you
can do with the server now that it has been installed.

After the Installation — Managing the Server

The NetWare 5 server's primary function is to run the network. A variety of
utilities exist on the server to help you see how well it's doing its job. You can
also use these utilities to change how the server is working.

The following sections discuss:

▶ The types of utilities that run on the server itself

▶ How to access and control the server from your workstation

▶ How to bring down and reboot the server

▶ The error log files you may want to read periodically

Console Utilities and NLMs

There are two primary types of utilities (helpful programs or tools) that run on the NetWare 5 server: console utilities and NetWare Loadable Modules.

Console utilities are commands you type at the server's console (keyboard and monitor) to change some aspect of the server or view information about it. These console utilities are built into the operating system, just as internal DOS commands are built into DOS. To read online help for console utilities, type the following command at the server's keyboard:

HELP

NetWare Loadable Modules (NLMs) are software modules that you load into the server's operating system to add or change functionality. Many NLMs are automatically installed with the NetWare 5 operating system. Others are optional; you can load them if your particular situation requires them.

You can use four different types of NetWare Loadable Modules to add different types of functionality to your server:

▸ NLMs

▸ Name space modules

▸ LAN drivers

▸ Storage drivers

These NLMs are described in Table 2.2. Many third-party software manufacturers create different types of NLMs to work on NetWare 5.

TABLE 2.2   *Different Types of NLMs*

TYPE OF NLM	FILENAME EXTENSION	DESCRIPTION
NLM	.NLM	Changes or adds to the server's functionality. Such an NLM might allow you to back up network files, add support for another protocol, or add support for devices such as a CD-ROM drive or a UPS (uninterruptible power supply).
Name space module	.NAM	Allows the operating system to store Macintosh, OS/2, Windows NT, Windows 95/98, or NFS files, along with their long file names and other characteristics.

TYPE OF NLM	FILENAME EXTENSION	DESCRIPTION
LAN driver	.LAN	Enables the operating system to communicate with a network board installed in the file server.
Storage driver	.CDM and .HAM	Enables the operating system to communicate with a storage device (such as a hard disk or CD-ROM drive) and its controller board (also called host adapter) installed in the server. The .CDM driver (custom device module) drives the storage device. Its accompanying .HAM driver (host adapter module) drives the storage device's adapter. You need both drivers for a single storage device. The .CDM and .HAM drivers replace the older .DSK drivers used in previous versions of NetWare.

You can load and unload NLMs while the server is running.

Many NLMs have their own status screen that displays on the server. Because several NLMs may be running on the server simultaneously, several different screens may be active on the server (similar to having multiple windows open on a Windows workstation). There are two ways to move between active NLM screens on the server's console:

▸ Use Alt+Esc to cycle through the available NLM screens.

▸ Use Ctrl+Esc to bring up a list of available screens, from which you can select one.

To work with NLMs, you can use commands from the server console. These commands are shown in Table 2.3. (The server console may be either the physical console or the Remote Console, as explained in the next section.)

TABLE 2.3	NLM Commands
COMMAND	**DESCRIPTION**
LOAD *nlmname*	Loads the NLM. You do not need to type the NLM's filename extension. In most cases, if an NLM requires that other NLMs also be loaded, it will automatically load them.
UNLOAD *nlmname*	Unloads the NLM.
MODULES	Lists all the currently loaded NLMs. If you want to see the version number of a single NLM (such as DS.NLM, for example), you can add the NLM's name at the end of the command, as in MODULES DS.

NetWare 5 does not require the LOAD command before the NLM name. It is now optional, especially for those who always type in LOAD. Novell changed it just for you.

NOTE

Using Remote Console to Control the Server from a Workstation

To control the server from a workstation, you can temporarily transform your workstation into a "remote console." With the Remote Console feature running, you can enter console utilities and load NLMs, and the commands you execute will work just as if you were using the server's real keyboard and monitor. Using Remote Console allows you to access the server from any workstation on the network, which gives you greater freedom when administering your network.

NetWare 5 contains two different versions of Remote Console: a Java version and a DOS version. The Java version can run on any workstation or server that is running a Java engine, whereas the DOS version can run on DOS workstations, or in a DOS box on a Windows workstation. In NetWare 5, the Java-based version of Remote Console and the DOS-based Remote Console can perform most of the same tasks, with the following exceptions:

▸ The Java-based version cannot be used to transfer files to a server, whereas the DOS-based version can.

▸ The Java-based version cannot be used to remotely install or upgrade a server, whereas the DOS-based version can.

▸ The DOS-based version requires an IPX connection, and the Java-based version requires an IP connection (but can access IPX servers through a proxy server).

▸ Only the Java-based version can control one server from another server. The DOS-based version cannot run on a server, so you can't control one server from another's console using the DOS-based version.

The following sections describe how to use the DOS version Remote Console. For information on how to use the Java version, see *Novell's NetWare 5 Administrator's Handbook* or the Novell online documentation.

Running Remote Console over a Direct Connection

To run Remote Console on a workstation that is connected directly to the network, complete the following steps:

1. Load RSPX.NLM (which automatically loads REMOTE.NLM) on the server by typing the following command at the server's console:

```
RSPX
```

2. When you load RSPX.NLM, you are asked for a password. Enter any password you choose. (You will have to supply this same password when you use Remote Console from the workstation.)

3. From the workstation, make sure a search drive is mapped to SYS:PUBLIC to give the workstation access to the Remote Console files.

4. Launch the Remote Console software from the workstation by using one of the following methods:

▸ From the NetWare Administrator utility, open the Tools menu, and then choose Remote Console.

▸ From the Windows Start or Run option, locate and execute the RCONSOLE.EXE file in the SYS:PUBLIC folder.

▸ From the workstation's DOS prompt (or from a DOS box inside Windows), type:

```
RCONSOLE
```

5. From the Connection Type menu, choose LAN.

6. Select the server to which you want to connect.

7. Enter the Remote Console password you assigned when you loaded RSPX.NLM.

8. When the console prompt appears on the workstation's screen, you can begin your Remote Console work.

Running Remote Console over a Modem

You can run Remote Console on a workstation that connects to the server via a modem (called an *asynchronous* connection). To run Remote Console over a modem, complete the following steps:

1. Load REMOTE.NLM on the server by typing the following command at the server's console:

   REMOTE

2. When you load REMOTE.NLM, you are asked for a password. Enter any password you choose. (You will have to supply this same password when you use Remote Console from the workstation.)

3. Load RS232.NLM on the server by typing the following command:

   RS232

4. When prompted, enter the COM port and baud rate that the modem will use.

5. Load a communications port driver on the server. You may have a driver from the modem's manufacturer, or you can use the driver supplied with NetWare 5 (AIOCOMX.NLM). For example, to load AIOCOMX.NLM on the server, type:

   AIOCOMX

6. Create a directory on the workstation, and copy the following files from their network directories to the new workstation directory to give the workstation access to Remote Console files:

   - RCONSOLE.EXE (located in SYS:PUBLIC)
   - IBM_RUN.OVL (located in SYS:PUBLIC)
   - _RUN.OVL (located in SYS:PUBLIC)
   - IBM_AIO.OVL (located in SYS:PUBLIC)
   - TEXTUTIL.IDX (located in SYS:PUBLIC)
   - RCONSOLE.HEP (located in SYS:PUBLIC\NLS\ENGLISH)
   - RCONSOLE.MSG (located in SYS:PUBLIC\NLS\ENGLISH)
   - TEXTUTIL.HEP (located in SYS:PUBLIC\NLS\ENGLISH)
   - TEXTUTIL.MSG (located in SYS:PUBLIC\NLS\ENGLISH)

7. Launch the Remote Console software from the workstation using one of the following methods:

  ▸ From the NetWare Administrator utility, open the Tools menu, and then choose Remote Console.

  ▸ From the Windows Start or Run option, locate and execute the RCONSOLE.EXE file in the SYS:PUBLIC folder.

  ▸ From the workstation's DOS prompt (or from a DOS box inside Windows), type:

    RCONSOLE

8. From the Connection Type menu, choose Asynchronous.

9. (Optional) If this is the first time you have run Remote Console from this workstation, choose Configuration. Enter the information about your modem. You also must enter a user ID (which can be any identifier you want to use, such as a name or phone number) and the Callback number (the modem's telephone number from which you are calling). When finished entering information, press Esc to exit the window, and answer Yes to save your data.

10. From the Asynchronous Options menu, choose Connect to Remote Location.

11. Select the server to which you want to connect and enter the remote console password you assigned when you loaded REMOTE.NLM.

12. When the console prompt appears on the workstation's screen, you can begin your Remote Console work.

Using Remote Console

When you are running a Remote Console on your workstation, you can use the keystrokes shown in Table 2.4 to navigate through the Remote Console screen.

Bringing Down and Rebooting the Server

If you need to shut down or reboot the server, try to make sure users have been notified and have been given time to close any files on that server that they were using. Then, shut down the server by typing:

    DOWN

T A B L E 2.4	Remote Console Keystrokes
KEYSTROKE	**DESCRIPTION**
F1	Displays help
Alt+F1	Displays the Available Options menu
Alt+F2	Quits the Remote Console session
Alt+F3	Moves you forward through the current server screens
Alt+F4	Moves you backward through the current server screens
Alt+F5	Shows this workstation's address

This will stop the NetWare server operating system from running on this computer, and will return the computer to DOS. From the DOS prompt, you can turn off the computer, reboot it, or restart the server.

If you want, you can reboot the server without first bringing the computer back to DOS. To simply reboot the server, instead of typing DOWN, type the following command at the server's prompt:

```
RESTART SERVER
```

To start the server from the DOS prompt, go to the NWSERVER directory and type the following command:

```
SERVER
```

Typing SERVER executes SERVER.EXE, which loads the NetWare operating system on the computer, turning it back into a server.

By default, the following commands are added to the computer's AUTOEXEC.BAT file during server installation so the server automatically starts up whenever the computer is rebooted:

```
CD NWSERVER
```

```
SERVER
```

If you do not want the server to automatically start when the computer is rebooted, you can edit the AUTOEXEC.BAT file to remove these commands. Then you will have to execute these commands manually to restart the server.

Modifying Server Startup Activities

When you start up or reboot the NetWare 5 server, several startup files work in sequence to start and configure the server. These boot files execute in the following order:

1. The DOS system files load, and then run AUTOEXEC.BAT. This boot file sets up a basic environment and can be set to execute SERVER.EXE automatically.

2. SERVER.EXE is the actual NetWare 5 operating system. When this file executes, the computer is turned into the server.

3. STARTUP.NCF automates the initialization of the NetWare 5 operating system. It loads disk drivers, loads name space modules to support different file formats, and executes some additional parameters that modify default initialization values. This file is created during the server installation, and contains commands that reflect the choices you made during the installation.

4. AUTOEXEC.NCF loads the server's LAN drivers, specifies the server name and server ID number, mounts volumes, loads any NLMs you want loaded automatically (such as MONITOR), and executes additional server parameters. This file is also created during the server installation, and contains commands that reflect the choices you made during the installation.

5. Additional .NCF files, if they've been created, can be called from the AUTOEXEC.NCF file or executed from the server's console. Optional products you install on the server may create these additional files, and they contain configuration information to make the server work better with the product that is installed on it.

You can edit the STARTUP.NCF and AUTOEXEC.NCF files after installation to add new commands or modify existing ones if you'd like. If you install other products on the server, those products' installation programs may edit these files automatically to add necessary commands. You can also edit these files manually, if you need to (however, it is seldom necessary to do this).

To edit either .NCF file, you can use EDIT.NLM, which is a simple text editor that runs on the server. To use EDIT.NLM, type the following command:

```
EDIT
```

Then, specify the file you want to edit. When the file opens, edit it like you would any other text file. Save it when you're finished, and then exit EDIT.

Monitoring the Server's Activities

MONITOR.NLM is a useful management utility for seeing how the server is performing. When you load MONITOR on the server, you can see a tremendous amount of information about the server, including its disk information, processor utilization, memory utilization, file activity, workstation connections, and the like. Figure 2.16 shows Monitor's main menu.

► . . . . ◄

F I G U R E 2.1 6 *Main menu of MONITOR.NLM*

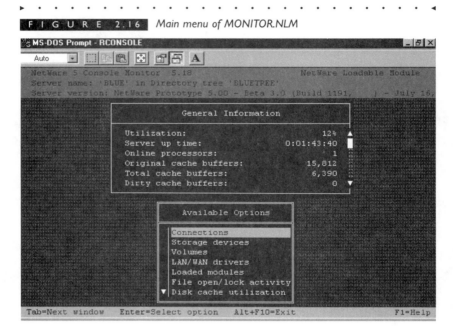

For the most part, the information that MONITOR displays is highly technical and useful primarily to advanced network administrators who know how to interpret the information and "tweak" it to optimize the server's performance.

If you'd like to learn more about all the information displayed in MONITOR, see the Novell documentation.

Monitoring the Error Log Files

You can monitor several different error log files to see if your network generated any error messages. You should make a practice of reviewing these files on a regular basis to ensure that nothing out of the ordinary is happening to your network.

- SYS$LOG.ERR logs error messages for the server. It is stored in the server's SYS:SYSTEM directory. All of the messages or errors that appear on the server's console are stored in this file.

- VOL$LOG.ERR logs error messages for a volume. Each volume has its own log file, which is stored at the root of the volume. Any errors or messages that pertain to the volume are stored in this file.

- ABEND.LOG tracks any abends that may have happened on the server. (An *abend*, short for "abnormal end," is a serious error that stops the server from operating.) NetWare 5 has a new feature that allows the server to shut it down and restart automatically after most abends, so you may not be aware that the server has abended unless you view this file. This file is created on the server's boot partition but gets copied to SYS:SYSTEM when the server restarts.

- TTS$LOG.ERR logs all data that is backed out by the NetWare Transaction Tracking System (TTS). This file is stored in the SYS volume. To allow this file to be created, use MONITOR.NLM to turn the TTS Abort Dump Flag parameter to On.

- BOOT$LOG.ERR logs all the errors that occur during server startup. This file is stored in the SYS:SYSTEM directory. To view any of these error log files, you can either use a text editor from a workstation, or you can use EDIT.NLM from the server. To use EDIT.NLM, enter the command:

  EDIT

- Then, specify the path and name of the desired log file.

Beyond the Basics

This chapter has described the simplest ways to install and upgrade your server. It also explained the basics of how to use the server's console commands and NLMs.

The following topics are addressed later in this book:

- For information on NDS, see Chapter 4.

- For instructions on installing workstations, see Chapter 3.

- For information on setting up printing services, see Chapter 8.

The default NetWare 5 installation options are adequate for many network setups, and network administrators rarely need much more information than what's included in this book. However, once you're comfortable with the NetWare 5 server basics, you may want to learn more about the advanced features of NetWare 5 servers. There is plenty to learn, because NetWare 5 is an incredibly powerful product — and in software lingo, "powerful" often goes hand-in-hand with "complex."

You can find more information about the following topics in Novell's online documentation (which came with your NetWare 5 package) and in *Novell's NetWare 5 Administrator's Handbook* (from Novell Press):

▸ Migrating previous NetWare data from an old server machine to a new one

▸ Understanding Ethernet frame types

▸ Managing the NetWare 5 server once it's installed

▸ Setting up the Java-based Remote Console and running Java applications on the server

TIP

Another useful resource for server management information is the *Novell AppNotes.* This is a monthly publication put out by the Novell Research Department, and each issue contains research reports and articles on a wide range of advanced topics. To order a subscription, call 800-377-4136 in the U.S. or 303-297-2725 worldwide.

CHAPTER 3

Installing Workstations

Workstations are the computers that a company's employees use for their daily work — writing memos, creating spreadsheets, sending e-mail, and other normal computer-related activities. After you've installed a server, the next logical step is to install the workstations.

To users, working on a network workstation doesn't appear much different than using the computer by itself (often called a *standalone computer*). This is because NetWare 5 takes care of the workstation's communications with the rest of the network without affecting how the computer's own operating system (such as Windows 95/98 or Windows NT) functions. Therefore, users can work with files — they can open files, run applications, and save files — in the same way they would if the computer weren't attached to a network. What makes a network workstation different from a standalone computer is the fact that users can access files, applications, printers, and other resources stored on the network, in addition to the files stored on the computer's own disks. Workstation users can also share those applications, files, and printers with other users throughout the network.

Workstations on a NetWare 5 network can be running any of the following operating systems:

- Windows 95/98
- Windows NT
- Windows 3.1*x*
- DOS

You don't need to have all workstations running the same operating system, either. You can have Windows 95/98, Windows 3.1, and Windows NT workstations all running on the same network, all accessing the same printers, files, and so on.

To make a workstation function on a NetWare 5 network, you have to install a special set of NetWare 5 workstation software. This software, called the NetWare 5 *client software*, allows the workstation to communicate with the rest of the network. (On a NetWare 5 network, workstations are often called *clients* because they request services from the network.)

Each type of workstation operating system requires a particular type of NetWare 5 client software. (For example, a Windows 95/98 workstation uses a different set of client software than a Windows NT workstation.) This chapter explains how to obtain the latest version of client software. It also explains how to install NetWare 5 client software on the following (most common) types of workstations:

- ▸ Windows 95 (and 98) and Windows NT
- ▸ Windows 3.1*x* and DOS

Getting the Latest Client Software

Most of the different types of client software are included on the NetWare 5 CD-ROM that you purchased. However, Novell updates client software on a fairly regular basis (every few months or so). Therefore, the client software on your CD is older software, and newer versions of the client software exist on the World Wide Web.

If at all possible, you should try to use the updated client software from the Web. Generally, each new update of the client software includes both bug fixes and new features that make it easier to use, more efficient, or easier to install. In addition, new LAN drivers for newly created network boards may also be included.

To obtain the newest versions of client software, visit Novell's Web site at www.novell.com. Periodically, Novell changes the organization of material on its Web site, but downloadable client files are usually located in the technical support section of the Web site.

When you locate the area of the Web site that contains the downloadable client files, select the link to the platform you want (such as Windows 95/98, Windows NT, Windows 3.1*x*, or DOS). Follow the instructions on the screen for downloading your desired client files.

NOTE

When downloading files, be sure you select the option to download a single ZIP file (a compressed file that contains all of the client software), rather than downloading the files individually. It is much faster to download a single ZIP file. A single client ZIP file can be very large — up to 39MB or 40MB. It will unzip and extract hundreds of files, taking much more than 60MB to 75MB of disk space. If you are asked whether you want to open the file or save it to a disk, it's faster to save it to your hard disk (or other storage device that has plenty of disk space available) and then unzip the file on that disk.

You can unzip files by using commonly found ZIP programs such as those produced by PKWare. There are shareware versions of ZIP programs that you can download for free, as well as full-featured versions that you can purchase. For more information about ZIP programs, search the Web for zip programs, or see PKWare's Web site at www.pkware.com.

Once you've downloaded (and unzipped) the client files, you will see a set of executable files. Double-click each of these files to execute them. This will cause each of the files to decompress and extract dozens of additional files. When all those files are extracted, you're ready to run the NetWare 5 client installation program.

Installing NetWare 5 Client Software

The installation program for the NetWare 5 client software changes slightly with a new graphical user interface (GUI) for each new update of the software. In addition, the screens that appear during the installation program will vary from workstation to workstation, depending on the workstation's particular hardware setup, the operating system, any pre-existing client software already installed on it, and other such conditions.

The fundamental steps of the client installation are fairly consistent from version to version, however, and the typical installation is simple regardless of the version. The following instructions describe the basic flow of the installation program, along with explanations of the screens you will most likely see. Don't panic if your installation process doesn't show all of the same types of information described here. When asked to choose from multiple options, the default option is usually recommended, and you'll usually be safe selecting the default.

NOTE

Remember that you can use the Help button or online documentation to get help at any time during the client installation program.

You can choose one of the following three methods to install the NetWare 5 client on your workstation:

- ► You can download the latest client software from Novell's Web site. This is the recommended method because it ensures that you get the latest version with the most recent updates. You can download the files directly into a folder on the workstation, and run the installation program from there. You can also download the files onto one workstation, run a special program to make a set of installation diskettes, and then run the installation program from those diskettes. This is useful if you have several computers, not all of which are connected to the Internet.

► You can install the client directly from the *NetWare 5 Z.E.N.works* CD-ROM, if the workstation has a CD-ROM drive. This version of the NetWare 5 client software could be older than that available on the Web.

► If you are upgrading an existing NetWare workstation to a newer version of the NetWare 5 client, you can install the client from the CD-ROM or from a network directory on the server. To use the network directory method, you must put the client installation files into a directory on the server. If you've downloaded the updated client files from the Internet, copy those files to a network directory on the server. If you're using the client files from the CD-ROM, copy the DOSWIN32, WIN95, and WINNT directories from the *NetWare 5 Z.E.N.works* CD-ROM under the SYS:\PUBLIC\CLIENT directory.

NOTE

The NetWare 5 client installation program automatically copies all necessary NetWare 5 files to the workstation. It also edits any DOS, Windows 3.1*x*, or Windows 95/98 files that require modifications.

If you're installing the client software that came in your NetWare 5 Z.E.N.works CD-ROM package, the client software is called *NetWare Client for Windows 95/98* (or Windows NT, depending on the flavor you're using).

Windows 95/98 and Windows NT Workstations

This section explains how to install the Novell client software from a Windows 95/98 or Windows NT workstation. Before you can install the client, though, your workstation must meet certain requirements:

► To install the client software on a Windows 95 workstation, the computer should have at least 16MB of disk space available on drive C. It must also be running the Windows 95 Service Pack 1 or better. (You can download Microsoft's Service Pack 1 from Microsoft's Web site, at www.microsoft.com.) Windows 98 workstations should meet all the requirements for running Windows 98.

▶ To install the Novell client software on a Windows NT workstation, the computer should meet all the requirements for running Windows NT. In addition, it should be running Windows NT version 4.0, with Service Pack 3 or later installed on it. Again, see Microsoft's Web site for more information about downloading their service packs.

▶ For either platform, you will also need a CD-ROM drive if you're installing the client directly from the CD-ROM, or a connection to the Internet if you're downloading the client. If you're upgrading an existing workstation that already has a connection to the network, you can run the installation program from a network directory instead.

The Novell client software for both Windows 95/98 and Windows NT will work on IP, IPX, or mixed networks. You specify the protocol you want to use during the client installation. (See Chapter 1 for more information on protocols.)

If all these requirements are met, then you're ready to install the client software. To install the Novell client software on a workstation that is running Windows 95/98 or Windows NT, complete the following steps:

NOTE

You can use the following procedure whether you're installing a network workstation or upgrading an existing one. If you are upgrading an existing workstation, the installation program will detect existing settings (such as the protocol used, the network board, and optional features) and use those same settings as the default settings for the upgraded workstation.

1. Install a network board in the workstation according to the manufacturer's documentation. Record the board's configuration settings, such as its interrupt and port address.

2. Cable the network board to the network using the correct cabling hardware, including terminators, hubs, or any other hardware required by your topology. See Chapter 1 and your hardware manufacturer's documentation for more information about limitations and guidelines for installing network hardware.

3. (Optional, if not installing from the network) If you are planning to upgrade a workstation and want to run the installation program from the network, create a directory called CLIENT under SYS:PUBLIC, and then create a directory called WIN95 (or WINNT) under CLIENT. Then, copy all the files from the PRODUCTS\WIN95\

IBM_ENU (or PRODUCTS\WINNT) folder on the CD-ROM to your newly created network directory. Also, copy the WINSETUP.EXE file from the root of the CD-ROM to the new installation directory. (The IBM_ENU folder contains the English version of the client files. If you need another language, use the corresponding IBM_*language* folder.)

4. Run WINSETUP.EXE.

- If you're installing from the CD-ROM, insert the Client CD-ROM in the workstation's drive. WINSETUP.EXE, which is located at the root of the CD-ROM, will start automatically.

- If you're upgrading an existing workstation and are running the installation program from the network, run WINSETUP.EXE from the SYS:PUBLIC\CLIENT\WIN95 (or WINNT) directory.

5. Click the language you want to use.

6. Click Windows 95/98 Client (or Windows NT Client); these choices are shown in Figure 3.1.

7. Click Install Novell Client (see Figure 3.2).

FIGURE 3.1 *Selecting a Client installation*

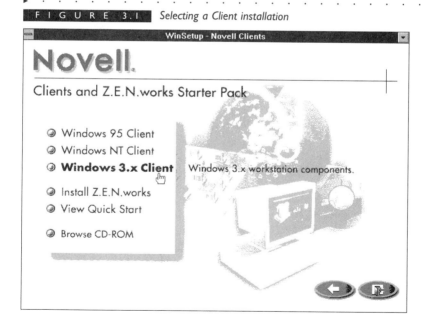

FIGURE 3.2 *Selecting Install Novell Client*

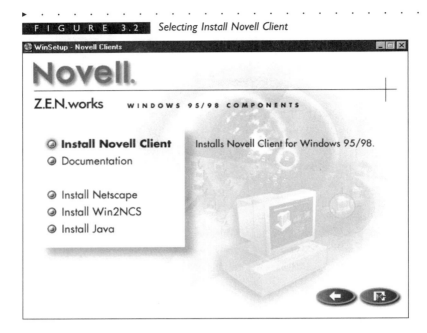

 NOTE

If the "Install Novell Client" line is grayed out, then you have chosen the wrong client (for example, a Windows NT Client selected on a Windows 98 OS computer).

8. After you've read the license agreement, choose Yes to accept it.

9. A screen entitled "Welcome to the Novell Client for Windows 95/98 Install" appears (see Figure 3.3). Choose Custom, and then click Next.

10. Choose the protocol you want this workstation to use (see Figure 3.4).

   • *IP Only* — Installs only the IP protocol. The workstation will be able to communicate only with IP servers, and will not be able to communicate with IPX servers.

   • *IP with IPX Compatibility Mode* — Installs the IP protocol, but allows the workstation to communicate with IPX networks if the servers have IPX Compatibility Mode and a Migration Agent installed.

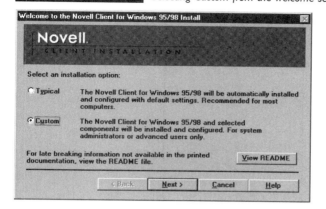

FIGURE 3.3 *Selecting Custom from the welcome screen.*

- *IP and IPX* — Installs both protocols, allowing the workstation to communicate with either type of server.
- *IPX* — Installs only the IPX protocol, allowing the workstation to communicate with IPX servers, but not directly with IP servers.

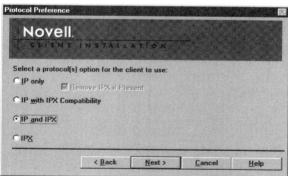

FIGURE 3.4 *Selecting the protocol this workstation will use*

11. Choose whether you want to log in to NDS or to a bindery, and then click Next (see Figure 3.5). (Only select the bindery option if you need to log in to a NetWare 3.x server.)

FIGURE 3.5 *Establishing an NDS connection*

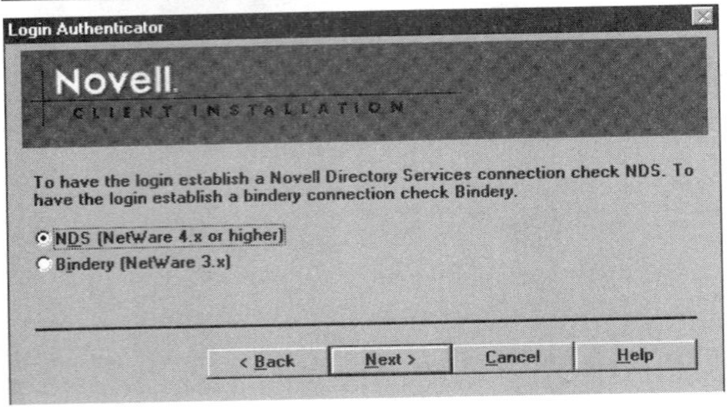

Login Authenticator

Novell.
C L I E N T   I N S T A L L A T I O N

To have the login establish a Novell Directory Services connection check NDS. To have the login establish a bindery connection check Bindery.

● NDS (NetWare 4.x or higher)
○ Bindery (NetWare 3.x)

| < Back | Next > | Cancel | Help |

12. Select any optional components you also want to install. (If the installation program detects that any of these options are already installed on this workstation, those options will be checked, as shown in Figure 3.6.) At minimum, you will probably want to select the Novell Distributed Print Services (NDPS) option. (See Chapter 8 for more information about NDPS.)

FIGURE 3.6 *Selecting optional components to install*

Novell Client for Windows 95/98 Custom Options

Novell.
C L I E N T   I N S T A L L A T I O N

In addition to the Novell Client, select any optional components to install:

☑ Novell Workstation Manager
☑ Novell Distributed Print Services
☐ Novell NetWare/IP Protocol
☐ Novell SNMP Agent
☐ Host Resources MIB for the Novell I
☐ Network Management Responder fo
☐ Novell Target Service Agent for Wir
☐ Novell Remote Access Dialer
☑ Novell NDS Provider - ADSI

Description
Novell Workstation Manager allows all user account and desktop information to be centrally managed within NDS using a single administrative utility.

Configure

Reset Components

| < Back | Install > | Cancel | Help |

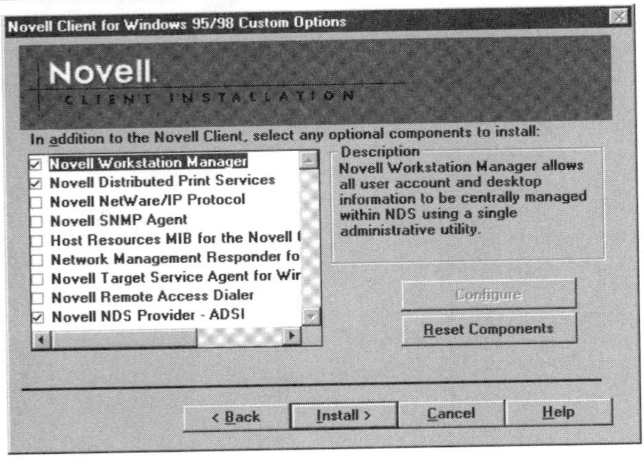

13. Click Install.

14. The client installation program can automatically detect and load many LAN drivers for common network boards (which the program calls network adapters). If it cannot detect your network board, it will prompt you to select one. You will need to insert a diskette (or specify another location) for the LAN driver your network board requires.

15. If you are prompted to set a Preferred Tree and Name Context, enter the name of your tree, your name context, and the first network drive. This will make it easier for you to log in later — you won't have to specify this information every time. You do not need to specify a preferred server unless you want to log in to a NetWare 3.*x* server. When you've finished entering this information, click Finish.

16. You will be asked if you want to reboot after the installation completes. Choose Reboot to restart the workstation so the Novell CLIENT files can take effect (see Figure 3.7).

F I G U R E 3 . 7 *Selecting Reboot to enable Novell Client files to take effect*

When the workstation reboots, it will automatically connect to the network and present you with a Login screen. See the section "Connecting to the Network and Logging In" later in this chapter for more information on logging in to the network.

Windows 3.1x and DOS Workstations

The following sections explain how to install the client software on a Windows 3.1x or DOS workstation. Both the Novell client installation program for DOS (INSTALL.EXE) and for Windows 3.1x (WINSETUP.EXE) accomplish the same tasks during installation. You can choose whichever version you prefer. Before you can install the client, however, make sure your workstation meets the following requirements:

- The workstation computer should have a 386 or better processor, and at least 8MB of RAM. It should also have at least 16MB of disk space available on drive C.

- The workstation should be running a memory manager, such as HIMEM.SYS, EMM386.EXE, QEMM, or 386MAX.

- You will also need a CD-ROM drive if you're installing the client directly from the CD-ROM, or a connection to the Internet if you're downloading the client. If you're upgrading an existing workstation that already has a connection to the network, you can run the installation program from a network directory instead.

The following instructions guide you through the installation steps for each platform.

Installing the Client Software from Windows 3.1x

To install the Novell client software from Windows 3.1x, complete the following steps:

1. Install a network board in the workstation according to the manufacturer's documentation. Record the board's configuration settings, such as its interrupt and port address.

2. Cable the network board to the network using the correct cabling hardware, including terminators, hubs, or any other hardware required by your topology. See Chapter 1 and your hardware manufacturer's documentation for more information about limitations and guidelines for installing network hardware.

3. (Optional) If you are planning to upgrade a workstation and want to run the installation program from the network, create a directory called CLIENT under SYS:PUBLIC, and then create a directory called DOSWIN32 under CLIENT. Then, copy all the files from the PRODUCTS\DOSWIN32 folder on the CD-ROM to your newly created network directory. Also, copy the WINSETUP.EXE file from the root of the CD-ROM to the new installation directory.

4. Run WINSETUP.EXE.

- If you're installing from the CD-ROM, insert the Client CD-ROM in the workstation's drive. WINSETUP.EXE, which is located at the root of the CD-ROM, will start automatically.

- If you're upgrading an existing workstation and are running the installation program from the network, run WINSETUP.EXE from the SYS:PUBLIC\CLIENT\DOSWIN32 directory.

5. Click the language you want to use.

6. Click Windows 3.*x* Client.

7. Click Install Novell Client.

8. After you've read the license agreement, choose Yes to accept it.

9. Click Next to begin the installation.

10. Select any optional components you also want to install, and then click Next. (If the installation program detects that any of these options are already installed on this workstation, those options will be checked.) At minimum, you will probably want to select the Novell Distributed Print Services (NDPS) option. (See Chapter 8 for more information about NDPS.)

11. Choose the destination directory on the workstation, and then click Next. The default is C:\NOVELL\CLIENT32.

12. The install program displays the disk space required to install your selections. If this is acceptable, click Begin Copy.

13. Select the first network drive letter (a letter that is not already assigned to a local drive or a CD-ROM drive). Then click Next.

14. Choose a Program Group for the client software, and then click Next. The default program group is Novell Client.

15. Choose the manufacturer and model of your network board. Use the pull-down menus to select yours from the list. If yours isn't on the list, you will have to load your LAN driver from a diskette supplied by the manufacturer. (For more information on configuring a particular network board, contact the network board manufacturer.) Then click Next.

16. Choose the settings for your network board (also called a LAN adapter).

17. When asked, "Would you like to connect to network servers?" choose Yes. Then enter the name of your tree and your name context. This will make it easier for you to log in later—you won't have to specify this information every time. You do not need to specify a preferred server unless you want to log in to a NetWare 3.x server. Click Next.

18. (Optional) Select any additional protocol you want to use, such as TCP/IP. Click Next.

19. Remove any diskettes from the workstation's drives, keep the Restart Computer option marked, and click Finish. This will restart the workstation so the Novell Client files can take effect.

When the computer reboots, the Novell Login icon will appear in the Novell Client program group on your Windows desktop. See the section "Connecting to the Network and Logging In" later in this chapter for more information on logging in to the network.

Installing the Client Software from DOS

To install the Novell client software on a DOS computer, complete the following steps:

1. Install a network board in the workstation according to the manufacturer's documentation. Be sure to record the board's configuration settings, such as its interrupt and port address.

2. Cable the network board to the network using the correct cabling hardware, including terminators, hubs, or any other hardware required by your topology. See Chapter 1 and your hardware manufacturer's documentation for more information about limitations and guidelines for installing network hardware.

3. (Optional) If you are planning to upgrade a workstation and want to run the installation program from the network, create a directory called CLIENT under SYS:PUBLIC, and then create a directory called DOSWIN32 under CLIENT. Then copy all the files from the PRODUCTS\DOSWIN32 folder on the CD-ROM to your newly created network directory.

4. Run INSTALL.EXE.

- If you're installing from the CD-ROM, insert the Client CD-ROM in the workstation's drive. Then go to the PRODUCTS\DOSWIN32 directory on the CD-ROM, and type **INSTALL**.

- If you're upgrading an existing workstation and are running the installation program from the network, map a drive to the SYS:PUBLIC\CLIENT\DOSWIN32 directory, then type **INSTALL**.

5. After you've read the license agreement, press Enter to accept it.

6. Select the components you want to install and press F10. At minimum, select the Novell Client for DOS (see Figure 3.8). If this workstation will run Windows 3.1*x*, also select Novell Client Windows Support and the Novell Distributed Print Services option. Use the Spacebar to mark each option you want to install. Press F10 to save your selections and continue.

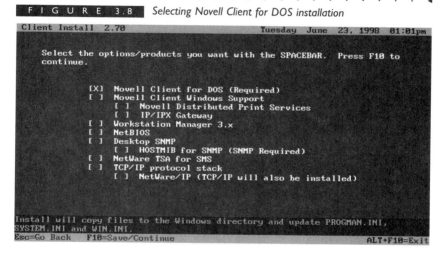

FIGURE 3.8 *Selecting Novell Client for DOS installation*

7. Specify if you want to use more country codes than the one currently installed on this machine (in most cases, answer No).

8. Network administrators are asked if they want to set the shared Windows path. (In most cases, answer No, unless you are an administrator who does want to set up a shared Windows path.) Then press F10 to continue.

9. Choose whether you want to install a 16-bit or 32-bit driver (see Figure 3.9). Select a 32-bit driver if one is available for your network board.

FIGURE 3.9
Selecting the LAN driver to install

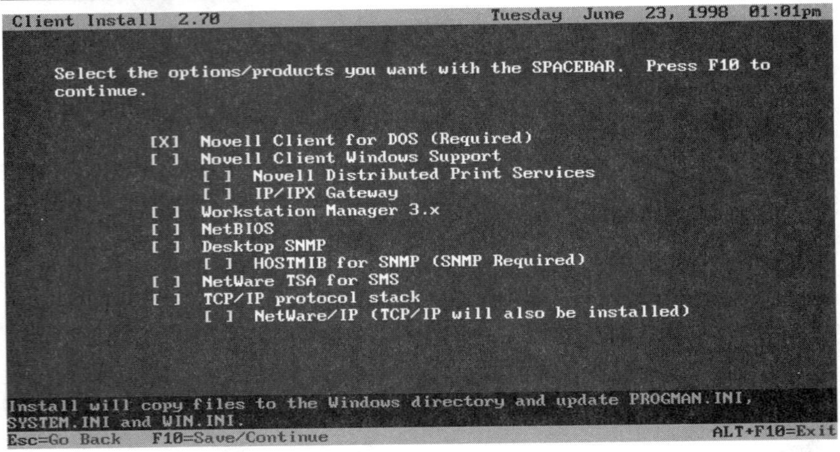

```
Client Install  2.70                    Tuesday  June  23, 1998  01:01pm

    Select the options/products you want with the SPACEBAR.  Press F10 to
    continue.

         [X]  Novell Client for DOS (Required)
         [ ]  Novell Client Windows Support
              [ ]  Novell Distributed Print Services
              [ ]  IP/IPX Gateway
         [ ]  Workstation Manager 3.x
         [ ]  NetBIOS
         [ ]  Desktop SNMP
              [ ]  HOSTMIB for SNMP (SNMP Required)
         [ ]  NetWare TSA for SMS
         [ ]  TCP/IP protocol stack
              [ ]  NetWare/IP (TCP/IP will also be installed)


Install will copy files to the Windows directory and update PROGMAN.INI,
SYSTEM.INI and WIN.INI.
Esc=Go Back   F10=Save/Continue                          ALT+F10=Exit
```

10. Allow the installation program to edit the AUTOEXEC.BAT and
    CONFIG.SYS files on the workstation.

11. Accept the default client directory (the location on the workstation
    where the client files should be installed) and the workstation's
    Windows directory.

12. Select your LAN driver. If the driver you need isn't on the CD-ROM,
    you will need to have it on a diskette. (Drivers are available from the
    network board's manufacturer.)

13. Press F10 to accept all the defaults (or your changes) and continue.
    Client files will now be installed on the workstation.

14. After the installation is complete, restart the computer to make the
    new client take effect.

After the workstation reboots, you can log in to the network. See the next
section, "Connecting to the Network and Logging In," for more information on
logging in to the network.

Connecting to the Network and Logging In

When the workstation reboots after you install the client software, it automatically connects to the network. Now you can log in to the network. How you log in depends on the type of workstation you're using. The following sections describe the different ways you can log in.

Logging In from Windows 95/98

When you reboot a Windows 95/98 workstation after installing the NetWare 5 client software, the Novell Login (or NetWare Login) screen appears. (Whether the name *NetWare* or *Novell* appears depends on the version of client software you installed.)

When the Login screen appears, as shown in Figure 3.10, enter your login name (your username) and password. By default, a screen will appear showing the results of the login request. The client software will authenticate you to the network. When the login is completed, you can close this screen. You're now logged in to the network. Your workstation is connected, and you are ready to work.

FIGURE 3.10 *The login screen (on a Windows 95/98 workstation)*

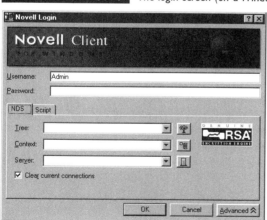

Windows 95/98 includes an icon on your desktop called Network Neighborhood. The NetWare 5 client software modifies the information this icon's program sees, so that Network Neighborhood can recognize the NetWare 5 tree and server.

Double-click the Network Neighborhood icon to see what your NetWare 5 network looks like from Windows 95/98. Figure 3.11 shows an example of a simple Network Neighborhood — you can see the BlueSky Directory tree and the server named Blue. You'll also see a file icon called BlueSky. This isn't really a file; it's the Organization object at the top of the Directory tree. Because Windows 95/98 doesn't recognize NDS objects, it displays the file icon by default.

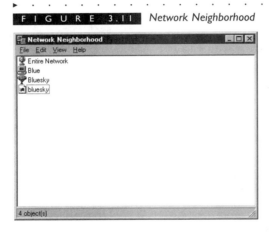

FIGURE 3.11 *Network Neighborhood*

If you double-click the server's icon (called Blue in this example), you will see the server's volumes. In this case, server Blue has a single volume called SYS. You can open the volume by double-clicking it and see the folders and files it contains, just as though you were opening folders on your own work-station (see Figure 3.12).

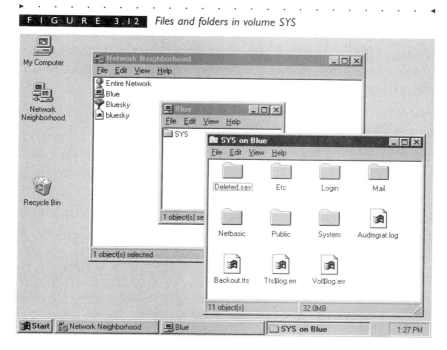

FIGURE 3.12 *Files and folders in volume SYS*

The client installation program for NetWare 5 places a red "N" in the System Tray, which is, by default, located on the right end of the Windows taskbar. You can log in to the network from the workstation by right-clicking the "N" icon and then clicking NetWare login.

You can also log in from the Network Neighborhood of Windows 95/98 by right-clicking the Network Neighborhood icon from the Windows desktop and then clicking NetWare Login.

By double-clicking the tree or server to which you want to log in, you can automatically start the NetWare login process. You can also right-click the desired tree or server and then select Authenticate or Login.

Logging In from Windows NT

When you reboot a Windows NT workstation after installing the NetWare 5 client software, the Novell Login (or NetWare Login) screen will appear after you start the WINLOGON process (using the Ctrl+Alt+Del keys).

When the Login screen appears, enter your login name and password. By default, a screen will appear showing the results of the login request. When the login is completed, you can close this screen. You're now logged in to the network.

Windows NT also uses the Network Neighborhood Icon on the desktop. It will perform the same functions as it did in Windows 95/98.

Logging In from Windows 3.1x

If you're using Windows 3.1, the NetWare 5 Login (or NetWare Login) icon will appear in the NetWare 5 Tools (or NetWare Tools) program group on your Windows desktop. (Whether the name NetWare or NetWare 5 appears depends on the version of client software you installed.)

To log in to the network, double-click the Login icon, and then enter your login name (your username) and password when prompted. The client software will authenticate you to the network. When it's finished, your workstation will be connected, and you will be logged in and ready to work.

NOTE   You can't use a login name unless it has already been defined on the server. If this is the first workstation installed on the network, the only username available so far will be Admin. Chapter 5 explains how to create additional users on the network.

You can set up the LOGIN program so it executes automatically whenever you start up the NetWare 5 client in Windows 3.1. This way, whenever you first load Windows, the Login screen will prompt you for your username and password.

To make the LOGIN program execute automatically, double-click the NetWare User Tools icon on your desktop. Then click the Hot Key button (the button that shows a picture of a key with flames). Click the Startup tab to open the Startup page, then mark the Launch on Startup button under the Windows Login heading. Under the Login tab, you can set whether the Login window, by default, logs you into a tree or into a server. When you're finished, close the User Tools.

Now, when you start Windows (which automatically launches the NetWare 5 client software) the Login screen appears. Enter your name and password, then click OK. To change the server or tree you want to log in to, click the Connection tab to open that page, and enter your desired tree or server.

Logging In from DOS

To log in from a DOS workstation, be sure you first have the F:\ prompt on your screen. Type **LOGIN**, and then enter your full login name (your username) and password when prompted. The client software will authenticate you to the network. When it's finished, your workstation will be connected, and you will be logged in and ready to work.

You can also add the Login command and your username to the AUTOEXEC.BAT file, so it will execute the Login command automatically for you whenever you reboot the workstation. For example, if your login name is SWalsh, enter the following command in the AUTOEXEC.BAT file:

```
LOGIN SWALSH
```

You will still have to enter your password each time the workstation reboots, however, for security reasons.

Beyond the Basics

In this chapter, you learned how to install workstations on the network. The following topics are addressed later in this book:

▶ For information on viewing and working with the objects in the Directory tree, see Chapter 4.

▶ For information on creating additional user accounts on the network, see Chapter 5.

▶ For information on working with network files and applications, see Chapter 7.

You can find more information about installation, configuration, and removal of the client software in Novell's online documentation (which came with your NetWare 5 package) and in *Novell's NetWare 5 Administrator's Handbook* (from Novell Press).

CHAPTER 4

Managing Novell Directory Services (NDS)

Novell *Directory Services* (NDS), in simplest terms, is a database of network information. It contains information that defines every object on the NetWare 5 network, such as users, groups, printers, print queues, servers, and volumes. For every NDS object, the NDS database describes the type of object it is, where it resides, what level of security the object can exercise, who can access it, and other similar types of information.

As discussed in Chapter 1, the NDS database is not confined to a single server. Instead, all the NetWare 5 servers in a network tree share a single, distributed database. This greatly simplifies your network management life. For example, with NDS, you only have to create a user or other object once in the network tree, and every server will automatically recognize that same user or object. You can allow a user to access different servers simply by granting him or her the appropriate rights to the necessary volumes on each server.

Chapter 1 also explained that NDS uses a hierarchical database structure. With this type of structure, you can group objects together under categories and subcategories. This makes it easier to locate specific objects. It also allows you to control objects as a group, such as when you're modifying the security levels of those objects.

The NDS database is often referred to as the Directory tree. Figure 4.1 is a simple illustration of a Directory tree, showing how the tree begins with a Root object at the top. Beneath the root, objects are divided into branches and subbranches that fan out beneath it.

FIGURE 4.1 *Directory tree*

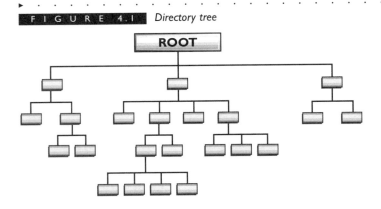

NDS Objects

For each type of network entity that will operate on the network, you will create an NDS object. This object may represent a real entity, such as a user, or it may represent a service, such as a print server.

Each NDS object contains several *properties*, which are the pieces of information that define the object. For example, a User object contains properties that define the user's full name, his or her ID number, an e-mail address, group memberships, and so on. (Properties are also called *attributes*.) Each type of object, such as a Server or Printer object, may have different properties than another type of object. Each type of object, such as User, Print Queue, or Server, is referred to as an *object class*.

Categories of Object Classes

Object classes fall into three basic categories, as follows:

- ▸ *Root object* — The Root object is unique and is situated at the very top of the Directory tree. All other objects in the tree are located beneath the Root object. When the first NetWare 5 server is installed in a company, the installation program creates a new Directory tree with the Root object at the top. Subsequent servers will be installed underneath the original Root object.

- ▸ *Container objects* — Container objects are, simply put, objects that contain other objects. For example, a container object called Sales could contain all the users who work in the Sales department, their workstations, and their printers.

- ▸ *Leaf objects* — These objects represent the individual entities on the network. Leaf objects, such as users, servers, and volumes, cannot contain other objects.

You can use these three types of object classes to place your NDS objects into a manageable organization. The Root object resides at the top of the tree. The container objects form branches and subbranches. The leaf objects are the individual users, printers, servers, and so on, that populate those branches.

Figure 4.2 shows how these three categories of object classes appear in the Directory tree.

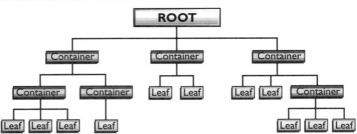

Root, container, and leaf objects in a Directory tree

The following are the most common container object classes available, though you will probably only use one or two of them:

► Country (seldom used in NDS trees)

► Locality (seldom used in NDS trees)

► Organization (always used in NDS trees)

► Organizational Unit (often used in NDS trees)

NOTE

Country and Locality objects are used primarily for compliance with X.500 naming specifications, but are seldom used in NDS trees. The X.500 specifications, which were created by organizations seeking standards for Directory Services, include a standardized form of naming restrictions for all Directory Services applications. (Some NetWare 5 utilities don't even recognize the Locality object. In most cases, Organization and Organizational Unit objects are all you will need to organize your NDS tree.)

You can have only one level of Country objects (if you use them at all), which fall immediately below the Root object. A Country object is often designated by the abbreviation "C," such as "C=US."

You can have only one level of Organization objects. This falls below the Country object if one is specified, or the Root object if no Country object is specified. You need at least one Organization object. During the server installation, you're asked to specify an Organization name for this mandatory object. Organization objects are assigned the abbreviation "O," as in "O=BlueSky."

Finally, you can have multiple levels of Organizational Unit objects, which fall below the Organization objects. Organizational Unit objects have the abbreviation "OU," as in "OU=Sales."

The Locality object, if used, can be located under any of the other container objects. It is assigned the abbreviation "L."

Unlike container objects, all leaf objects use the same abbreviation, regardless of the type of objects they may be. All leaf objects use the abbreviation "CN," which stands for "Common Name." This designation is required by the X.500 specifications. Therefore, all leaf objects, such as printers, users, servers, and print queues, use the abbreviation CN, as in "CN=ServerA" or "CN=Fred."

Figure 4.3 shows the simplest form of Directory tree you can have. It has only one level of Organization objects (it is mandatory to have at least one Organization object — the example shows two), and all leaf objects (which use the abbreviation "CN") reside immediately beneath it.

FIGURE 4.3 *Simplest Directory tree format*

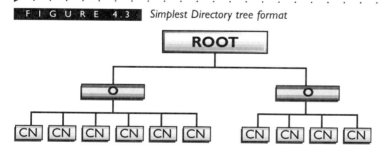

Figure 4.4 shows a tree that uses Organizational Unit objects to subdivide all the objects.

Common Directory tree format, using Organizational Unit objects

Figure 4.5 shows a less-common tree format, which includes Country objects and Locality objects. (Remember, some NetWare 5 utilities don't recognize Locality objects, so these are rarely used in NetWare 5 networks.)

Complex Directory tree format, using Country and Locality objects

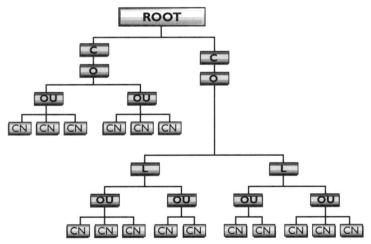

NDS Object Classes

In NetWare 5, many different types of object classes are available. Table 4.1 lists most of the object classes available in NetWare 5. The table also indicates which objects are commonly used in the average NetWare 5 network; some NDS objects exist for specific — but less common — needs, so it is likely that your network will not include many of these. These lesser-used NDS objects are generally aspects of some of the more advanced, specialized features of NetWare 5. See the Novell online documentation if you'd like to learn more about them.

TABLE 4.1	Object Classes Available in NetWare 5	
OBJECT CLASS	**COMMONLY USED**	**DESCRIPTION**
Address Range		This object defines a range of IP addresses used by DHCP. Used with Novell DNS/DHCP Services.
Administrator Group		This object represents a group of users who have access to DNS/DHCP Locator objects. These users can use the DNS/DHCP Administrator utility to create and manage DNS and DHCP objects. Used with Novell DNS/DHCP Services.
AFP Server		This object is an AppleTalk File Protocol (AFP) server that is a node on the network.
Alias		This object is a representation of another object that is really located in a different part of the Directory tree. Aliases let you place duplicate icons for an object in multiple locations in the tree. This enables users to get to the object from wherever they are in the tree. For example, if you want the Sales users to be able to access a printer in the Marketing office, you could put an Alias object for that printer in the Sales container, while the original printer object remains in the Marketing container.

Continued

T.A B L E 4.1	Object Classes Available in NetWare 5 (continued)	
OBJECT CLASS	**COMMONLY USED**	**DESCRIPTION**
Application	X	This object is a pointer to an application installed on the network. There are different variations of this object, depending on the type of application: DOS, Windows 3.x, Windows 95, and Windows NT. An Application object can be "associated" with users or groups. Then that application can easily be executed from each user's NetWare Application Launcher. (See Chapter 7 for more information on using Application objects.)
Application Folder		This object represents multiple Application objects. Application Folder objects are used with the Application Launcher in Z.E.N.works.
Audit File		This object manages an audit trail's configuration and access rights, and is used only if the auditing feature is used. (The auditing feature tracks various types of network usage, which can then be audited by an independent auditor, much like having your financial books audited. This feature is seldom used in ordinary situations.)
Bindery Object		This object represents an object that was upgraded from a bindery-based server, but that could not be converted into a corresponding NDS object.

OBJECT CLASS	COMMONLY USED	DESCRIPTION
Bindery Queue		This object represents a print queue that exists outside the NDS tree (either on a NetWare 3.x server or in another NetWare 4 tree). This object lets you manage this queue, even though it's outside of your current NDS tree.
Certificate Authority		This object stores a certificate authority, used with security applications. It is used with the Novell PKI (Public Key Infrastructure) Services.
Computer		This object indicates any computer that exists on the network. It can be a server, workstation, or any other type of computer.
Country		This optional container object represents the country where a portion of your company is located.
DHCP Server		This object represents a DHCP server and contains a list of subnet ranges this server can service. Used with Novell DNS/DHCP Services.
Directory Map	X	This object is a representation of a directory path that typically points to an application or directory. (See Chapter 5 for more information about using Directory Map objects.)
Distribution List		This object contains a list of e-mail recipients; it is used if Message Handling Services (MHS) is installed. (MHS is a type of communications protocol that is used by some older e-mail packages. See the documentation on your e-mail package for more information.)

Continued

TABLE 4.1		Object Classes Available in NetWare 5 (continued)
OBJECT CLASS	COMMONLY USED	DESCRIPTION
DNS Resource Record Set		This object represents an individual . domain name in a DNS zone. Used with Novell DNS/DHCP Services.
DNS Server		This object represents a DNS server and contains configuration information about the DNS server, such as its IP address and zone list. Used with Novell DNS/DHCP Services.
DNS/DHCP Group		This object represents a group of DNS and DHCP servers that all need rights to DNS and DHCP data in the tree. Used with Novell DNS/DHCP Services.
DNS/DHCP Locator		This object describes DNS and DHCP information, such as DNS servers, global defaults, DHCP options, subnets, and zones. Used with Novell DNS/DHCP Services.
External Entity		This object stores information about non-NDS entities for other applications or services. It is used if Message Handling Services (MHS) is installed.
Group	X	This object contains a list of users who have at least some identical characteristics, such as the need for access rights to the same application. Users listed as group members receive a security equivalence to the group. (See Chapter 5 for more information about Group objects.)
IP Address		This object represents a single IP address on the network. Used with Novell DNS/DHCP Services.

OBJECT CLASS	COMMONLY USED	DESCRIPTION
Key Material		This object stores a server's security information so that security applications can find and use that information. It can store a server's public key, private key, public key certificate, and certificate chain. Used with the Novell PKI (Public Key Infrastructure) Services.
LAN Area		This object contains a list of servers that all use the same WAN Traffic Policy (which determines how often NDS traffic is transmitted between those servers).
LDAP Group		This object stores configuration information for a server or group of servers that provide NDS information to LDAP clients. Used with LDAP Services for NDS.
License Container	X	This object contains the licenses for applications enabled with NetWare Licensing Services (NLS). It can also contain metered certificates. All NetWare 5 trees have these.
License Catalog		This object gathers and provides information about licenses that exist on the network, so the administrator can access that information quickly through the NLS Manager utility.
License Certificate	X	This object represents a product license certificate. When an application that uses NLS is installed, that product's certificate is added as an object in the License Product container object. All NetWare 5 trees have these.

Continued

T A B L E 4.1	Object Classes Available in NetWare 5 (continued)	
OBJECT CLASS	**COMMONLY USED**	**DESCRIPTION**
List		This object simply contains a list of other objects. Objects that are list members do not have a security equivalence to the List object. (For more information about security equivalences, see Chapter 6.)
Locality		This optional container object represents a location.
LSP Server	X	This object represents a License Service Provider server. It is used only if NLS is used. Each NetWare 5 server has an LSP object in the tree representing it as being an LSP (License Service Provider).
Message Routing Group		This object represents a group of message servers. The individual servers are connected directly to each other so that e-mail messages can be routed between them. It is used if Message Handling Services (MHS) is installed.
Messaging Server		This object represents a server that receives and transfers e-mail messages.
NDPS Broker		This object represents the NDPS Broker installed on a server. The NDPS Broker object controls three NDPS printing services: the Resource Management Service, the Event Notification Service, and the Service Registry Service. (See Chapter 8 for more information about NDPS printing.)
NDPS Manager		This object represents the NDPS Manager, which is a software program that controls all the printer agents on a server. (See Chapter 8 for more information about NDPS printing.)

OBJECT CLASS	COMMONLY USED	DESCRIPTION
NDPS Printer		This object represents a network printer that uses the NDPS printing system. (See Chapter 8 for more information about NDPS printing.)
NDSCat:Master Catalog		This object represents a master catalog, which is an easy-to-search database of specified NDS object types and information, such as an employee phone directory. Catalogs are discussed later in this chapter.
NDSCat:Slave Catalog		This object represents a copy of a master catalog, which can be placed on a server in another geographic location. Catalogs are discussed later in this chapter
NetWare Server	X	This object indicates a NetWare server installed on the network.
Organization	X	This object is simply an organization's name (such as a company name).
Organizational Role	X	This object is a position (such as director, project leader, or recreation coordinator) that various users can occupy. (It allows you to assign rights to the position rather than to specific users).
Organizational Unit	X	This container object can form a subdivision under an Organization. Examples of this include division, department, project team, or workgroup.
Policy Package		This represents a policy package for use with Z.E.N.works.

Continued

T A B L E 4.1		*Object Classes Available in NetWare 5 (continued)*
OBJECT CLASS	**COMMONLY USED**	**DESCRIPTION**
Print Queue	X	This represents a print queue. Used in queue-based printing. (See Chapter 8 for more information about queue-based printing.)
Print Server (Non-NDPS)	X	This object is a NetWare print server that provides print services. (See Chapter 8 for more information about printing.)
Printer (Non-NDPS)	X	This object is a printer attached to the network. (See Chapter 8 for more information about printing.)
Profile	X	This object has the sole function of providing a login script. The script can be used by several users — not all of whom need to be in the same container. (See Chapter 5 for more information about login scripts.)
Root	X	This object is the highest point — the starting point — of the Directory tree. (It contains no information.)
Security		This object holds security-related objects.
SLP Directory Agent		This object is used by the Services Location Protocol (SLP), which manages how services are advertised and located on the network.
SLP Scope Unit		This object is used by the SLP.
Subnet		This object represents a subnet and holds configuration information that applies to all the IP Address and Address Range objects under the Subnet container object. Used with Novell DNS/DHCP Services.

OBJECT CLASS	COMMONLY USED	DESCRIPTION
Subnet Pool		This object provides support for multiple subnets. Used with Novell DNS/DHCP Services.
Template		This object is used to define common characteristics for all users created using this template. (See Chapter 5 for more information about user templates.)
Unknown		This represents an object that the server couldn't restore because the object's class is no longer defined in the current schema. (Schemas are explained later in this chapter.)
User	X	This object represents a network user. (See Chapter 5 for more information about users.)
Volume	X	This object indicates a network volume. (See Chapter 7 for more information about volumes.)
Workstation		This object is created automatically when you register and import workstations for Z.E.N.works (a workstation management program included in NetWare 5).
Workstation Group		This object represents a group of Workstation objects. Used with Z.E.N.works (a workstation management program included in NetWare 5).
Zone		This object represents a DNS zone and holds all information about that zone. Used with Novell DNS/DHCP Services.

The NDS Schema

The overall plan that defines and describes the allowable types of NDS objects, their properties, and the rules that govern their creation and existence is called the *NDS schema*. The schema also determines how objects can inherit properties and trustee rights of other container objects above it. In addition, the schema defines how the Directory tree is structured and how objects in it are named.

Software developers who create applications that work with NDS objects can expand or change the schema by identifying new classes of objects (say, for example, a database server). They can also add more properties to existing object classes (such as adding a property called *Pager Number* to a User object).

 NOTE When you install or upgrade to NetWare 5, you may notice messages indicating that the NDS schema is being extended. This is done to support some of the features of NetWare 5 that require additional object classes in the schema.

Working with NDS Objects

Once you've installed a server and a workstation, you can log in to the NetWare 5 network and look at the NDS tree you've created so far. As you create new users and groups, or install new printers or servers, you can see the tree grow.

The primary tool for looking at the Directory tree, and for creating or modifying NDS objects, is the NetWare utility called *NetWare Administrator*. The NetWare Administrator utility (sometimes referred to as NWAdmin) runs in Windows 95/98 and Windows NT.

Typical tasks you can do with NetWare Administrator are as follows:

▶ Create new NDS objects (such as users, groups, or printers)

▶ Delete objects

▶ Move objects to different parts of the Directory tree

▶ Search for objects by particular properties (such as all users in a given department)

▶ Change an object's properties

▶ Rename objects

NOTE

If you have upgraded your network from NetWare 4.1 or NetWare 4.11, you will discover that the old version of NetWare Administrator, called NWADMIN.EXE or NWADMN95.EXE, is still in your SYS:PUBLIC directory.

If you want to use the new NetWare Administrator utility that comes with NetWare 5, you must first upgrade your workstation to the client software that comes with NetWare 5. The new version of NetWare Administrator requires new files that are contained in the new client software. If you don't upgrade your client software, you will have to continue using the older NetWare Administrator utility.

To set up NetWare Administrator on a Windows 95/98 or Windows NT workstation, simply create a shortcut or icon on your desktop that points to the file NWADMN32.EXE, located in the SYS:PUBLIC/WIN32 folder:

1. From the Windows 95/98/NT desktop, right-click your mouse and choose New.

2. Select Shortcut.

3. Choose Browse, open the SYS volume and then the PUBLIC folder, followed by the WIN32 folder. Select the file NWADMN32.EXE.

4. Choose Next.

5. Enter a name for the shortcut, or use the default name provided (NWADMN32.EXE).

6. Choose Finish.

NetWare Administrator will now appear as a shortcut icon on the desktop. Double-click the shortcut icon to launch NetWare Administrator.

Now you can use NetWare Administrator to create and manage all NDS objects, including users and groups.

NDS Replicas and Partitions

As explained earlier, the NDS database is common to all servers on the network. If the database was stored on only one server (with all other servers accessing it from that server), the entire network would be disabled if the server went down.

To prevent this single point of failure, NetWare 5 can create *replicas* of the NDS database and store those replicas on different servers. Then, if one server goes down, all other servers can still access the NDS database from another replica of the database.

If your NDS database is large enough, you may not want to store the entire database on each server. In this case, you can create Directory *partitions,* which are portions of the database that can be replicated on different servers. A Directory partition is a branch of the Directory tree, beginning with any container object you choose. Partitions can also hold subpartitions beneath them (called *child partitions*). If you have a smaller NDS database, the whole database can reside in a single partition. Using partitions can improve network performance, especially if the network spans across a wide area network (WAN). Partitions can also make it easier to manage portions of the tree separately.

Figure 4.6 shows the same network that was illustrated in Figure 4.4. In this drawing, its NDS database is divided into two partitions.

FIGURE 4.6 *NDS tree with two database partitions*

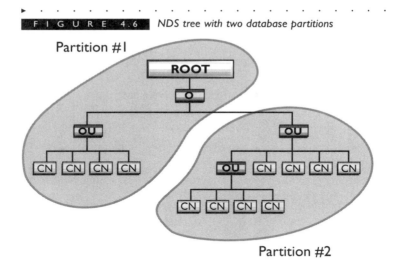

Partition #1

Partition #2

Managing NDS replicas and database partitions is an advanced feature of NetWare 5. In large, complex networks, administrators can create different types of replicas and partitions to better control the amount of information being updated and synchronized on the network. However, the NetWare 5 installation program automatically detects and sets up replicas and partitions that work well for most networks. This is a feature that many network administrators of average networks do not need to change.

To create, delete, or merge Directory partitions, you can use a utility called *NDS Manager*. This utility can be executed by itself, or it can be added to the NetWare Administrator utility so it appears as an option under the NetWare Administrator's Tools menu. For more information about this utility, see the Novell online documentation.

Planning the NDS Directory Tree

To plan your Directory tree, you can take advantage of the Organization and Organizational Unit container objects. With them, you can make the tree resemble your company's organization — organized by departments, geography, or some other logical scheme.

The key to planning your Directory tree is to decide how best to group objects together so that:

- Users can quickly and easily find the resources they use most often.

- You can easily manage all the resources, including responding to changes in the corporation.

The following sections offer some tips for planning your Directory tree.

Starting at the Top

The Root object resides at the very top of the tree. Immediately beneath the Root object lies the first level of container objects — the Organization objects.

For most companies, having a single Organization object at the top of the tree is the most logical move, especially if users will need to have access to all parts of the tree. Under this single Organization object, you can use Organizational Unit objects (OU objects) to subdivide the tree into useful groupings, if necessary.

Deciding whether you need to use OU objects at all is the first decision. If your company is small, you may want to have a single Organization object (representing your company) with all leaf objects directly beneath that container. Figure 4.7 shows how a tree for a small company, named BlueSky Research, might look.

FIGURE 4.7   *Sample Directory tree for a small company*

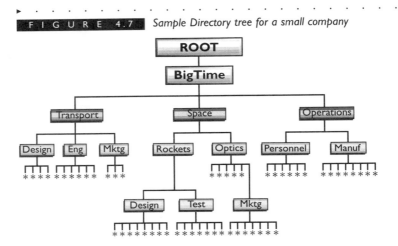

If your company is larger, you may want to use OU objects to divide the tree into more manageable chunks. (You can use multiple levels of OU objects if you need to.)

First, consider how many different locations you have that connect to each other across WAN (wide area network) links — in other words, over phone lines. If you have sites across town from each other, or in different cities or countries, you should probably create an OU object to represent each site.

Because the NDS database resides on multiple servers in a NetWare 5 network, changes made to the database must be synchronized across the network to all the affected servers (that is, servers with a copy, or replica, of that partition). If you have servers at different geographical sites connected by phone lines, the data being transferred during synchronization can keep those phone lines very busy at times.

Using OU objects to divide the tree according to geographical sites helps cut down on the amount of synchronization traffic that goes across the phone lines. You can make each geographical site fall into its own OU object, and specify that a new partition of the database begin at that OU object.

Now you have planned the top of your NDS tree. You either have a single Organization object, or you have a layer of OU objects representing WAN sites. Next, you will plan where to put all the leaf objects.

Organizing by Departments versus Locations

Your goal with the NDS tree is to make network objects easy for users to find, and easy for you to manage. The two most common ways to organize a tree are by department and by location.

For some companies, organizing by departments or divisions is the most logical way to set up the NDS tree. If all the Marketing users need access to completely different resources (such as servers, volumes, and printers), individual users, printers, and so on can be placed inside the OU object that corresponds to their department. (These individual objects are all leaf objects.) Figure 4.8 shows how a large company, called BigTime Engineering, might set up its Directory tree based on departments. Note the different levels of OU objects. The asterisks beneath the container objects represent various types of leaf objects (CN objects).

F I G U R E   4 . 8   *Sample Directory tree for a large company divided by departments*

On the other hand, you may find that users access resources based more on where they're located than on their department. For instance, suppose the second floor of your building contains the engineering department, the maintenance people, and your inside sales representatives. They all use the same three printers, access files and applications on the same server volumes, and so on. Dividing these users by department probably won't accomplish anything for you—you'll just have two or three unnecessary OU objects.

Instead, all those users and resources could be located under a single OU called Floor2. Then, they could easily locate resources they need, and you don't have to maintain three separate groups.

Figure 4.9 illustrates a Directory tree for a large company, called Yippy Skippy Toys, divided by location instead of departments.

▶ · ◀

FIGURE 4.9 *Sample Directory tree for a large company, divided by locations*

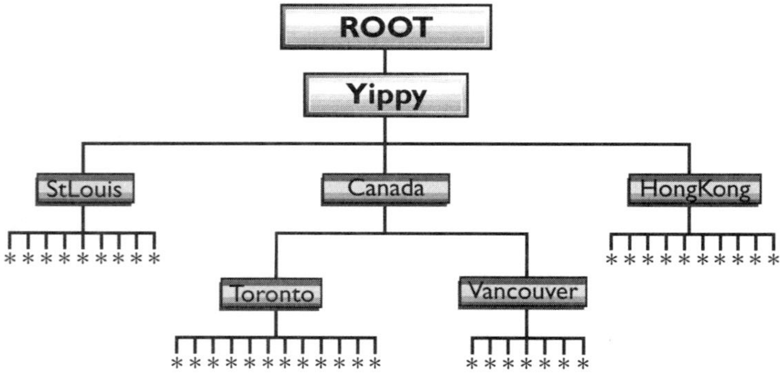

```
                    ┌──────────────┐
                    │     ROOT     │
                    └──────┬───────┘
                    ┌──────┴───────┐
                    │    Yippy     │
                    └──────┬───────┘
        ┌──────────────────┼──────────────────┐
   ┌─────────┐        ┌─────────┐        ┌───────────┐
   │ StLouis │        │ Canada  │        │ HongKong  │
   └─────────┘        └────┬────┘        └───────────┘
  *********          ┌─────┴─────┐         *********
               ┌─────────┐   ┌──────────┐
               │ Toronto │   │ Vancouver│
               └─────────┘   └──────────┘
              ***********      *******
```

You can, of course, mix the two methods, using both location and departmental OU objects, if that makes the most sense for your network.

TIP

When planning your NDS tree structure, try to make it flexible enough so you can easily change it if your company makes organizational changes. Consider the type of organizational changes your company is most likely to make. Does it reorganize departments on a frequent basis? Are you expecting the company to move to a new location soon? Is the company expanding, adding on new buildings, or leasing new floors of an existing building? The answers to these questions may help you decide on the most efficient way to set up your NDS tree.

Using Naming Standards

Another planning aspect that can make your NDS tree management go more smoothly is to plan a standard way to name objects such as users, servers, and printers. By establishing some naming standards up front, you make it easier for users to locate the resources they need. The following suggestions and tips may help you decide how you want to standardize your naming guidelines:

- ▶ If several people will be responsible for creating and managing NDS objects, make sure they're all committed to using the same standards.

- ▶ Get naming standards approved by management, if necessary.

- ▶ In general, keep names as short as possible, to make it easier to type full names. It's easier to type "BigTime" (or even "BT") than "BigTimeEngineering."

- ▶ Decide on a standard for usernames, such as last names only, first name and last initial, first two initials and last name, or some other logical format for your situation. Many companies make their usernames conform to the restrictions specified by their e-mail package, so users only need to remember one username.

- ▶ Decide how you will handle objects with similar names. For instance, if you've settled on using the first initial and last name for usernames, how will you deal with John Smith and Jill Smith?

- ▶ Do you want to make some object names indicate the types of object they are, such as using SERV_xxx for all server names?

- ▶ Do you want the names of printers and similar objects to indicate information such as the type, location, or owner? For example, you could specify that a printer be named P1-HP3si-Mktg to indicate that it is Printer #1 in the marketing department, and that it is a particular type of Hewlett Packard laser printer.

Name Context — Your Location in the Tree

Each object in the Directory tree exists in a specific location of the tree. This location is called the object's *name context*.

A name context is really a sort of "address" for that object's location, consisting of the names of any container objects over that object. An object's *full name* (also called the *full distinguished name*) consists of the object's name, plus its name context. Each of the names in a name context is separated by periods.

For example, suppose user Doug is located under the Organization object called BlueSky. Knowing where Doug is located, you can determine the following information about him:

► His name context is BlueSky, because that's the only container object above him.

► His common name is Doug.

► His full name is Doug.BlueSky.

Figure 4.10 shows Doug's location in the Directory tree.

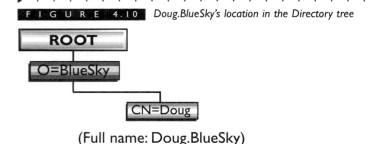

F I G U R E   4 . 1 0   *Doug.BlueSky's location in the Directory tree*

ROOT

O=BlueSky

CN=Doug

(Full name: Doug.BlueSky)

The name context of an object is useful because it lets you know exactly where that object is in the Directory tree. In addition, it lets you uniquely identify two objects that may have the same common name (such as "Doug"), but that reside in two different parts of the tree.

Within a single container, no two objects can have the same name. However, two objects can have the same name if they are in separate containers. This is because their name context is different, so each one has a unique full name.

For example, at BigTime Engineering, in the Transport Organizational Unit, there can be only one user with the common name Eric located within the container called Mktg. However, there can be other users named Eric in the tree if they are within other containers. Say there's an Eric in Mktg, and another Eric in Design, both of whom work in the Transport division of BigTime Engineering.

The Marketing Eric's full name would be Eric.Mktg.Transport.BigTime. Each container name is added to Eric's common name (separated by periods) to spell out his address in the Directory tree, clear back to the Organization's name. His name context, or location in the tree, is Mktg.Transport.BigTime.

The Design Eric's full name would be Eric.Design.Transport.BigTime. Because his full name is different from the other Eric's full name, NDS can keep them both straight.

Figure 4.11 shows where each Eric is located in the Directory tree at BigTime Engineering.

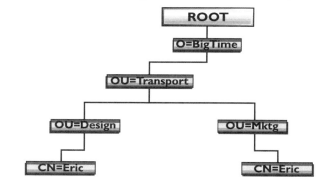

FIGURE 4.11 *Two users with the same common name can reside in different containers in the Directory tree*

(Full name: Eric.Design.Transport.BigTime)   (Full name: Eric.Mktg.Transport.BigTime)

NOTE   In some cases, you may see a full name (or a name context) that includes the object abbreviations. For example, you may see CN=Eric.OU=Design.OU=Transport.O=BigTime. This is the official, formal way to show full names; however, most NetWare 5 utilities let you eliminate the object abbreviations and use just the names instead.

Specifying objects in the Directory tree is similar to specifying subdirectories in a DOS file system. In the file system, if you are at the root of the volume or disk or in a completely separate directory path, you have to specify a full directory path to get to the subdirectory you want (such as D:\REPORTS\SALES\1998).

In the same way, if you are at the root of the Directory tree or in a completely different branch of the tree, you have to specify an object's full name to find it (such as .Eric.Design.Transport.BigTime).

However, if you are already somewhere in the subdirectory's directory path, you only need to specify the portion of the path that will get you to the desired subdirectory (such as SALES\1998). You don't need to specify the subdirectory's full path.

Similarly, if you are already within a container over an object's location, you only need to specify the portion of the Directory tree address that exists between you and the object (such as Eric.Design). You don't need to specify the object's full name back to the root. This is called specifying a *partial name* (or a *relative distinguished name*).

You may want to locate an object that is in a completely different place in the tree. If you do want to specify an object's full name back to the root, place a period at the beginning of the object's name (in any commands you type). This indicates to the utility you're using that it is a full name and shouldn't be interpreted as a partial name. For example, you would type **.Eric.Design.Transport.BigTime** to indicate that this is Eric's full name.

To move around in the Directory tree's context, moving up and down through containers, you use the NetWare Administrator utility. You open and close containers in the NetWare Administrator just as you open and close folders in Windows.

Using Additional Services with NDS

NetWare 5 includes three other features that you can use to enhance the functionality of NDS:

- ▶ Catalog Services
- ▶ LDAP Services for NDS
- ▶ Novell DNS/DHCP Services

Using Catalog Services to Search the Tree

One of the benefits of NDS is that you can search the NDS tree for objects you want to locate. One method of searching the tree is to simply use the NetWare Administrator's Browser screen and navigate your way through the tree, opening containers and looking for your desired object.

Another way to search for objects is to use Catalog Services. Catalog Services is a feature of NDS that enables you to group together specific types of objects and information into a smaller database, so you can quickly locate the objects you want. A good example of this would be an employee phone directory — you could define a "catalog" that would gather an up-to-date list of all the User objects in the tree and their telephone number properties. Then, you could search that catalog and see a list of all those employees without having to navigate the tree itself.

By default, such catalogs are updated daily by a process called a *dredger*, which simply goes through the NDS tree looking for new information that should be added to the catalog. (You can manually update a catalog at any time, or you can change the automatic update interval.)

Applications, such as e-mail packages, can also create catalogs of information for their own use.

There are two types of catalogs: a master catalog and a slave catalog. The master catalog is the main catalog. Slave catalogs are copies of the master. The slave catalogs can be placed on remote servers so users in those locations can quickly access the same information as in the master catalog.

See the Novell documentation for more information about Catalog Services.

Using LDAP Services for NDS

LDAP (Lightweight Directory Access Protocol) is a communications protocol currently being developed for use on the Internet. The goal is for LDAP to eventually become the standard protocol for accessing directory information over the Internet. NDS provides a strong directory service for LDAP to access and use.

LDAP Services for NDS is an optional feature of NetWare 5. You can install it during the server installation as an additional product. LDAP Services enables LDAP clients to access information stored in NDS. You can specify what types of information are available to those LDAP clients.

For more information about using LDAP with your network, see the Novell documentation.

Using Novell DNS/DHCP Services

Novell DNS/DHCP Services is an optional feature of NetWare 5 that integrates DNS and DHCP addressing and management into NDS. DNS (Domain Name System) and DHCP (Dynamic Host Configuration Protocol) manage the assignment and discovery of IP addresses on a network. By integrating this information into NDS, network administrators can now manage both DNS/DHCP information and regular NDS information from a single, centralized location. The DNS/DHCP information is stored in an NDS database, so it is distributed and replicated just like other NDS data, making it easier to access and manage.

When you install DNS/DHCP Services as an optional product during the server installation, an IP client can establish a connection with the network by using DHCP. A DHCP server sends the address of an NDS server to the client, along with an IP address and NDS context that the client can use to log in. DHCP enables a workstation to be "leased" an IP address from a pool of available addresses, rather than requiring that the workstation be assigned a fixed address individually. This can make the maintenance of IP addresses much easier on a network.

For more information about DNS/DHCP Services, see the Novell documentation.

Keeping Your NDS Software Up to Date

Periodically, Novell releases updated versions of DS.NLM (the NDS database program) and its management utilities on the Novell Web site (www. novell.com). These updates may add minor features or fix problems. You should try to keep your network updated with these new versions whenever possible.

If you obtain an updated version of DS.NLM, install it on all the NetWare 5 servers in your network. All servers must be running the same version of DS.NLM to use any new features of DS.NLM. Keeping all your servers running the same version will help simplify your support of the Directory tree.

Beyond the Basics

This chapter explained the basics of NDS, and showed you how Directory trees are set up. The following topics are explained in other sections of this book:

▶ For instructions on creating NDS objects, such as User objects, using the NetWare Administrator utility, see Chapter 5.

▶ For information about NDS object security features, see Chapter 6.

▶ For instructions on installing NDS when you install a server, see Chapter 2.

NDS is another aspect of NetWare 5 that has a number of advanced features that let you customize the network to fit your needs. After you've mastered the fundamentals of NDS, you may want to learn more. If so, some resources you can use include Novell's online documentation, *Novell's NetWare 5 Administrator's Handbook* from Novell Press, or *Novell's Guide to NetWare 5 Networks* by Jeff Hughes and Blair Thomas from Novell Press (which describes NDS design in detail). In these resources, you can learn more about the following topics:

- ▶ Understanding database replicas and partitions
- ▶ Using NDS Manager to work with replicas and partitions
- ▶ Using the SET NDS TRACE and DSREPAIR utilities to identify and fix NDS problems
- ▶ Using Bindery Services to allow bindery-based applications to use the objects in the NDS database
- ▶ Working with multiple NDS trees
- ▶ Merging multiple NDS trees

TIP

As mentioned in Chapter 2, another useful resource for NetWare 5 management information is the Novell *AppNotes*. This monthly publication contains research reports and articles on a wide range of advanced topics, including NDS management. To order a subscription, call 800-377-4136 in the U.S., or 303-297-2725 worldwide.

CHAPTER 5

Creating and Managing Users

Even if all the hardware and software is set up for your network, a new user can't just log in and begin using the network. He or she must first obtain a user account on the network.

Each person who will use the network should have his or her own user account. That way, each user can log in using his or her own name. (Although users can share a login name, this is generally not as safe, and can cause unnecessary confusion.)

Of course, after a brand-new installation, the only User object that will exist in the tree is the Admin User object.

Therefore, before the users can begin using the network, you (as the network administrator) must create user accounts for each of them. In addition, there are several other tasks you can perform to make life easier for the users:

- ▶ You may want to create some Group objects, and organize the users into those groups. Groups allow you to manage security, printer assignments, and other issues that may affect many (or all) of the users in the same way.

- ▶ To make the network easier to use for DOS or Windows 3.1 users, you can create login scripts. Login scripts automatically set up the users' workstation environments with necessary drive mappings and other types of useful environmental settings. (Windows 95/98 or Windows NT users can use the Network Neighborhood to modify their environments, instead.) Login scripts are used by the user for whom they were created, no matter which version of DOS or Windows is implemented.

- ▶ You can use the NetWare Application Launcher to set up an icon on users' desktops that points directly to network applications. Then, the users can simply launch the application from their desktops without having to know where the application is located, which drives to map, and so on.

What Do Users Need?

Creating a user's account means creating a new object for the user in the NDS tree. However, it involves more than that.

Before a user can really work on the network, you must set up many of the following tools or characteristics (some are optional, depending on your situation):

- The user's account (which is an NDS object for the user with its associated properties filled in, such as the user's last name, full name, telephone number, and so on)
- The user's group memberships
- A home directory (folder) for the user's work files
- A login script that maps drives to the directories and applications to which the user will need access
- NDS security (rights that control how the user can see and use other NDS objects in the tree)
- File system trustee rights to the files and directories the user needs to work with (to regulate the user's access and activities in those files and directories)
- Account restrictions, if necessary, to control when the user logs in, how often the user must change passwords, and so on
- Access to the network printers
- An e-mail account, if necessary

The following sections of this chapter describe how to create user and group accounts on the network, how to create user home directories, how users can log in and log out, as well as the basics of login scripts.

NOTE NDS security, file system security, and account restrictions are explained in Chapter 6. Chapter 8 explains how to give users access to network printers. For information on creating an e-mail account for a user, see the documentation that came with your e-mail program.

Creating Users and Groups

Users are the individuals who have accounts on the network. Each real-life user has a specific User object defined in the NDS Directory tree. This User object is the account that defines when the user can log in, what rights the user has to work on the network, what the user's full name is, and other types of information. Each piece of information that defines the User object is called a *property*.

A Group object is a single object that is assigned a list of users. Whenever one of the Group object's properties is changed (such as a new security assignment), every user in the Group's list is suddenly changed the same way.

Using Group objects is a fast, efficient way to assign security levels to groups of users who have the same needs, but who may not be in the same container object. You can also use Group objects when some — but not all — of the users in a container have similar needs.

TIP

If all users in a container object (such as an Organization) have the same needs, you probably don't need to use a Group object. Just change the container object's properties to affect all the users in the container.

Because you can use container objects to assign rights and login scripts to all the users in those containers, you may find that you don't need to use as many groups as you may have in NetWare 3.1x or earlier versions.

To create a new user or group on the network, you use the NetWare Administrator utility from a workstation. The NetWare Administrator is a NetWare 5 utility that can run on either Windows 95/98 or Windows NT. (If you have not yet installed the NetWare Administrator on your workstation, see Chapter 4 for instructions.)

In previous versions of NetWare, the NetWare Administrator utility was found in SYS:\PUBLIC\WIN95\ or SYS:\PUBLIC\WINNT\ and was called NWADMIN.EXE for Windows 95/98 or Windows NT. NetWare 5 uses a newer NetWare Administrator. NWADMN32, found in SYS:\PUBLIC\WIN32\, is used for both Windows 95/98 and Windows NT.

NOTE

To create any new NDS object, including users and groups, you have to be logged in as the Admin user, or as another user that has been given the rights necessary for creating or changing objects. See Chapter 6 for more information about security rights.

Creating a User

Before creating a new User object for a user, answer the following questions:

- Under which container will the user's object be placed?
- Where will the user's home directory (folder) be placed?

NOTE

In many cases, network administrators create a directory, called USERS, on a server's volume. Then, the administrator creates a home directory for each user underneath USERS. Users have all rights to their home directory, so they can store applications, work files, or personal files there. Users can create additional directories underneath their home directory — it's just like any other directory or folder on their workstation's hard disk. You can specify whether to create a home directory automatically, and where to put it, when you create a new user.

To create a new User object, complete the following steps:

1. Create a directory for all users' home directories. For example, you might want to create a network directory called USERS on volume SYS.

2. Start up the NetWare Administrator utility by double-clicking its icon. The NetWare Administrator's browser window should appear, as shown in Figure 5.1. (If the browser window doesn't appear, choose NDS Browser from the Tools menu.)

FIGURE 5.1 *NetWare Administrator browser window*

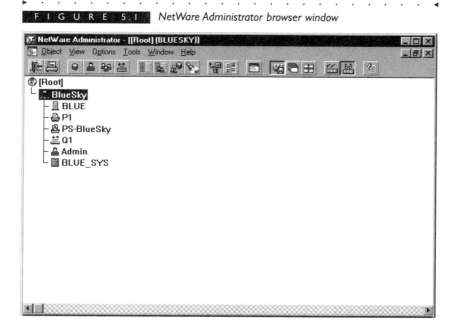

3. Select the container object (an Organization or Organizational Unit object) that will hold the new user.

4. From the Object menu, choose Create.

5. From the New Object dialog box that appears (see Figure 5.2), choose User, and then choose OK.

► · ◄

| F I G U R E   5 . 2 | *Creating a New User object in the New Object dialog box* |

New Object   ☒

Parent:
BlueSky

[OK]
[Cancel]
[Context...]
[Help]

Class of new object:

- Organizational Unit
- Print Queue
- Print Server
- Printer
- Profile
- Template
- User
- Volume

6. In the Create User dialog box, enter the user's login name and last name. The login name is the name you want this user to type when he or she logs in.

7. Create a home directory for this user:

   a. Mark the checkbox next to Create Home Directory.

   b. Click the Browse button to specify a path to the home directory. (The button isn't actually labeled "Browse," but it has an icon resembling a directory structure on it. The button is located below the Home Directory area on the screen.)

   c. From the Directory Contents panel on the right, double-click the container and then the volume that will hold the user directories.

   d. When the directory you created in Step 1 appears in the left panel (under Files and Directories), select that directory and click OK. The path to that directory should now appear in the Create User dialog box.

8. Mark the Define Additional Properties checkbox. (This will allow you to see and modify more information about the User object after you create it in the next step.)

9. Choose Create.

10. The user's Identification page appears, as shown in Figure 5.3. The Identification page will appear every time you use the NetWare Administrator utility to look at this object in the future. Along the right side of the screen are large rectangular buttons with turned-down corners. Each of these buttons represents a different page of information about the user. You can fill in some, none, or all of the information on these pages depending on your needs. If you have entered new information in one of these pages that needs to be saved, the turned-down corner will appear black. Fill in any information you want to specify, and then choose OK when finished.

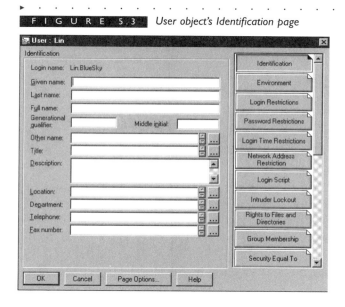

F I G U R E   5 . 3   *User object's Identification page*

11. Create another user by following the same steps.

After you've created a new User object, that User object will appear in the Directory tree. You can use the NetWare Administrator's browser to see where the object is in the tree and to see, or change, the User object's information.

Creating Groups and Assigning Group Membership to Users

Creating a Group object is similar to creating a user. The following steps show how to create a Group object and assign group membership to a user:

 1. Start up the NetWare Administrator utility by double-clicking its icon. The NetWare Administrator's browser window should appear, as shown in Figure 5.4. (If the browser window doesn't appear, choose NDS Browser from the Tools menu.)

FIGURE 5.4 *NetWare Administrator's browser window*

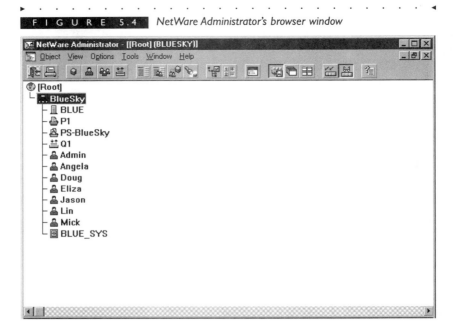

 2. Select the container object that will hold the new group.
 3. From the Object menu, choose Create.
 4. From the New Object dialog box that appears (see Figure 5.5), choose Group, and then choose OK.

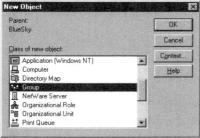

FIGURE 5.5 *Creating a new Group object in the New Object dialog box*

5. In the Create Group dialog box, enter the Group object's name.

6. Mark the checkbox next to Define Additional Properties.

7. Choose Create.

8. The group's Identification page appears. Enter any information you desire on the Identification page, such as a description of the Group object.

9. Choose the Members page and click Add.

10. From the screen that appears, specify any existing users who should be members of this group. From the right panel, open the container that holds the user you want. From the left panel, select the user, and then choose OK. The user's name now appears as a member of the group. (To select multiple users, use Shift+Click or Ctrl+Click.) You must click OK to save the selected user information. The information on the black "dog-eared" tabs show the changed items that need to be saved.

TIP

If the group already exists, you can also assign a user to that group by selecting the User object, opening the user's Group Membership page, and adding the group.

Opening an Object's Information Pages

There are three ways to open an object's information pages in NetWare Administrator:

► If the object is a leaf object (such as a user or group), double-click the object's icon.

▸ Highlight the object, and then choose Details from the Object menu (which appears in the menu bar across the top of the NetWare Administrator's window).

▸ Right-click the object, then choose Details from the menu that appears, as shown in Figure 5.6.

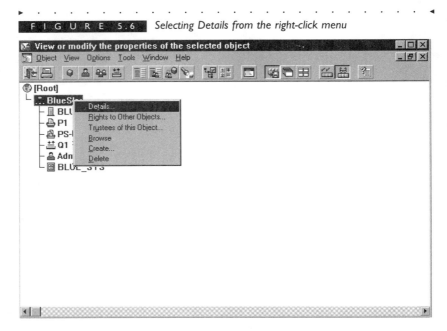

F I G U R E   5 . 6   *Selecting Details from the right-click menu*

Double-clicking a container object won't show you the container's detail pages. Instead, double-clicking the icon will just open the object in the Browser, showing the objects underneath it. Therefore, to see a container object's detail pages, you must choose the Details option from either the Object menu or the right-click menu.

User Network Activities

Once users have been created, they can begin working on the network. In most cases, users on a network will notice very little difference from working on a standalone computer. They still use the applications they were used to before. They still open, save, and delete files the same way. They can still play the same games — if they can get away with it.

Most users will only notice the following primary differences:

- ▸ They have to enter a login name and password.
- ▸ They have more drives and directories available to them.
- ▸ They are restricted from accessing some files.
- ▸ Their print jobs go to the same printer as everyone else's.

Whether you want them to be able to control most of these network activities themselves is up to you.

For most users, the following NetWare 5 and Windows utilities will take care of their networking tasks:

- ▸ LOGIN (from either the DOS command line or from Windows 3.1, 95/98, or NT) lets users log in to the network.
- ▸ LOGOUT (from either the DOS command line or from Windows 3.1, 95/98, or NT) lets users log out of the network.
- ▸ NetWare User Tools (from Windows 3.1) lets users perform many networking tasks, such as logging in and out, mapping drives, and changing passwords.
- ▸ Windows Network Neighborhood (from Windows 95/98 or NT) lets users perform many network tasks, such as logging in and out, mapping drives, and changing passwords.
- ▸ NetWare Administrator (from Windows 95/98 or NT) lets users browse the NDS tree, see information about network objects, manage their printers, and so on.

Logging In

To log in to the network, the user must use NetWare 5's LOGIN program to enter a login name and a password. The network verifies the name and password. If the name and password match, the network lets the user in to the network. If the name and password don't match, the network prevents the user from logging in.

How you log in to the network depends on what operating system you're running on your workstation.

DOS users type the following command at the DOS prompt, substituting either a Directory tree or server name for *tree* or *server* (this is not necessary if the user wants to log in to the default tree or server), and their login name for *user* (and entering a password when prompted):

```
LOGIN <tree>/<user>
```

or

```
Login <server>/<user>
```

Windows 3.1, Windows 95/98, or Windows NT users can use the LOGIN program that is installed as part of the NetWare 5 Client software. To log in using the graphical LOGIN program, use one of the following methods (depending on the workstation's OS):

- ▶ To log in to the network from Windows 3.1, double-click the Novell Login icon (located in the Novell Client program group), and specify a login name and a password.

- ▶ From Windows 95/98 or NT, the LOGIN program is usually set to execute automatically whenever the workstation is rebooted. Enter a login name and password when the utility appears (see Figure 5.7).

▶ . . . . ◀

F I G U R E   5 . 7   *Novell Client login*

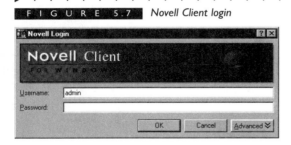

- ▶ From Windows 95/98 or NT, you can also log in from the Network Neighborhood. Open the Network Neighborhood by either double-clicking the Network Neighborhood icon or right-clicking the N logo in the system tray. Then right-click the desired tree or server, click either Authenticate or Login to NDS Tree, and then enter a login name and password. You can also open the Login program by opening the Start menu, selecting Programs, then Novell, and then NetWare Login.

By default, users must enter their full names when they log in. For example, Eric's full name might be Eric.Design.Transport.BigTime; he would have to enter that name every time he logged in.

This occurs because the LOGIN utility doesn't know the NDS name context in which the user was created. It assumes the default context is at the root of the Directory tree. If you've created the user in a container beneath the root (which is sometimes the case), LOGIN won't find the user in the tree if the user enters only his or her common name. If LOGIN can't find the user, the user can't log in to the network.

However, there is an easy way to store the user's name context (location in the tree) on the workstation, so that the user can simply enter his or her short name (such as Eric) instead:

▶ DOS and Windows 3.1 users can add a command to a file on their workstation named NET.CFG.

▶ Windows 95/98 and Windows NT users can configure the NetWare 5 Client software to store the user's name context in the client software.

The following sections explain how to set the name context.

Specifying a Name Context in DOS and Windows 3.1

On DOS and Windows 3.1 workstations, the NetWare 5 Client software creates a file called NET.CFG. You can use any text editor (such as Windows' NotePad) to edit this file.

Locate the file by opening first the Novell directory, and then the Client32 directory. When you've opened the NET.CFG file in the text editor, scroll down through the file until you see the heading, "NetWare DOS Requester." Under this heading, type the following command, substituting the user's name context for *username*:

```
NAME CONTEXT="username"
```

For example, to specify Eric's context, enter the following command in the NET.CFG file:

```
NAME CONTEXT="Design.Transport.BigTime"
```

Then, save the file. You will have to reboot the workstation to make this new command take effect. After you've rebooted the workstation, Eric can just log in using his common name, Eric, which is obviously going to be easier for him to remember.

To simplify the user's life even more, you may also want to put the LOGIN command in the user's AUTOEXEC.BAT file so that it executes every time the user boots the workstation.

Specifying a Name Context in Windows 95/98

When you installed the NetWare 5 Client software on a Windows 95/98 or Windows NT workstation, you may have taken the opportunity to specify a name context during the installation.

If you didn't specify a name context during the installation, or if you want to change the name context to something different, you can easily specify a new name context by completing the following steps:

1. Right-click the Network Neighborhood icon on your Windows 95/98 or Windows NT desktop.

2. Choose Properties.

3. From the list that appears, highlight Novell NetWare Client (or Novell NetWare Client32, if you're using an older version of the client software), and then click Properties.

4. The screen that now appears (see Figure 5.8) lets you specify a preferred server, a preferred tree, and a name context. In the Name Context field, enter the context for this user. (If your network has more than one tree, you can also enter a preferred tree, to indicate which one you want to log in to on a regular basis. In most cases, you don't need to indicate a preferred server, because NetWare 5 lets you log in to the entire tree — not to a specific server, as earlier versions of NetWare required.)

► . . . . ◄

FIGURE 5.8   *Entering a name context for the user*

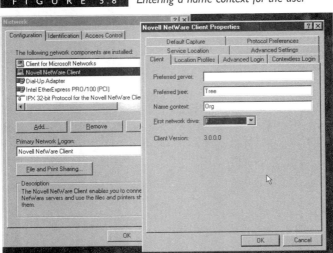

5. Click OK to save the name context information.

6. Exit the Network Neighborhood properties.

Now the user can simply enter his or her login name instead of a full name whenever the Login screen appears. Eric will be able to log in using just his common name, Eric, instead of his full name.

Specifying a Name Context in Windows NT

To set Windows NT users' default name contexts so they don't have to enter a full name each time they log in, use the Control Panel:

I. From the Windows NT Start menu, choose Settings.

2. Choose the Control Panel, then Network, then Services.

3. From the Network Services list, choose Novell Client for Windows NT, and then click Properties.

4. Put the user's context in the Name Context field. If it isn't already filled in, also indicate a Preferred Tree for the user.

5. When finished, click OK.

Now the user can simply enter his or her login name instead of a full name whenever the Login screen appears.

Logging Out

When you finish working on the network, you should log out of it to make sure no one else accesses the network using your account. Always ensure that you log out before you leave your desk, even if you leave your computer turned on. How you log out depends on the operating system you're using on your workstation:

▶ If you're using a DOS workstation, simply type the following command at the DOS prompt:

```
LOGOUT
```

▶ If you're using a Windows 3.1 workstation, you can either go to DOS and type **LOGOUT** at the DOS prompt, or you can use the NetWare User Tools utility to log out. Double-click NetWare User Tools, select NetWare Drive Connections, choose the server or tree from which you want to log out, and choose Logout. (The NetWare User Tools utility is explained in the following section.)

▶ If you're using a Windows 95/98 or Windows NT workstation, double-click the Network Neighborhood icon (or open the Network

Neighborhood by clicking the N logo in the system tray), right-click the NDS tree or server from which you want to log out, and choose Logout.

Using NetWare User Tools

Novell's NetWare 5 includes a utility, called NetWare User Tools, that allows Windows 3.1 users to perform their most common network tasks. The NetWare 5 Client installation program automatically places the icon for NetWare User Tools in the NetWare Tools program group on your Windows 3.1 desktop.

With NetWare User Tools, users can do the following:

► Set up print queues and control how their print jobs are printed on the network. (See Chapter 8 for more information about printing.)

► Send short messages to other network users.

► Map drive letters to network directories. (Drive mappings are explained later in this chapter.)

► Change passwords.

► Log in to and out of Directory trees and network servers.

► Change their own name contexts in the Directory tree.

To use NetWare User Tools, double-click the NetWare User Tools icon, which is automatically placed in the Novell Client program group when the Novell client software is installed. Use the icons along the top of the utility to perform different network tasks.

When you make changes in NetWare User Tools (such as mapping drives to directories, or changing your printer port to point to a print queue), you can click the Permanent button. This will make those assignments permanent; if you don't make the changes permanent, they will be erased when you log out.

Use the Help button to read about the tasks you can do with this utility.

Network Tasks from Windows 95/98 and Windows NT

Most Windows 95/98 and Windows NT users will use the Network Neighborhood to accomplish most common networking tasks, such as logging in and out of the network and mapping drives. (See the section titled "The MAP Login Script Command" later in this chapter for more about drive mapping.) Users can also right-click the N logo in the system tray to choose network tasks from a menu. (The system tray usually appears at the bottom right-hand corner of the Windows screen.)

For example, to map a drive from the Network Neighborhood, open the Network Neighborhood and double-click a server to display its volumes. Open a volume, and keep opening folders until you find the one to which you want to map a drive. Then right-click the folder and select Novell Map Network Drive. Choose a drive letter and mark the options you want, such as Map Root, Reconnect at Logon (which maps the drive permanently so it continues to be mapped every time you log in), or Map Search Drive (see Figure 5.9). Then click Map. The new drive mapping will appear when you open My Computer.

FIGURE 5.9 *Mapping a drive*

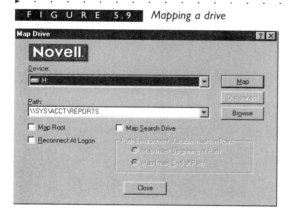

To map a drive from the N logo in the system tray, right-click the N logo. From the menu that appears, choose Novell Map Network Drive. The same Map screen appears as in the procedure from Network Neighborhood. You choose the drive letter, mark the options you want, and click Map.

To delete a drive mapping, open My Computer. Right-click the drive mapping, and choose Disconnect.

Making Applications Easy to Access

NetWare 5 includes a feature called the Z.E.N.works Starter Pack, which you can use to make your applications easier to access. This is a subset of the full-featured Z.E.N.works, which can be purchased separately. The Starter

Pack includes primarily the Application Launcher, which existed in NetWare 4.11, but which has been enhanced for NetWare 5. The Starter Pack also includes some basic workstation management functionality.

NOTE The full-featured Z.E.N.works product includes advanced workstation management features, such as Help Request management tools and workstation registration tools so you can remotely access a user's workstation to diagnose problems. The full-featured product is available separately. Only the Starter Pack is included in NetWare 5.

Once you have the Z.E.N.works Starter Pack installed on a server and the Application Launcher set up on each user's workstation, you can use NetWare Administrator to make an application become an object in the NDS tree. Then, the icon for the Application object will appear automatically on the desktop of each user you assign to that application.

The users don't need to know where the application is, they don't need to map drives or enter launch parameters, and you don't need to update login scripts. When you update the application, the icons in all the desktops will continue to point to the new application. You can make an application simply run from the network, or you can even make the application install itself automatically on each workstation.

To install Z.E.N.works on the server, you need to run the installation program on the Z.E.N.works CD-ROM. This is the same CD-ROM that contains the Novell Client software. When Z.E.N.works is installed, it extends the NDS schema to add Application objects (and other related objects). In addition, it automatically adds a snap-in module to the NetWare Administrator utility so you can manage Application objects.

After you've installed Z.E.N.works on the server, you can create an Application object to represent a particular application. Then, you put a command in each user's login script to execute the Application Launcher (for Windows 3.1) or Application Explorer (for Windows 95/98 or NT). The Application Launcher/Explorer is a window that appears on the user's desktop. This Window contains any Application objects you assign to that user.

For Windows 95/98 and NT, you can also specify that the Application object appears on the user's desktop, in Windows Explorer, or in the System Tray.

If you want the application to install itself automatically on the workstation, you can run the application's installation program on a single representative workstation and capture all the installation information and settings with a program called snAppShot. Then you can use that captured information when you create the Application object. The object will use that captured information to run the installation program on every other workstation. This captured information is stored in a file with an .AOT extension (Application Object Template). You can also create a text file with this type of information, and store it in a file with the extension .AXT; however, in most cases it is easier to use the .AOT file.

Z.E.N.works requires that each workstation using the Application object must be running the Novell client software that came on the Novell Client and Z.E.N.works CD-ROM. Earlier versions of the client software won't work with Z.E.N.works.

In addition, you must use the NetWare Administrator utility that came with NetWare 5 (NWADMN32.EXE). The same utility is included on the Novell Client and Z.E.N.works CD-ROM, for your convenience.

The following sections explain how to:

▶ Install Z.E.N.works on the server.

▶ Run snAppShot to create an .AOT file to capture installation options and settings if you want the application to install itself on workstations.

▶ Create an Application object and assign it to users, groups, or containers.

Installing Z.E.N.works on the Server

To install Z.E.N.works on the server, complete the following steps:

1. From a workstation, insert the Novell Client and Z.E.N.works CD-ROM. The installation program should start up automatically.

2. Choose English.

3. Choose Install Z.E.N.works.

4. At the Welcome screen, click Next.

5. At the License Agreement screen, read it and click Yes.

6. From the screen that appears, choose Typical to install application management software, desktop management software, and NetWare Administrator (see Figure 5.10). If you only want to install one or two of these options, choose Custom and select the ones you want. Click Next to continue.

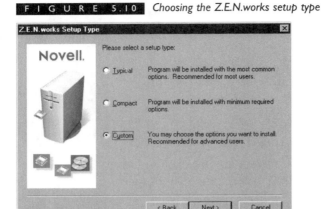

7. Choose the tree and server upon which you want to install Z.E.N.works. Click Next to continue.

8. Choose the language you want to install, and click Next.

9. Confirm the installation summary, which shows the components you've selected. If you want to keep the selections, click Next. To change some selections, choose Back.

10. Select a context to which all users will have rights, so they can write a workstation registration entry to their container. Select the default, or specify another container. Then click OK to continue.

11. When a message appears saying rights were successfully set up, click OK.

12. If you want to view the README file and the SETUP log file, leave the boxes next to those options checked, and click Finish. If you don't want to view them, unmark the boxes, and click Finish.

13. When you receive an informational message telling you to distribute new client software on all workstations, click the Exit button (at the bottom right corner of the screen) to exit the installation program.

The Z.E.N.works Starter Pack has now been installed on the server. If you go into NetWare Administrator, you can see that Z.E.N.works has successfully been installed by choosing Tools — you'll see Application Launcher Tools listed as an option.

Running snAppShot

If you want the application to install itself on workstations, you can use snAppShot to capture all the installation options and parameters in an .AOT file. Many applications make modifications to a variety of workstation files while being installed. For example, an application may modify the Windows Registry file, .INI files, system configuration files, and so on. SnAppShot captures all those modifications by running twice — once before the application's installation program runs, and once after. Then snAppShot compares the two images of the workstation and creates a template file (with the extension .AOT) showing the differences.

SnAppShot also captures all the files that the application installs on the workstation, and copies them to a network directory that you specify. It renames all the files numerically and gives them the extension .FIL. The Application object will use these files when it installs itself on other workstations.

Then, when you create the Application object, you can tell it to use the .AOT file, and it will automatically know which changes to make to all subsequent workstations.

NOTE

An .AOT file will work best on applications that don't require specific hardware choices that may vary between workstations on your network. If your application requires that you choose a video driver, for example, and your workstations have different video drivers, you may not be able to run a single .AOT file for all your workstations. You may need to set up different application objects, using different .AOT files, for each different type of workstation.

To run snAppShot, complete the following steps. You will need to run snAppShot on a workstation that adequately represents the other workstations on which the Application object will run later. You will install the application on this workstation as part of the snAppShot process.

1. From a representative workstation, log in to the network.

2. Run the file SNAPSHOT.EXE from the SYS:PUBLIC\SNAPSHOT folder.

3. (Optional) When the introductory screen appears, you can click Getting Started if you want to read an overview of snAppShot. When finished reading the overview, close the online help screen to return to the introductory snAppShot screen.

4. Choose the type of discovery process you want to use. In most cases, choose Standard, which runs the discovery process using default settings. (After you have become familiar with using snAppShot, you may want to choose one of the other options instead. The Custom option lets you specify the particular drives, files, folders, Registry hives, and shortcuts that snAppShot discovers. The Express option lets you scan for any changes using a snAppShot Preferences file created during a previous discovery session.)

5. Enter the name you are going to give the Application Object, and then enter an Application Icon Title (the name of the icon that will appear on users' workstations), as shown in Figure 5.11. Then click Next.

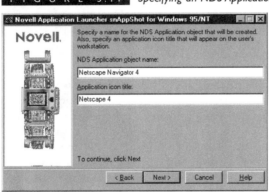

F I G U R E   5.11   *Specifying an NDS Application object name*

6. Enter the location where you want the application files to be captured. The default path will be to the C: drive on the workstation, but change the path to a network directory on the server, so that all workstations will be able to access those files. (You should create a unique network directory for each application you install.) Click Next when finished.

7. Accept the filename and location for the .AOT file. (The location should be the same as the directory you specified in Step 6.) Click Next to continue.

8. Choose the drives you want snAppShot to scan for installation changes. Click Add if you want to add more drives than those that are listed. Then click Next to continue.

9. Review the summary of your selections (see Figure 5.12), and click Next to continue. (If you want to make changes, click Back.)

FIGURE 5.12 Reviewing a summary of snAppShot settings

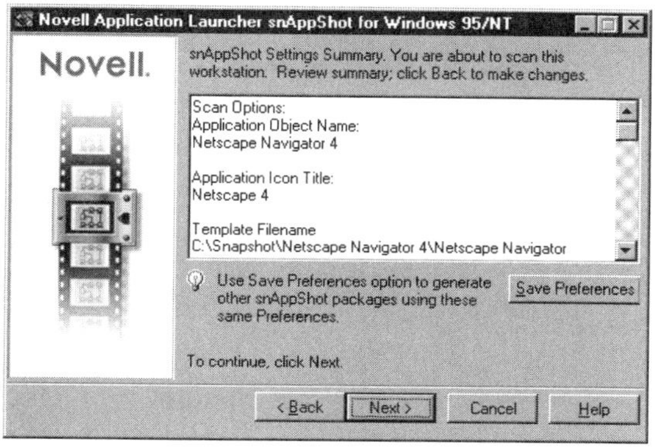

10. When snAppShot finishes scanning the workstation for the preinstallation image, click Run Application Install. You will now run the application's regular installation program. Browse for the application's installation (or Setup) program, and go through the normal installation procedures. When the installation is finished, be sure you note the location of the application's executable file on the workstation.

11. When the installation finishes, you are returned automatically to snAppShot. Enter the path to the executable, and then click Next to continue. SnAppShot will now re-scan the workstation to capture the post-installation image. Then it will compare the two images to create a template of the changes.

12. When snAppShot is finished, review the Completion Summary to see where snAppShot put the installation files.

Now you are ready to create the application object.

Creating an Application Object

To create an Application object for a network application, complete the steps in the following checklist:

1. Start up NetWare Administrator.

2. Select the container object that will hold the Application object.

3. From the Object menu, choose Create.

4. From the New Object dialog box that appears, choose Application and then choose OK.

5. Choose whether to create the object using an .AOT file (see Figure 5.13), and then click Next.

▶ · · · · · · · · · · · · · · · · · · ◀

F I G U R E   5.13 *Creating an Application object*

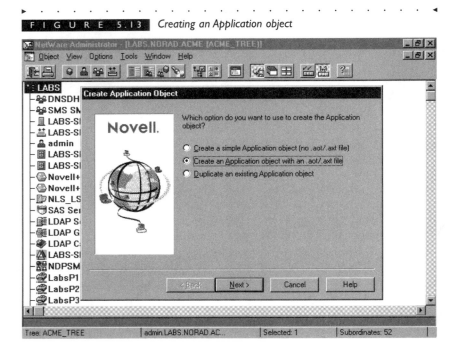

6. If you chose to create the object using an .AOT file, enter the path to the .AOT file.

7. When the Application object's dialog box appears, enter its name, source path (the network directory that contains the application files), and the target path on the workstation (where you want the application installed).

8. Review your choices, and mark the checkbox next to Display Details After Creation. Then click Finish.

9. Open the Application object's Associations page. In this page, click Add to assign this Application object to users, groups, or containers that you want to have access to this application.

10. Open the System Requirements page, and choose the platforms on which this application will run.

11. Enter any additional information necessary on other pages for this application. When finished, click OK to save your changes and exit the object's property pages.

12. From the NetWare Administrator Browser, select the user, group, or container object that will use this application, and choose Details from the Object menu.

13. (Optional) Open the Launcher Configuration page. In this page, you can click Edit to specify any particular settings you want for the Application Launcher or Application Explorer when it appears on this user's (or group's) desktop.

14. Open the Login Script page. Add a command to the login script that will execute the Application Launcher or Application Explorer. Use one of the following sets of login script commands:

   ▶ For Windows 3.1 workstations, add this command to launch the Application Launcher, substituting the name of the server for *server*:

   ```
   @\\server\sys\public\nal.exe
   ```

   ▶ For Windows 95/98 and NT workstations, add these commands to launch the Application Explorer, substituting the name of the server for *server* (and change "w95" to "w98" if you are using Windows 98):

   ```
   if platform = "w95" then

       @\\server\sys\public\nalexpld.exe

   end

   if platform = "wnt" then

       if os_version = "v4.00" then

           @\\server\sys\public\nalexpld.exe

       end

   end
   ```

15. (Windows 95/98 and Windows NT only) Open the Applications page. Here, you can change where the Application object appears on Windows 95/98 and NT workstations. Click Add if necessary to add an application to the list. Then, in the list, mark the checkbox under each location option: Force Run, Application Launcher (marked by default), Start Menu, Desktop, or System Tray.

16. Click OK to save all your changes and exit the object's property pages.

Now, when the user boots the workstation, the Application object should appear in the Application Launcher (or Application Explorer) window, and in any other location you may have specified in Step 15.

NOTE For more information about using Z.E.N.works Starter Pack and its application management and desktop management features, see the Novell online documentation or the Z.E.N.works help file. To read the Z.E.N.works help file from the Z.E.N.works CD-ROM, browse to locate the file called DMPOLICY.HLP, located in the PRODUCTS\ZENWORKS\PUBLIC\NLS\ENGLISH folder. You can also read the help file by opening the NetWare Administrator utility, choosing Help, opening Help Topics, and selecting Z.E.N.works.

Login Scripts

Login scripts are tools similar to batch files that you can use to set up users' workstation environments automatically. Each time a user logs in, the LOGIN utility executes the login scripts. These can set up frequently used drive mappings, capture the workstation's printer port to a network print queue, display connection information or messages on the screen, or do other types of tasks for the user.

NOTE In NetWare 5, you can assign a drive letter (such as G or H) to point to a specific network directory. This works the same way as making drive C point to your hard disk, or drive E point to a CD-ROM. When you assign a drive letter to a directory, it's called *mapping a drive*. The resulting drive assignment is called a *drive mapping*.

When you log in, you see a series of commands scroll by automatically. Those are the commands being executed by your login script.

Login scripts are a fairly advanced feature of NetWare 5. However, this chapter will explore the basics of login scripts and the most common commands used in those scripts.

A default login script is set up when NetWare 5 is installed. This script contains some very basic drive mappings, so you can get to the NetWare 5 utilities on the server. However, you can create your own login scripts if you'd like to set up more drive mappings for your workstation.

In previous versions of NetWare (3.1*x* and 2.*x*), there were two types of login scripts: user login scripts and system login scripts. The system login script was a file on the server. It executed for every user who logged in to that server, so it was a good place to store drive mappings or other information that was common to all users. The user login script was a separate file for each user, stored in users' MAIL subdirectories. In the user login script, you could create drive mappings or other items that were specific to that user only.

TIP

Login scripts are primarily for users of DOS and Windows 3.1 workstations. Windows 95/98 or Windows NT users can use the desktop features on their own workstations to set up many of the things login scripts set up. For example, Windows 95/98 or Windows NT users can set up shortcuts to their applications or frequently used folders. Therefore, if you use Windows 95/98 or Windows NT, you may not want — or need — to use more than the default login script.

In NetWare 5, there are three types of login scripts:

▶ *Container (System) Login Scripts* — The container login script (also called the *system login script* in previous versions of NetWare) is a property of a container object. All the commands in the container login script execute for every user within that container who logs in. Therefore, this is a good place to put commands that are common to all users within the container.

▶ *Profile Login Scripts* — With a profile script, you can create a script that will apply to several users who don't necessarily have to be in the same container. It's kind of a group login script. The profile login script is a property of a Profile object, which defines a list of users who belong to the Profile. (A Profile object exists solely to support these profile login scripts. If you don't want to use a profile login script, you don't need to create any Profile objects.) A user can have only one profile login script execute upon login.

▶ *User Login Scripts* — A user's login script is a property of his or her User object. If there are specific drive mappings or other commands that this particular user needs (but others don't), you can store those commands in the user login script. If the user does not have a specific user login script, the default login script will execute instead, setting up the most basic drive mappings.

These three types of login scripts work together to set up each user's environment upon login. They execute in the following order:

1. Container login script
2. Profile login script
3. User login script (or default login script, if a user login script doesn't exist)

All three are optional. If you don't create one of them, the LOGIN program will skip to the next in the list. If no login scripts exist, the default script will be the only one that runs when a user logs in. Figure 5.14 shows three different users in the BlueSky tree, and the objects in the tree that contain login scripts.

FIGURE 5.14 *Login scripts located in the BlueSky tree*

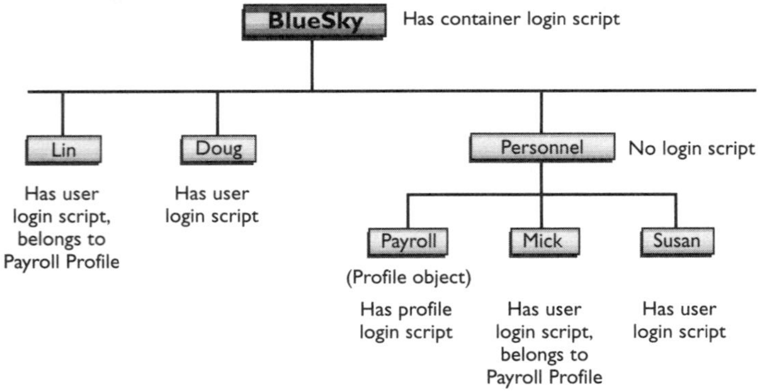

When user Lin logs in, three login scripts will execute for her. First, the container login script that belongs to the container immediately above her (BlueSky) executes, followed by a profile script (because she belongs to the Payroll Profile object) and then her own user login script.

When user Doug logs in, two login scripts execute for him. First, the container login script that belongs to his container (BlueSky) executes, followed by his own user login script.

When user Mick logs in, two login scripts execute for him. A profile login script executes first (because he belongs to the profile Payroll); then, his own user login script executes. The container immediately above him (Personnel) does not have a login script, so no container script will execute for Mick.

When user Susan logs in, only one script executes for her: her own user login script. She doesn't belong to the profile Payroll, and her container doesn't have a login script, so neither a profile nor container script will execute for her.

Because up to three different login scripts can execute for a given user, conflicts between the login scripts may occur. If they do, the final login script to execute wins. Therefore, if the container login script maps a directory to drive letter G, and then the user script maps a different directory to drive letter G, the user script's mapping overwrites the container script's mapping.

NOTE

Container login scripts only apply to the users immediately within that container. They don't apply to users in a subcontainer. If the container that holds user Susan in Figure 5.14 doesn't have a login script, no container login script will execute when Andrea logs in, even if a container higher up in the tree has a login script.

To simplify the administration of your network's login scripts, try to put as much common information as possible (such as drive mappings to application directories) in the container and profile login scripts. It's much easier to change a drive mapping in one script and have it apply to all your users than to make the same change dozens or hundreds of times for every user script.

Creating a Login Script

You use the NetWare Administrator utility to create login scripts just as you assign any other properties to NDS objects. Open the object's Details page (choose Details from the Object menu), and then click the button for the Login Script page.

When you open up the Login Script property for a User, Profile, or container object, you are presented with a blank screen (or the previous login script, if one already exists). In this screen, type any commands you want the login script to hold: drive mappings, printer port captures, messages, environment settings, and so on.

In general, you can only change your own login script if you're an ordinary user. If you're the Admin user, you can change login scripts for other users and for containers. (Even if you aren't the Admin user, you can be given rights to modify other objects' login scripts, if necessary. For more information about the rights you need for changing other objects' properties, see Chapter 6.)

Assigning Profile Login Scripts to Users

To create a profile login script, you create a Profile object just as you create any other NDS object. Create its script in the Profile object's Login Script property. After you've created the script, you must assign it to individual users. To do this, complete the following steps:

1. Use the Browser to select a User object.

2. Choose Details from the Object menu, and then open the Login Script page.

3. Enter the name of the Profile object in the Profile field beneath the login script text window.

4. Save the information and return to the Browser.

5. From the Browser, select the Profile object. A warning will pop up informing you that read rights must be assigned so the user can access the profile script.

6. From the Object menu, choose Trustees of This Object.

7. In the Trustees window that appears, click the Add Trustee button and then enter the name of the user who will use this profile login script.

8. Make sure the Browse object right and Read property right are checked, and then choose OK to assign those rights to the user.

The Most Common Login Script Commands

You can use more than 30 commands in login scripts. However, the three main reasons people use login scripts are to execute an external command or program, to redirect parallel ports to print queues, and to map drives to network directories. Therefore, it's likely that you will only see, or use, three different login script commands. These three commonly used commands are:

- ▶ @ command
- ▶ #CAPTURE command
- ▶ MAP command

The @ Login Script Command

This command executes an external command or program, such as a NetWare utility or a Windows-based application, from the login script. Use this command only on Windows-based workstations. To execute the program, use the @ symbol at the beginning of the command. (The @ command will allow the login script to finish while letting the application continue running.)

For example, to execute the NetWare Administrator utility from within the login script, include the following command in the script:

```
@SYS:\PUBLIC\WIN32\NWADMN32
```

The #CAPTURE Login Script Command

This command redirects the workstation's parallel port, so that it points to a network print queue instead of to a printer attached directly to the workstation. (This concept is explained more fully in Chapter 8.)

To execute the CAPTURE program, remember to put the pound (#) symbol at the beginning of the command. When the CAPTURE program is finished executing, the login script will take over again and continue running, executing other commands as necessary.

For example, to capture a user's LPT1 port to use a network print queue named LaserQ, you might put the following command in the login script:

```
#CAPTURE L=1 Q=.LaserQ.Sales.BlueSky NB NT NFF TI=5
```

The MAP Login Script Command

Use this command to map drive letters to network directories. When you put a MAP command in a login script, a drive letter will be mapped to the specified network directory every time the user logs in.

To map a drive letter to a directory in a login script, type the MAP command using the following format:

```
MAP letter:=path
```

For example, to map drive L to VOL1:APPS\WP, the command would be as follows:

```
MAP L:=VOL1:APPS\WP
```

You can also use MAP to map search drives. Search drives are special types of drive mappings that act like DOS path commands. Search drives are used to indicate directories that contain applications or utilities. A search drive lets users execute an application without having to know where the application is located. The network searches through all the available search drives for the application so the user doesn't have to search for it.

To map a search drive, you don't designate a specific drive letter. Instead, you use the letter S, followed by a number. Novell's NetWare 5 will assign search drives their own letters in reverse order, starting with the letter Z. (You can have up to 16 search drives mapped, so those drives would be letters Z through K.) For example, if you already have one search drive mapped, and you want to map the second search drive to the SYS:MSWORD directory, enter the following line in the login script:

```
MAP S2:=SYS:MSWORD
```

TIP

Search drive mappings are added to the workstation's DOS PATH environment variable. This means that if you specify that a search drive is S1, that search drive mapping will overwrite the first DOS path that had already been set. To avoid overwriting a path setting, use the INS option (which stands for "insert"). For example, you can type MAP INS S1: instead of MAP S1:.

By using the INS option, the search drive mapping for the SYS:PUBLIC directory will be inserted at the beginning of the DOS path settings. This moves the original first path setting to the second position.

In login scripts, the first search drive should be mapped to the PUBLIC directory. This directory contains the NetWare 5 utilities and other files that users need.

To map the first search drive to the PUBLIC directory (which is in the SYS volume), use the following command:

```
MAP INS S1:=SYS:PUBLIC
```

Because NetWare 5 assigns drive letters for search drives starting at the end of the alphabet, this command will assign the drive letter Z to the SYS:PUBLIC directory. If you go to the Z drive, you'll see the PUBLIC files listed.

TIP

Instead of mapping search drives in order (S3, S4, S5, and so on), you can use MAP S16 for all subsequent mappings that don't require an exact position or a specific drive letter. Each MAP S16 command will insert its drive mapping at the end of the list, pushing up the previous mappings. This just makes the list of search drives more flexible. For example, if you delete one, the others will reorder themselves automatically. Also, you don't run the risk of overwriting a search drive that may have been specified in another login script.

You can use several variations of the MAP command to accomplish different tasks, as shown in Table 5.1.

TABLE 5.1 *MAP Command Option*

TASK	DESCRIPTION
Map drives in order, without specifying drive letters	If you don't want to specify exact drive letters, you can map each available drive, in order. This is useful if you don't know which drive letters have already been mapped in a system or profile login script. To assign drive letters this way, use an asterisk, followed by a number. For example, to get the first and second available drives, you could use the following commands: MAP *1:=VOL1:APPS\WP MAP *2:=VOL1:DATA\REPORTS
Map the next available drive	To map the next available drive, use the letter N (without a colon), as in the following command: MAP N VOL1:APPS\WP
Delete a drive mapping	To delete a mapping for drive G, for example, use the following command: MAP DEL G
Turn off MAP's display	Whenever a MAP command is executed in the login script, it will display the new drive mapping on the workstation screen unless you specify otherwise. To turn off this display, use the following command: MAP DISPLAY OFF
Turn on MAP's display	At the end of the login script, you may want to turn MAP's display back on and show a listing of all the completed drive mappings. To do this, put the following commands at, or near, the end of the login script: MAP DISPLAY ON MAP

Continued

TABLE 5.1	*MAP Command Option (continued)*
TASK	**DESCRIPTION**
Map a fake root	Some applications must be installed at the root of a volume or hard disk. If you would rather install the application in a subdirectory, you can do that, and then map a fake root to the application's subdirectory. A *fake root* mapping makes a subdirectory appear to be a volume, so that the application runs correctly. (See Chapter 7 for more information about fake roots.) You can map a fake root in a regular drive mapping or in a search drive mapping. To map drive H as a fake root to the VOL1:APPS\CAD subdirectory, use the following command: MAP ROOT H:=VOL1:APPS\CAD
Map a drive to a Directory Map object	You can create an NDS object, called a Directory Map object, that points to a particular directory. Then you can map drives to that object instead of to the actual directory path. This way, if you later move the directory to another part of the file system, you can just change the Directory Map object's description instead of updating all the affected login scripts. Preferably, use Directory Map objects in the user's current context. If the Directory Map object is in another part of the NDS tree, create an Alias object for the Directory Map object in the user's current context. To map a search drive to a Directory Map object named Database, use the following command: MAP S16:=DATABASE

Beyond the Basics

This chapter explained how to create users and groups, how to log in and out of the network, and how to use the NetWare Application Launcher.

The following topics, mentioned in this chapter, are explained more fully in other chapters in this book:

▶ To install NetWare Administrator on your workstation, see Chapter 4.

▶ For more information about NDS objects and name contexts, see Chapter 4.

▶ For information about NDS security, file system security, see Chapter 6.

▶ To set up passwords and account restrictions, see Chapter 6.

▶ To give users access to network printing, see Chapter 8.

For more information on the following topics, refer to Novell's online documentation or *Novell's NetWare 5 Administrator's Handbook* (from Novell Press):

▶ Using login scripts and their commands

▶ Using the NET.CFG file

Managing Network Security

One of the aspects of NetWare that sets it apart from other network operating systems is its high level of security. How you implement this security is up to you. You can make your NetWare 5 network as open as you need, or as secure as Fort Knox.

Some people may not think they need to worry about network security. It's easy to think that only banks and government agencies need to worry about it. However, network security doesn't just mean preventing spies and hackers from breaking into your network. For example, network security can:

- ▶ Prevent employees from seeing each other's personnel or salary files.
- ▶ Keep employees from accidentally erasing each other's files.
- ▶ Keep viruses from spreading.
- ▶ Let other users see some of your personal files, without letting them see the files you'd rather they didn't see.
- ▶ Prevent users from changing other users' security levels.
- ▶ Protect applications from being inadvertently deleted or copied over.
- ▶ Allow certain users to manage printers and print queues, while preventing other users from messing with them at all.
- ▶ Allow users to read public documents without letting them modify or erase them.
- ▶ Let key people have rights to manage certain groups of users, portions of the Directory tree, or all the files on a volume or in a directory, so you can distribute the workload of network management.

These are only a few of the ways network security can protect and simplify your network. If you think about your network situation for a while, you may come up with additional ways that network security can benefit you and your users.

Novell's NetWare 5 uses three basic security features to allow you to control your network's security:

- ▶ Login security, which ensures that only authorized users can log in to the network
- ▶ NDS security, which controls whether NDS objects (such as users) can see or manipulate other NDS objects and their properties
- ▶ File system security, which controls whether users can see and work with files and directories

Each of these types of security is described in this chapter.

Login Security

Login security is NetWare 5's first line of defense, ensuring that only authorized users can get into the network.

The three main aspects of login security are:

▸ Ensuring that all users have valid user accounts and valid passwords (required)

▸ Using account restrictions (optional) to limit the times that users can log in, the workstations they can use, and such things as the length of their passwords and how frequently they must change their passwords

▸ Using intruder-detection features (optional) to recognize when someone may be trying to break into the network by guessing passwords

User Accounts and Passwords

Everyone who accesses the network should have his or her own user account. While it may seem convenient to have several people use a single user account, or to allow someone else to log in using your account, this can be a potential security problem. For example, you may not want all those users to have rights to access all the same files. If they are all using the same account, you cannot control their individual access, you cannot control the password they are using, and you may end up with unexpected conflicts.

It's a much better plan to give users their own individual user accounts. Then, once users have their own accounts, they each have their own passwords as well.

If passwords are to be a useful form of security, you should ensure that they are being used, that users are changing them frequently, and that users aren't choosing passwords that can be guessed easily.

You can set these types of password restrictions by using the NetWare Administrator utility. (For instructions on how to set up the NetWare Administrator utility on a workstation, see Chapter 4.) To set password restrictions for a user, open the NetWare Administrator's Browser and select the User object. Then, from the Object menu, choose Details, select the Password Restrictions page, and enter the restrictions you want to apply to the user. Figure 6.1 shows the Password Restrictions page for a User object.

► · ◄

F I G U R E   6 . 1   *A User object's Password Restrictions page in NetWare*
Administrator

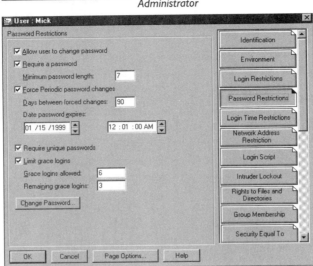

Users can change their own passwords in any of the following ways:

► Type the command **SETPASS** at the DOS prompt, and enter the new password when prompted for it.

► Open the Password Restrictions page in the NetWare Administrator utility, and specify a new password there.

► Specify a new password while logging in. If the password has expired, the LOGIN utility will tell the user, and allow him or her to type in a new password at that time.

Preserving Password Security

The following tips can help preserve password security (and you can enforce most of them by using password restrictions):

► Require passwords to be at least five characters long (seven or eight is better). The default minimum is five characters.

► Require that passwords be changed every 30 days or less.

► Require unique passwords so users can't reuse a password they've used before.

- Do not allow unlimited grace logins. Limit the number of grace logins to three. (A *grace login* allows you to log in using an expired password.)

- Remind users not to tell others about their passwords or allow others to use their accounts.

- Tell users to avoid choosing passwords that can be guessed easily, such as birthdays, favorite hobbies or sports, family member names, pet names, and so on. Instead, tell users to mix words and numbers together to form words that can't be found in a dictionary, such as BRAVO42 or ST66CL.

Account Restrictions

With user account restrictions, you can limit how a user can log in to the network.

Password restrictions, as explained in the previous section, are one form of account restriction. You can also implement the following three additional types of account restrictions:

- *Login Restrictions* specify whether the account has an expiration date (which might be useful in settings such as schools, where the authorized users will change with each semester), and whether the user can be logged in from multiple workstations simultaneously.

- *Login Time Restrictions* dictate the times of day that users must be logged out of the network. (By default, users can be logged in at any time — there are no restrictions.)

- *Network Address Restrictions* specify which network addresses (workstations) a user can use to log in. (By default, there are no restrictions on addresses.)

You can set each of these types of account restrictions for individual users, or you can set them in a user template so they apply to all users you create in a particular container. If you set them up in a user template, the restrictions will apply to any new users you create from that point on. They aren't retrofitted to users who already exist. Managing account restrictions for all new users in a user template can save you time if all your users need the same types of restrictions.

To set any of these account restrictions, you use the NetWare Administrator utility. (For instructions on setting up the NetWare Administrator utility on a workstation, see Chapter 4.)

To set account restrictions for a user, use the NetWare Administrator utility and select the User object. Then, choose Details from the Object menu. You'll see an Information page for each type of account restriction listed along the right side of the Details screen. Open the Information page for the type of restriction you want to set, and specify the limits you want.

As an example, Figure 6.2 shows the Login Time Restrictions page for a user named Mick. By default, users are not restricted from logging in at any time. However, in Mick's case, the network administrator has restricted Mick's account so that he cannot log in at all on Saturdays or Sundays, nor can he log in between 9 p.m. and 6 a.m. (Gray cells in the grid indicate times that the user cannot be logged in. To change a cell from gray to blank, simply click the cell.)

F I G U R E 6 . 2 *A User object's Login Time Restrictions page in NetWare Administrator*

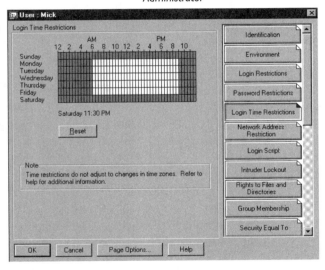

To set account restrictions for all new users you create, use the NetWare Administrator utility and select the appropriate Template object. Then select Details from the Object menu, open the appropriate restriction pages, and specify the correct restrictions. (Changes to the Template object apply only to users you subsequently create. These changes do not apply to users who already exist.) For more information about using Template objects, see Chapter 5.

Intruder Detection

Enforcing account restrictions and passwords can keep unauthorized users from breaking into the network. However, we've all seen movies where the bad guys (and sometimes the good guys) hack into a computer by repeatedly guessing at passwords. Novell's NetWare 5 provides a feature that can keep such hackers from trying over and over again until they guess correctly. This feature is called *intruder detection*.

With NetWare 5, you can set the network so that users are locked out after a given number of failed login attempts. This helps ensure that users don't try to break into the network by simply guessing another user's password, or by using programs that automatically generate passwords.

To set up intruder detection, you use the NetWare Administrator utility and assign intruder detection for a container. Then, any user account within that container is subject to being locked if a set number of login attempts fail.

To enable intruder detection, complete the following steps:

1. From the NetWare Administrator's Browser, select the container for which you want to set up intruder detection, and then choose Details from the Object menu.

2. Open the Intruder Detection page shown in Figure 6.3.

FIGURE 6.3 *Intruder Detection page*

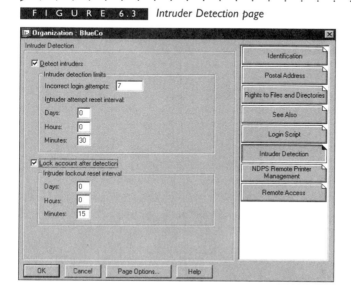

3. To detect intruders, mark the Detect Intruders checkbox. Then, specify the intruder detection limits. The Incorrect Login Attempts and Intruder Attempt Reset Interval allow you to specify how many incorrect login attempts will be allowed in a given time. If you mark the Detect Intruders checkbox, the default values that appear allow seven incorrect attempts within a 30-minute interval. You may want to reduce the number of attempts to four or five, depending on how likely your network is to have such an intruder.

4. If you want the user's account to be locked after an intruder is detected, mark the Lock Account After Detection checkbox. Then, specify how long you want the account to remain locked. The default locks the account for 15 minutes after the given number of failed login attempts. After 15 minutes, the account will be reopened automatically (intruder detection for that account will be reset). You may want to increase this time if you are concerned about intruders.

To see if a user's account has been locked, use the NetWare Administrator and select the user in question. Choose Details from the Object menu, and then open the user's Intruder Lockout page. This page shows whether the account is locked, as shown in Figure 6.4. If the Account Locked checkbox is marked, the account is locked. To unlock it, click the checkbox to clear it.

F I G U R E 6.4 *Intruder Lockout page*

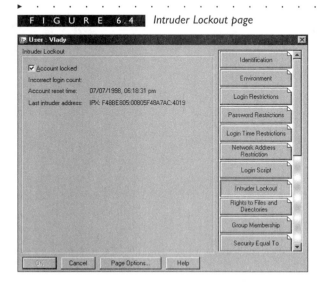

This page also shows when the user's account was locked. In addition, it shows the address of the workstation from which the failed login attempts were tried.

NDS Security

Once you've created your NDS Directory tree, you've probably invested a fair amount of time ensuring that the objects you've created contain all the right information in their properties. Now you can decide who gets to see that information and who can change it.

To make the information about the objects in your tree secure, you can use NDS trustee rights to control how objects in the tree can work with other objects and their properties. *NDS trustee rights* are permissions that allow users or objects to perform tasks such as viewing other objects, changing their properties, deleting them, and so on.

When you assign a user enough NDS trustee rights to work with another object, you've made that user a *trustee* of the object. Each object contains a property called the *Access Control List* (ACL), which is a list of all the trustees of this particular object.

When the network is first installed, the user Admin has all NDS trustee rights to all objects in the tree. This means that when you log in as user Admin, Admin's NDS trustee rights let you create and delete other objects, see them, read and modify all their properties, and so on. Admin is the only user who has full NDS rights to everything in the network immediately after installation.

By default, when all others users are created, they are granted only a subset of NDS rights, so they have limited abilities to work with other NDS objects. However, while logged in as Admin, you can add to or remove these NDS rights to customize your users' abilities. You can even grant other users the same NDS rights as the Admin user, so they can have the same control over all other objects.

For security reasons, you should be frugal with NDS rights. NDS rights are a tool to protect your network objects from both accidental and intentional tampering. You may want to assign two users full NDS rights to the network, such as Admin and another user account that only you can use. This way, there is a backup account you can use if, for example, you forget the Admin's password or delete the Admin user.

NDS Rights

There are two types of NDS trustee rights. *Object rights* control how the user works with the object (see Table 6.1). *Property rights* control whether the user can see and work with an object's properties (Table 6.2). (As explained in Chapter 4, an NDS object's properties are the defined characteristics of the object. For example, a User object's properties might include the user's full name, telephone number, trustee rights to other objects, login script, and title.)

TABLE 6.1	*NDS Object Rights*
NDS OBJECT RIGHT	**DESCRIPTION**
Supervisor	Grants the trustee all NDS rights to the object and all of its properties. If a trustee has the Supervisor right, the trustee can create, change, or delete any aspect of the object. The Supervisor right can be blocked by the Inherited Rights Filter (explained in the next section).
Browse	Allows the trustee to see the object in the NDS tree. If you don't have this right to an object, that object won't appear in the NetWare Administrator's Browser screen when you look at it.
Create	Allows the trustee to create a new object in this container. (This right only appears if you're looking at the trustee assignments for a container object.)
Delete	Allows the trustee to delete an object.
Rename	Allows the trustee to change the object's name.

TABLE 6.2	*NDS Property Rights*
NDS PROPERTY RIGHT	**DESCRIPTION**
Supervisor	Grants the trustee all NDS rights to the property. It can be blocked by the Inherited Rights Filter (explained in the following section).

NDS PROPERTY RIGHT	DESCRIPTION
Compare	Allows the trustee to compare the value of this property to a value the user specifies in a search. (For example, with the Compare right to the Department property, a user can search the tree for any object that has Marketing listed in its Department property.)
Read	Allows the trustee to see the value of this property. (The Read right automatically grants the Compare right, as well.)
Write	Allows the trustee to add, modify, or delete the value of this property. (The Write right automatically grants the Add or Delete Self right, as well.)
Add or Delete Self	Allows trustees to add or remove themselves as a value of this property. This right only applies to properties that list User objects as values, such as group membership lists or the Access Control List. (While this right is officially called the Add or Delete Self right, it usually appears on the screen as simply the "Add Self" right.)

To change object or property rights, refer to the "Seeing and Changing an Object's NDS Rights" section later in this chapter.

Inheriting NDS Rights

NDS object and property rights can be inherited. This means that if you have NDS rights to a parent container, you can inherit those rights and exercise them in an object within that container, too. Inheritance keeps you from having to grant users NDS rights at every level of the Directory tree.

However, it is sometimes desirable to block inheritance. For example, you may want to allow a user to delete objects in a parent container, but not let that user delete any objects in a particular subcontainer. Inheritance can be blocked in three ways:

▶ By granting a new set of NDS rights to an object within the container. Any new assignment will cause the inherited NDS rights from a parent container to be ignored. You can grant a new set of rights using the NetWare Administrator utility, as explained later in this chapter.

▶ By marking a container's trustee assignments as either inheritable or not. If you specify that a container's trustee assignments are not inheritable, none of the rights will be inherited at lower levels.

▶ By removing the right from an object's Inherited Rights Filter (IRF). Every object has a property called an *Inherited Rights Filter*, which specifies which NDS rights can be inherited from a parent container. By default, an object's IRF allows all NDS rights to be inherited. You can change the IRF, however, to revoke one or more NDS rights. Any rights that are revoked from the IRF cannot be inherited.

You can only inherit an NDS right if you've been assigned that right at a higher level. If you don't have the Supervisor right in the parent container, for example, you can't inherit it and use it in another object even though that right is allowed in the IRF. The IRF doesn't grant NDS rights; it just allows you to inherit them if they've already been assigned to you.

Figure 6.5 shows the NDS rights that Angela can inherit. In the container called Space, Angela has four trustee rights: Browse (B), Create (C), Delete (D), and Rename (R). Ordinarily, she would inherit all four of those rights in the sub-container called Rockets. However, the administrator has changed Rocket's IRF, and removed the Rename right. That means Angela cannot inherit that right, even though she has it at a higher level in the tree. Therefore, in the Rockets container, Angela only inherited three rights: Browse, Create, and Delete.

FIGURE 6.5 *One of Angela's inherited rights is blocked by the IRF*

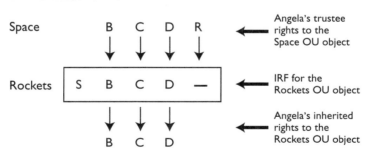

The NetWare Administrator utility prevents a user from cutting off all supervisor access to a branch of the NDS tree by searching for an object with supervisor rights to the given container. If an object

NOTE

with supervisor rights isn't found, NetWare Administrator warns you and prevents you from blocking rights.

NDS Security Equivalence

Sometimes, you may decide you want to give one object exactly the same NDS trustee rights as another object. You can do this easily by assigning the first object a *security equivalence* to the second object.

You assign a security equivalence by using the Security Equal To property. With security equivalence, you can make user Jason have the same NDS rights to the same NDS objects as user Erica, for example. (In fact, a security equivalence will give Jason the same file system rights as Erica, too. File system rights are explained later in this chapter.)

When you add a user to a Group object's membership list or to an Organizational Role object's list, the user really becomes security equivalent to that Group or Organizational Role object. Then, when you grant a right to the Group object, for example, all the users who belong to the Group get that same right because of their security equivalences.

When you are given *security equivalence* to another user, you only receive the same NDS rights (and file system rights) that the other user was explicitly granted. You do not get equivalences to that other user's equivalences. In other words, security equivalence doesn't travel. If Jason is equivalent to Erica, and Erica is equivalent to Mick, Jason doesn't end up being equivalent to Mick, too. Jason only receives whatever rights Erica received explicitly.

Effective NDS Rights

Because a user can be given NDS rights to an object and its properties through a variety of methods (explicit assignment, security equivalence, and inheritance), it can be confusing to determine exactly which NDS rights the user really has. A user's *effective NDS rights* are the combination of NDS rights that the user can ultimately exercise. The user's effective rights to an object are determined in one of the following two ways:

▶ The user's inherited NDS rights from a parent container, minus any rights blocked by the object's IRF.

▶ The sum of all NDS rights granted to the user for that object through direct trustee assignments and security equivalences to other objects. The IRF does not affect direct trustee assignments and security equivalences.

For example, suppose user Joanna has been given the Browse right to a container object. Joanna has also been given a security equivalence to user Mick, who has Create, Delete, and Rename rights to the same container. This means Joanna's effective NDS rights to this container are now Browse (B), Create (C), Delete (D), and Rename (R), as illustrated in Figure 6.6.

FIGURE 6.6 *Joanna's effective NDS rights are her explicit trustee assignment plus her security equivalence*

Mick's assignment   =   C D R

Joanna's assignment   =   B
                              + C D R   (security equivalence to Mick)

Joanna's effective rights   =   B C D R

Even if the container's IRF blocks the Delete right, Joanna still has that right. This is because the IRF only affects inherited rights, and inherited rights are completely ignored if the user has explicit trustee assignments to an object or a security equivalence that gives her NDS rights to that object.

Seeing and Changing an Object's NDS Rights

To work with the trustees of an object, and to see or change NDS trustee rights, use the NetWare Administrator utility, which runs in Windows 3.1 or Windows 95/98. (To set up NetWare Administrator on your workstation, see Chapter 4.)

Seeing an Object's Trustees, and Modifying the Trustees' Rights

From the NetWare Administrator's Browser, select the object whose list of trustees you want to see, and then choose Trustees of This Object from the Object menu. (You can also click the right mouse button to bring up a menu that contains some of the more frequently used tasks, and select Trustees of This Object from that menu.)

The Trustees of This Object screen appears, and you can see all the trustees of this object, as shown in Figure 6.7. If you click on each trustee, you can see the specific NDS object and property rights belonging to that trustee. You can also add or delete NDS rights from that trustee by marking the checkboxes next to each right.

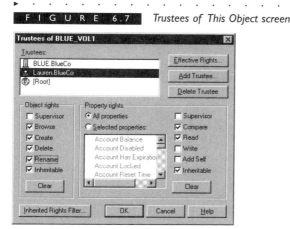

FIGURE 6.7 *Trustees of This Object screen*

Seeing and Changing the Inherited Rights Filter

From the NetWare Administrator's Browser, select the object whose IRF you want to see, and then choose Trustees of This Object from the Object menu. (You can also click the right mouse button and choose the same option from that menu.)

On the Trustees of This Object screen, click the Inherited Rights Filter button to bring up the IRF information, as shown in Figure 6.8.

FIGURE 6.8 *Object's Inherited Rights Filter*

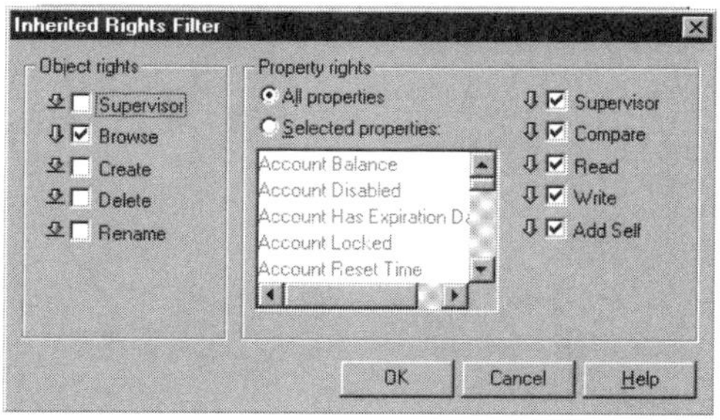

By default, any object or property rights can be inherited from the parent object. If you want to block an NDS right from being inherited, unmark the checkbox located beside that particular right. (Click a checkbox to mark or unmark it.)

Assigning Property Rights to an Object

To grant a user property rights to an NDS object's properties, select the NDS object, and then choose Trustees of This Object from the Object menu. (You can also click the right mouse button and choose the same option from that menu.)

On the Trustees of This Object screen, click the trustee to which you want to grant property rights. Once you've clicked the trustee you want, you can choose one of two ways to assign property rights:

▶ You can click the All Properties button, which is a quick way to give the user the same property rights to all the properties of that object. If you select All Properties, those property rights can be inherited.

▶ You can click Selected Properties and give the user different property rights to each individual property. Property rights assigned only to specific properties cannot be inherited.

Figure 6.9 shows the property rights that user Jason has been assigned for a print server object. His property rights apply for all of the print server's properties.

F I G U R E   6 . 9   *User's property rights*

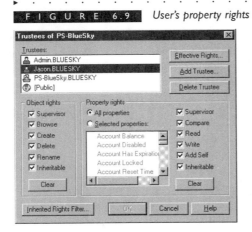

Seeing the List of NDS Objects to Which an Object Has Rights

To see all the objects to which a particular object has NDS rights, select the object. Then, from the Object menu, choose Rights to Other Objects (or click the right mouse button and select the same option from the menu that appears).

Specify the name context (location in the NDS tree) where you want to search for objects to which your selected object has rights. Then, the Rights to Other Objects screen appears. Figure 6.10 shows the Rights to Other Objects screen for the Admin user. The list of objects that Admin has rights to in this example includes print servers, print queues, other users, and so on.

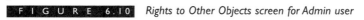

F I G U R E   6.10   *Rights to Other Objects screen for Admin user*

To change the rights this object has to another object, first click the name of the second object in the list. Then, to grant a right, click the checkbox beside the right to mark it. To remove a right, click the checkbox again to unmark it. (A marked checkbox indicates that the right is granted. A blank checkbox means the object cannot exercise that right.)

You can also give this object new trustee assignments to additional objects, by clicking the Add Assignment button. Likewise, you can delete trustee assignments by choosing Delete Assignment.

Seeing and Changing Security Equivalences

To see or change a user's security equivalence, select the user, and then choose Details from the Object menu (or right-click the user and select Details). Then open the Security Equal To page.

From this page, you can add or delete other objects to which this user has a security equivalence. You can add or delete security equivalences by clicking the Add or Delete buttons.

File System Security

File system security ensures that users can only access and use the files and directories you want them to see and use. The two different types of security tools you can implement in the file system (either together or separately) to protect your files are:

- *File system trustee rights*, which you assign to users and groups. Just as NDS object rights and NDS property rights control what users can do with other objects, file system trustee rights control what each user or group can do with the file or directory.

- *Attributes*, which you can assign directly to files and directories. Unlike file system rights, which are specific to different users and groups, attributes belong to the file or directory, and they control the activities of all users, regardless of those users' file trustee rights.

The next few sections explain file system trustee rights. File and directory attributes are explained later in this chapter, in the "File and Directory Attributes" section.

File System Trustee Rights

File system trustee rights allow users and groups to work with files and directories (folders) in specific ways. Each right determines whether a user can do things such as see, read, change, rename, or delete the file or directory.

When a user is given a file system right for a particular file, the right affects the user's allowable actions in that file only. When a user is given a file system right for a directory, the right affects the user's allowable actions on that particular directory, as well as on all the files within that directory.

As with NDS rights, when a user is given rights to a file or directory, the user is called a *trustee* of that file or directory.

NOTE

Although file system rights are similar in nature to the NDS rights for objects and properties (described earlier in this chapter), they are not the same. File system rights are separate from NDS rights. They affect only how users work with files and directories. NDS rights affect how users work with other NDS objects.

The only place where NDS rights and file system rights overlap is at the NetWare Server object. If a user is granted the Supervisor object right to a Server object, that user is also granted the Supervisor file system right to any volumes attached to that server. Because user Admin has full NDS rights to all objects in the tree after the installation (although you can limit Admin's rights later), user Admin has the Supervisor file system right to the entire file system, too.

There are eight different file system trustee rights. You can assign any combination of those file system rights to a user or group, depending on how you want that user or group to work with files and directories.

Table 6.3 lists the available file system rights. Because a trustee right may act a little differently when assigned for a file than when it is assigned for a directory, Table 6.3 also explains the difference.

TABLE 6.3 *File System Trustee Rights*

FILE SYSTEM RIGHT	ABBREVIATION	DESCRIPTION
Read	R	*Directory:* Enables the trustee to open and read files in the directory. *File:* Enables the trustee to open and read the file.
Write	W	*Directory:* Enables the trustee to open and write to (change) files in the directory. *File:* Enables the trustee to open and write to the file.

Continued

T A B L E 6.3	*File System Trustee Rights (continued)*	
FILE SYSTEM RIGHT	**ABBREVIATION**	**DESCRIPTION**
Create	C	*Directory:* Enables the trustee to create subdirectories and files in the directory. *File:* Enables the trustee to salvage the file if it was deleted.
Erase	E	*Directory:* Enables the trustee to delete the directory and its files and subdirectories. *File:* Enables the trustee to delete the file.
Modify	M	*Directory:* Enables the trustee to change the name, directory attributes, and file attributes of the directory and its files and subdirectories. *File:* Enables the trustee to change the file's name or file attributes.
File Scan	F	*Directory:* Enables the trustee to see the names of the files and subdirectories within the directory. *File:* Enables the trustee to see the name of the file.
Access Control	A	*Directory:* Enables the trustee to change the directory's IRF and trustee assignments. *File:* Enables the trustee to change the file's IRF and trustee assignments.

FILE SYSTEM RIGHT	ABBREVIATION	DESCRIPTION
Supervisor	S	*Directory:* Grants the trustee all rights to the directory, its files, and its subdirectories. It cannot be blocked by an IRF. *File:* Grants the trustee all rights to the file. It cannot be blocked by an IRF.

Inheriting File System Rights

Just like NDS rights, file system rights can be inherited. This means that if you have file system rights to a parent directory, you can inherit those rights and exercise them in any file and subdirectory within that directory, too.

Inheritance is a handy feature that keeps you from having to grant users new file system rights at every level of the file system. There are two ways to block inheritance:

▶ You can grant the user a new set of file system rights to a subdirectory or file within the parent directory. Any new assignment will cause the inherited rights from a parent directory to be ignored.

▶ You can remove the right from a file's or a subdirectory's Inherited Rights Filter (IRF).

Every directory and file has an Inherited Rights Filter that specifies which file system rights can be inherited from a parent directory. By default, a file's or directory's IRF allows all rights to be inherited. You can change the IRF, however, to revoke one or more rights. Any file system rights that are revoked from the IRF cannot be inherited.

You can only inherit a file system right if you've been assigned that right at a higher level. If you don't have the Create right in the parent directory, for example, you can't inherit it and use it in another subdirectory — even though that right is allowed in the IRF. The IRF doesn't grant rights; it just allows you to inherit file system rights if they've already been assigned to you at a higher level.

For instructions on assigning file system rights or changing the IRF, see the "Seeing and Changing a User's File System Rights" section later in this chapter.

File System Security Equivalence

Security equivalence for file system rights works the same way as security equivalence for NDS rights (explained earlier in this chapter). You can assign one user the same NDS rights and file system rights as another user by using the

Security Equal To property. With security equivalence, you can make user Lin have the same rights to the same NDS objects, files, and directories as user Erica.

When you add a user to a Group object's membership list, or to an Organizational Role object's list, the user then becomes security equivalent to that Group or Organizational Role object. Then, when you grant a right to the Group object, for example, all of the users who belong to the Group get that same right because of their security equivalences.

NOTE

Remember, when you are given security equivalence to another user, you only receive the same rights that the other user was explicitly granted. You do not get equivalences to that user's other equivalences.

For example, assume Don has explicit rights to folder A, and a security equivalence to Janet that gives him rights to folder B. If another user, Anthony, is security equivalent to Don, Anthony will automatically get Don's rights to A. However, Anthony won't get rights to folder B, because Don's security equivalence to Janet cannot be transferred to Anthony.

Effective File System Rights

Just as with NDS rights, determining which file system rights a user can actually exercise in a file or directory can be confusing at first. A user's effective file system rights are the file system rights that the user can ultimately execute in a given directory or file. The user's effective rights to a directory or file are determined in one of two ways:

- The user's inherited rights from a parent directory, minus any rights blocked by the subdirectory's (or file's) IRF

- The sum of all rights granted to the user for that directory or file, through both direct trustee assignment and security equivalences to other users

A file's or directory's IRF does not affect direct trustee assignments and security equivalences. Therefore, if you have been given an explicit trustee assignment in a file or directory, any rights you might have inherited from a parent directory will be completely ignored.

On the other hand, if you have not been given an explicit trustee assignment or security equivalence that specifically gives you rights in a file or directory, then you can use inherited rights in that file or directory. You will automatically inherit any rights you had in a parent directory, minus any rights blocked by the current file's or directory's IRF.

Seeing and Changing a User's File System Rights

To see a user's file system rights, use the NetWare Administrator utility (which runs in Windows 3.1 and Windows 95/98). To use the NetWare Administrator utility, you can either select a user and see the user's trustee assignments (a list of the files and directories of which that user is a trustee), or you can select a file or directory and see a list of all its trustees.

Seeing and Changing a User's Trustee Assignments

To see or change a user's trustee assignments, complete the following steps:

1. From the NetWare Administrator's Browser, select the user and choose Details from the Object menu.

2. Open the Rights to Files and Directories page.

3. To see the user's current file system rights, you must first select a volume that contains directories to which the user has rights. To do this, click the Show button. Then, in the Directory Context panel on the right side, navigate through the Directory tree to locate the desired volume. Select the volume from the Available Objects panel on the left side, and then click OK.

4. Now, under the Files and Directories panel, a list appears showing all the files and directories of which the user is currently a trustee (see Figure 6.11).

F I G U R E   6.11   *Trustee's rights to files and directories*

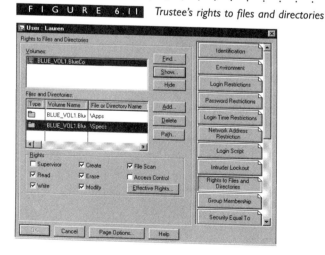

5. To see the user's assigned file system rights to one of these directories or files, select the directory or file, and then look at the list of rights below. A mark in the checkbox next to each right means that the user has rights to the given file or directory. To change the user's rights, click each desired checkbox to either mark it or clear it.

6. To see the user's effective file system rights to this file or directory, click the Effective Rights button.

7. To assign the user file system rights to a new file or directory, click the Add button. In the Directory Context panel on the right side, navigate through the Directory tree to locate the desired volume or directory. Then, select the volume, directory, or file from the left panel, and click OK. Now the newly selected file, directory, or volume appears under the Files and Directories panel. Make sure the new file, directory, or volume is selected, and then assign the appropriate file system rights by marking each desired checkbox.

8. To see or change a user's security equivalence, open the user's Security Equal To page. There, you can add or delete other objects to which this user has a security equivalence. Remember that security equivalence affects both NDS and file system rights.

Seeing and Changing a Directory's List of Trustees

To use the NetWare Administrator utility to see all the trustees of a directory (or a file or volume), complete the following steps:

1. From the NetWare Administrator's Browser, select the directory and choose Details from the Object menu.

2. Open the Trustees of this Directory page. This page shows the containers and users that have trustee rights to this directory (see Figure 6.12). This page also shows the directory's IRF. By default, the IRF allows any file system rights to be inherited from the parent directory.

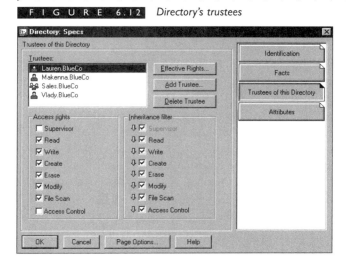

FIGURE 6.12 *Directory's trustees*

3. To change the IRF to block a file system right from being inherited, click the checkbox next to that right to clear its box.

4. To see a particular trustee's effective file system rights to the directory, click the Effective Rights button, and then select the trustee. (You can click the Browse button next to the Trustee field to navigate the NDS tree and select the trustee that way.) That trustee's effective rights will appear in boldface type.

5. To add a trustee to the directory, click the Add Trustee button. Navigate through the Directory tree in the right panel, and then select the user you want from the Objects panel on the left side. That user now appears in the Trustees list. Select that user, and then mark the checkboxes next to the file system rights you want the user to have.

File and Directory Attributes

Another important NetWare security tool for securing files and directories is attributes. *Attributes* are properties of files and directories that control what can happen to those files or directories. Attributes, which are also called *flags*, are different from trustee rights in several ways, including:

▶ Attributes are assigned directly to files and directories, while rights are assigned to users.

▶ Attributes override rights. In other words, if a directory has the Delete Inhibit attribute, you can't delete the directory even if you've been granted the Erase right.

▶ Attributes don't grant rights. Just because a file has the Read-Write attribute doesn't mean you can write to it if you don't have the Write right.

▶ Attributes affect all users, including the Admin user.

▶ Attributes affect some aspects of the file that rights do not, such as determining whether or not the files in a directory can be purged immediately upon deletion. (Purging is explained in Chapter 7.)

File and directory attributes are a very powerful security feature of NetWare 5. They are explained here in this chapter so you can understand them should the need arise. However, you will probably find that you seldom need to change or even be aware of attributes.

In some cases, applications will automatically set attributes needed to protect their executable files from being erased accidentally. This is often the only time you may encounter these attributes.

NOTE   Some available attributes are used by the more advanced features of NetWare 5 that aren't explained in this book, such as file compression, file migration, or block suballocation (advanced features used for maximizing the usage of disk space on a server). Should you decide to implement these advanced features in the future, you will need to use some of these attributes. See the Novell online documentation for more information about these features.

Types of File and Directory Attributes

There are eight attributes that apply to both files and directories. An additional eight apply only to files. All of the attributes are listed in Table 6.4. The table also shows the abbreviations used for each attribute, and whether the attribute applies to both directories and files, or only to files.

TABLE 6.4 File and Directory Attributes

ATTRIBUTE	ABBREVIATION	FILE	DIRECTORY	DESCRIPTION
Delete Inhibit	Di	X	X	Prevents users from deleting the file or directory.
Hidden	H	X	X	Hides the file or directory so it isn't listed by the DOS DIR command or in the Windows File Manager, and can't be copied or deleted.
Purge or Purge Immediate	P	X	X	Purges the file or directory immediately upon deletion. Purged files can't be salvaged. (Purging is explained in Chapter 7.)
Rename Inhibit	Ri	X	X	Prevents users from renaming the file or directory.
System	Sy	X	X	Indicates a system directory that may contain system files (such as DOS files). Prevents users from seeing, copying, or deleting the directory (However, does not assign the System attribute to the files in the directory.
Don't Migrate	Dm	X	X	Prevents a file or directory from being migrated to another storage device. (See the Novell documentation for information about file migration.)
Immediate Compress	Ic	X	X	Compresses the file or directory immediately. (See the Novell documentation for more information about file compression.)
Don't Compress	Dc	X	X	Prevents the file or directory from being compressed.

Continued

TABLE 6.4   File and Directory Attributes (continued)

ATTRIBUTE	ABBREVIATION	FILE	DIRECTORY	DESCRIPTION
Archive Needed	A	X		Indicates that the file has been changed since the last time it was backed up. (See Chapter 7 for more information about backing up files.)
Execute Only	X	X		Prevents an executable file from being copied, modified, or deleted. Use with caution! Once assigned, it cannot be removed, so assign it only if you have a backup copy of the file. You may prefer to assign the Read-Only attribute instead of the Executable Only attribute.
Read-Write	Rw	X		Allows the file to be opened and modified. Most files are set to Read-Write by default.
Read-Only	Ro	X		Allows the file to be opened and read, but not modified. All NetWare files in SYS:SYSTEM, SYS:PUBLIC, and SYS:LOGIN are Read-Only. Assigning the Read-Only attribute automatically assigns Delete Inhibit and Rename Inhibit.

Shareable	Sh	X	Allows the file to be used by more than one user simultaneously. Useful for utilities, commands, applications, and some database files. All NetWare files in SYS:SYSTEM, SYS:PUBLIC, and SYS:LOGIN are shareable. Most data and work files should not be shareable, so that users' changes do not conflict.
Transactional	T	X	When used on database files, allows NetWare's Transactional Tracking System (TTS) to protect the files from being corrupted if the transaction is interrupted. (See the Novell documentation for more information about TTS.)
Copy Inhibit	Ci	X	Prevents Macintosh files from being copied. (Does not apply to DOS files.)
Don't Suballocate	Ds	X	Prevents a file from being suballocated. Use on files, such as some database files, that may need to be enlarged or appended to frequently. (See the Novell documentation for more information about suballocation)

Assigning File and Directory Attributes

To assign attributes to a file or directory, use the NetWare Administrator utility (which runs in Windows 95/98 and Windows NT).

To use NetWare Administrator, select the file or directory and choose Details from the Object menu. Then select the Attributes page. The marked checkboxes show which attributes have been assigned to the file or directory. To change the attributes, click the checkboxes to mark or unmark them. Figure 6.13 shows a directory's attributes.

▶ ・ ◀

F I G U R E   6 . 1 3   *Directory's attributes*

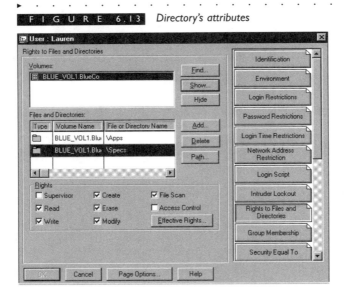

Beyond the Basics

This chapter explained the fundamentals of NetWare 5 security. The following topics, mentioned in this chapter, are explained more fully in other chapters in this book:

▶ For more information on NDS objects, see Chapter 4.

▶ For more information on creating and managing users, see Chapter 5.

▶ For information on managing files and directories (such as purging and salvaging files), see Chapter 7.

Some of the topics mentioned in this chapter deal with advanced features of NetWare 5. For more information on the following topics, refer to Novell's online documentation or to *Novell's NetWare 5 Administrator's Handbook* from Novell Press:

▶ Advanced file management features, such as block suballocation, file migration, and file compression

▶ Additional utilities you can use to work with rights and attributes

▶ Additional security features, such as NCP packet signing

CHAPTER 7

Managing Network Files

One of the most visible characteristics of a network, that network users can take advantage of, is the capability to access files and applications that aren't located on their own workstations. Having network applications and files stored in a central location also makes life easier for the network administrator.

The following are just a few of the benefits of storing applications and files on the network. You can probably think of additional benefits for your particular situation:

▶ Many of today's applications have multi-user licenses available, which makes it much easier to install and update applications for all the users on a network. Instead of installing the application on every user's workstation, you can install it once on a server, and let each user access the application there.

▶ Users can share files and folders with each other, without having to trade diskettes or e-mail them to each other.

▶ If users store all of their files on the network instead of on their workstations, the network administrator can make sure all files get backed up (archived) on a regular basis, without depending on each individual user to back up his or her own files each night.

▶ The network administrator can implement file system security features that protect the network files and applications. (Files stored on a local workstation hard disk cannot be protected by NetWare 5 security.)

This chapter explains how the NetWare 5 file system can work for you, and the tools you can use to manage your network files.

Understanding Server Volumes

To understand and plan your network file system, begin at the top — with volumes. A *volume* is the highest level in the file system hierarchy, and it contains directories and files. A NetWare 5 volume is just like a root directory on a floppy diskette or a hard disk.

Each NetWare 5 server has at least one volume, SYS, which contains all the NetWare 5 files and utilities. You can have additional volumes on a server if you want. Volumes help you organize files on the server, as shown in Figure 7.1.

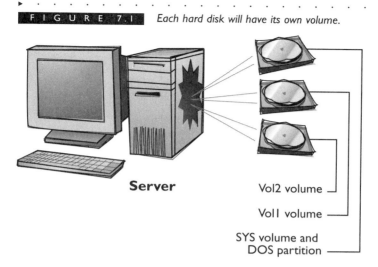

Each hard disk will have its own volume.

Server

Vol2 volume

Vol1 volume

SYS volume and
DOS partition

With NetWare 5, you can choose to create two different types of volumes: a traditional volume or a Novell Storage Services (NSS) volume. NSS is a new feature in NetWare 5. NSS volumes use a new type of NetWare file system that allows NSS volumes to mount much faster than traditional volumes. However, NSS volumes currently don't support some of the features that traditional NetWare volumes support.

The SYS volume, which is required on all NetWare servers, must be created as a traditional volume. Any other volumes on the server can be created as either type of volume, depending on your needs. You can even have both types of volumes on the same server. If you plan to have very large volumes that you want to mount quickly, NSS may be the right choice. If you need to use some of the traditional volume features of NetWare, however, you may want to use the traditional volume format instead.

The following sections explain the differences between traditional NetWare volumes and NSS volumes.

Traditional NetWare Volumes

If you have used previous versions of NetWare, you're familiar with traditional NetWare volumes. In NetWare 5, traditional volumes function exactly as they do in previous versions. A NetWare server can support up to 64 traditional volumes. In NetWare 5, volume SYS is always a traditional volume, because it requires some of the traditional volume features.

When a traditional volume is created on a disk, a "segment" is also created on the disk to hold the volume. If you create two volumes on the disk, the disk will have two segments (also called *volume segments*). If you later decide to merge the two volumes into one, you will discover that the new single volume contains two segments. If you create a volume that spans multiple hard disks, the portion of the volume on each disk will be contained in a different segment. One hard disk can hold up to eight volume segments that belong to one or more volumes. However, a single segment cannot span multiple disks.

When you create a traditional volume using the installation program or NWCONFIG.NLM, a Volume object is automatically created in the NDS tree at the same time. The Volume object is placed in the same context as the server. By default, the Volume object is named with the server's name as a prefix. For example, if the server's name is Sales, the Volume object for volume SYS is named Sales_SYS.

If you double-click a volume's icon in the NetWare Administrator Browser, the files and directories within the volume will appear. If you choose Details from the Object menu, you can see the Volume object's NDS information, as shown in Figure 7.2.

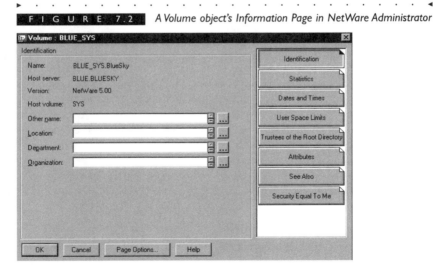

FIGURE 7.2 *A Volume object's Information Page in NetWare Administrator*

You can also open the volume from within your workstation's Windows File Manager (in Windows 3.1) or Windows Explorer (in Windows 95/98/NT) to see the files and directories within it, just as you open any other directory (folder). Your Windows utilities won't display the Volume object's NDS information, however.

NSS Volumes

NSS (Novell Storage System) is a new file system in NetWare 5 that is ideally suited for networks that require extremely large volumes, extremely large files, or huge numbers of files. NSS volumes can handle up to 8 trillion files, or a single file up to 8 terabytes (TB) in size.

In addition, NSS supports up to 255 volumes per server rather than the limit of 64 volumes supported by the traditional NetWare file system. NSS also allows up to one million files to be open simultaneously.

Aside from the large capacity provided by NSS volumes, another beneficial feature is the quick mounting and access times provided by NSS volumes. Volumes of any size, including 8TB volumes, can mount in less than one minute. NSS volumes are also frugal with memory — an NSS volume requires only 1MB of RAM to mount.

NSS also enables you to mount both CD-ROMs and the server's own DOS partition as NSS volumes.

The version of NSS that is included in NetWare 5 has some limitations, however. Some of the features available in traditional NetWare volumes are not available in NSS volumes at this time. However, many of them are slated to be delivered in future releases of NSS and NetWare. Currently, NSS volumes do not support the following features:

- ▶ File compression
- ▶ Block suballocation
- ▶ Data migration
- ▶ Novell Transaction Tracking System (TTS)
- ▶ NFS (Network File System, used in UNIX)
- ▶ FTP (file transfer protocol)
- ▶ Disk mirroring and duplexing
- ▶ Auditing
- ▶ File name locks
- ▶ Disk striping (although NSS does support disk spanning)

You can set up NSS volumes during the installation process, or you can set them up later. You must load support by typing **NSS** at the server prompt.

Planning Network Directories

On your network, you have at least one default volume, named SYS. You also will discover that several directories were created automatically within SYS.

You can create additional directories within SYS to hold all of your applications and regular working files. You can also create directories within other volumes (if other volumes exist on your server).

Before you begin adding directories to your network file system, you may want to plan your directory organization. You will need to decide which types of files you want to reside on the server, which ones should stay on workstations, and so on.

What Goes on the Server?

The types of files and directories that should be stored on the server can vary, depending on how much control you want your users to have over those files. In many cases, the difference between storing files in network directories and storing them on workstations is the amount of work you have to depend on the users to do, and the amount of work you have to do yourself. (Depending on users to do routine maintenance tasks is never a safe bet, even if they have the best intentions.) If users store the same files on the network, you can back up the files for them automatically. That way, you know you've archived all the necessary work files, and the users didn't even have to worry about them.

As another example, if you keep applications stored on the server, you can easily update the application for all your users *once*. If the application is stored on every workstation, you have to update the application multiple times instead of just once.

Another consideration when deciding where to store files is disk space. If your server disk space is limited, you'll probably want to limit the types of files that are stored on the network and tell users to store their files on their workstations.

If, however, you can install adequate storage space on the server, you'll probably want to encourage users to store everything on the server instead, for security and backup purposes. The following sections describe some of the types of network directories and files you can have on your server.

Directories Created Automatically

When you first install NetWare 5 on the server, some directories are created automatically in the SYS volume. These directories contain the files needed to run and manage NetWare 5. You can create additional directories and subdirectories in volume SYS, or if you created additional volumes during installation, you can create directories for your users in the other volumes.

The following directories are created automatically on volume SYS:

- ▸ *LOGIN* contains a few files and utilities that will let users change their current name context (location) in the NDS tree and log in to the network.

- ▸ *SYSTEM* contains NetWare Loadable Modules (NLMs) — programs that the network administrator can load to configure, manage, monitor, and add services on the NetWare server. It also contains LAN drivers, disk drivers, and other files needed for the server installation program (INSTALL.NLM).

- ▸ *PUBLIC* contains all the NetWare 5 utilities and related files. It also contains .PDF files (printer definition files) if you choose to install them on the server. In addition, PUBLIC contains the client subdirectories, which contain the files required for installing NetWare 5 client software on workstations.

- ▸ *MAIL* is empty when it is first created. It may be used by e-mail programs that are compatible with NetWare. In NetWare 3.1*x* and NetWare 2.*x*, the MAIL directory contained subdirectories for each individual user. Each of these subdirectories, named with the user's object ID number, contained the user's login script file. If you upgrade a NetWare 3.1*x* or 2.*x* server to NetWare 5, those existing users will retain their MAIL subdirectories in NetWare 5, but the login scripts will become properties of their User objects instead.

- ▸ *DELETED.SAV* is empty when it is first created. It will store directories that are deleted from the network, along with their files, until those directories are either salvaged (restored to the network), purged (completely erased), or until the space is needed and the system automatically saves new data over the deleted data. Salvaging and purging are explained later in this chapter.

- ▸ *ETC* contains files used for managing protocols and routers.

These directories contain the files required for running and managing your NetWare network. Be careful not to rename or delete any of them without making absolutely sure they're unnecessary in your particular network's situation.

Application Directories

Many of today's applications have been designed to work on networks and support multiple users. When you buy or upgrade an application, try to purchase a multiple user license for it, as those are sometimes less expensive than buying multiple copies of single-user programs.

It may be easier to assign file system trustee rights if you group all multiuser applications on the network under a single volume or parent directory. For example, by installing your word-processing, spreadsheet, and other programs into their own subdirectories under a parent directory named APPS, you can assign all users the minimum necessary rights to APPS. Then, the users will inherit those rights in each application's subdirectory. (For more information about file system rights, see Chapter 6.)

If different applications will be available to different groups of users, try to organize the applications' directory structures so you can assign comprehensive rights in a parent directory. This will eliminate the need to create multiple individual rights assignments at lower-level subdirectories.

If you install applications into subdirectories under a common parent directory, you can usually designate that daily work files of users be stored in their own home directories elsewhere on the network. This will allow you to grant more restrictive rights to the application directory (so that users can't accidentally delete any necessary application files). At the same time, it lets you grant broader rights to users in their own directories so that they can create, change, or delete the work files created from the application.

When planning network subdirectories for your applications, follow any special instructions from the manufacturer for installing the application on a network. Some applications can be run either from a local hard disk on the workstation or from a network directory.

In some cases, the instructions may indicate that the application has to be installed at the root of a volume. If your application requires this, you can still install it in a subdirectory under the APPS directory if you want, and then map a fake root to the application's subdirectory. A *fake root* mapping makes a subdirectory appear to be a volume, so that the application runs correctly.

For example, suppose you want to install an application called YOYO into a subdirectory under a directory called APPS on the volume called VOL1. However, the application's instructions say that YOYO must be installed at the root of the volume. Create a subdirectory called YOYO under VOL1:APPS, and install the application into YOYO. Then, you can map a fake root to the YOYO subdirectory and assign it to be a search drive at the same time by using the command:

```
MAP ROOT S16:=VOL1:APPS\YOYO
```

You can type this command at the workstation's DOS prompt if you only need the mapping to be in effect until the user logs out. If you want it to be in effect each time the user logs in, put the command in a login script. (For more information about mapping drives in login scripts, see Chapter 5.)

When you install an application, you may want to flag the application's executable files (usually files with the extension .COM or .EXE) with the Shareable and Read Only file attributes. This will allow users to simultaneously use the applications, but will prevent users from deleting or modifying them. (This is more typically controlled by assigning restrictive trustee rights to users in those applications' directories, however.) You can use the NetWare Administrator utility to assign file attributes. File and directory attributes are covered in Chapter 6.

Work Directories

When planning your network file system, decide where you want users' daily work files to reside. They can be stored in personal directories, in project-specific directories, or in some other type of directory structure.

All files related to Project Ace, for example, could be stored under a directory named ACE. Subdirectories could then be created for project-related files, such as status reports, billing information, and marketing publications. Project Zeus could have a parallel structure. Figure 7.3 shows a simple example of a directory structure for Project Ace.

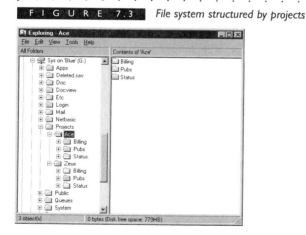

FIGURE 7.3 *File system structured by projects*

Allow ample network directory space for users to store their daily work files. Encourage your users to store their files on the network. This way, those files can be backed up regularly by the network backup process, and they can be protected by NetWare 5 security.

Home Directories

You must decide if you want users to have their own individual home directories. Users can store their work files in their home directories, as well as any other types of personal files (status reports, annual reviews, memos, and so on).

In general, you can allow users full control over their own home directories. If you let them keep a full set of rights to their home directories, they can create new subdirectories within them, delete and salvage files in them, give other users access rights to their files, and so forth.

You can create home directories automatically when you create new users, as explained in Chapter 5.

What Goes on the Workstation?

Again, the types of files that can be stored on users' workstations depend on how you want to manage your network. The following sections offer you some explanations and suggestions.

Directories Created Automatically

Many of the directories that exist on a workstation were created automatically by the workstation's own operating system (such as Windows or DOS).

When you install the NetWare 5 client software on a workstation, another directory (plus its related subdirectories) is added to the workstation. This directory is called NOVELL, and it contains all the necessary client files for that workstation to run. (The client installation program also modifies and installs various files in other pre-existing directories on the workstation.)

Application Directories

If you like, you can let users have their own copies of applications running locally on their workstations' hard disks. You might choose to install an application directly on a workstation instead of on the network, if you have one of the following situations:

> ▶ If your user has a laptop computer and needs to run the application when away from the network

▶ If you want your user to be able to run the application if the network is down

▶ If the application is not network-aware, and needs to be installed on a single computer

▶ If the application is used by only one user (especially if it requires access to a local device such as a CD-ROM)

Personal Directories
Many times, users store their personal files on their workstation's hard disk. Remind users that the network will not back up files stored on workstations, so any files on the workstation are at risk unless the users are diligent about making their own backups.

Managing Files and Directories

Many of the tasks you perform on network files and directories will be the same types of tasks you do on a standalone computer — copying files, deleting them, renaming them, creating new ones, and so on. Not surprisingly, you can use the same tools to do these tasks as you would with files on your workstation's hard disk — such as the File Manager (in Windows 3.1), Windows Explorer (in Windows 95/98 or Windows NT), or DOS commands such as COPY and MD.

Of course, network files and directories have additional characteristics with which you can work, such as trustee assignments and Inherited Rights Filters. To work with these aspects of network files and directories, you can use the NetWare Administrator utility.

Use the NetWare Administrator's Browser to select files and directories and view information about them. Select a file or directory and choose Details from the Object menu. From the Details screen that appears, you can open the Facts page, Trustees page, or Attributes page. Some of the types of information you can see about network files and directories include the following:

▶ Name spaces (explained in Chapter 2)

▶ Size restrictions of directories

▶ Creation dates and times

▶ Trustees

▶ Effective rights

▸ Inherited Rights Filters

▸ File and directory attributes

▸ File owners (the users who created the files)

Figure 7.4 shows the Facts page of information for a directory.

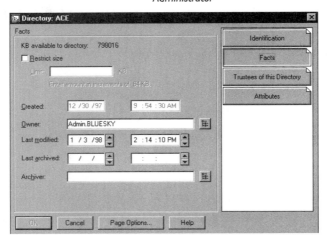

FIGURE 7.4   *A directory's information displayed in NetWare Administrator*

NOTE   You use the utility called NWCONFIG.NLM to manage volumes. See the online documentation for more information about NWCONFIG.NLM.

Purging and Salvaging Files

In NetWare 5, when files are deleted, they are not actually removed from the server's hard disk. Instead, they are retained in a salvageable state. Although you won't see a deleted file listed when you look at the file's directory (or folder), the file is really stored in a hidden state, in case you need to retrieve it later.

Deleted files are usually stored in the same directory from which they were originally deleted. If, however, the directory itself was also deleted, the deleted files are stored in a special directory called DELETED.SAV at the volume's root.

Deleted files are stored in this salvageable state until one of the following things happens:

- ▶ The file is salvaged and restored to its original form.

- ▶ The server runs out of free space on the disk and begins to overwrite deleted files. The oldest deleted files are overwritten first.

- ▶ The file is purged by the administrator or user. (When purged, a file is completely removed from the disk and cannot be recovered.) You can purge a file either manually, by using the NetWare Administrator utility or PURGE (a command-line utility), or you can use the Purge directory and file attributes to mark a file or directory to be purged immediately upon deletion.

- ▶ Assign the Purge directory attribute to the volume that contains files you want purged as soon as they are deleted. If you use this attribute, you cannot salvage files you delete from that volume.

You can only salvage or purge files to which you have adequate trustee rights. This prevents unauthorized users from salvaging files that they shouldn't see.

Purging and Salvaging Files with NetWare Administrator

To use the NetWare Administrator utility to either purge or salvage a deleted file or directory, complete the following steps:

1. From the NetWare Administrator's Browser, select the directory containing the files or directories you want to salvage or purge.

2. From the Tools menu, select Salvage. (This option will let you both salvage and purge files.)

3. In the Include field of the Salvage dialog box that appears, as shown in Figure 7.5, indicate which files you want to see displayed. Specify a filename or use wildcards to indicate several files. A blank line or the wildcard symbols will display all the deleted files in the selected directory.

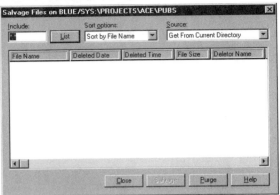

FIGURE 7.5 *The Salvage Dialog Box*

4. From the Sort Options drop box, specify how you want the displayed files to be sorted — by Deletion Date, Deletor Name, File Name, File Size, or File Type.

5. From the Source drop box, choose whether you want to see deleted files in your current directory or in a deleted directory.

6. Click the List button to display the files you've specified. Figure 7.6 shows an example of the Salvage dialog box with deleted files listed.

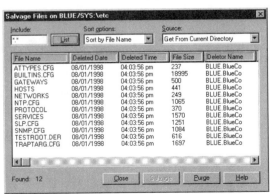

FIGURE 7.6 *The Salvage Dialog Box Shows Files That Have Been Deleted From This Directory*

7. From the displayed list, select the files you want to purge or salvage.

8. Click either the Salvage button or the Purge button, depending on what you want to do. If you salvage files from an existing directory, the files are restored to that directory. If you salvage files from a deleted directory, the files are restored into the DELETED.SAV directory under the root of the volume.

9. When finished, click the Close button.

Purging Files with PURGE

To purge deleted files, you can also use the PURGE command-line utility. To purge files using PURGE, use the following command:

```
PURGE path\filename /option
```

Replace *path* with the path to the files you want to purge, and replace *file-name* with a filename for the specific files. Wildcards are acceptable. The following options can be used with PURGE:

▶ /A — Purges all files in the current directory and all of its subdirectories.

▶ /VER — Displays the version number of PURGE.

▶ /? — Displays help screens for PURGE.

For example, to purge all the deleted files with the extension .BAT in the current directory only, use the following command:

```
PURGE .BAT
```

Backing Up and Restoring Files

Files can be lost or damaged in a variety of ways. They can be corrupted by viruses, accidentally deleted by users, overwritten by other applications, or destroyed when a hard disk fails. Despite all the best precautions, you can't always prevent files from being lost.

What you can do, however, is make sure that you always have current backup copies of your network data so you can restore files. If you have a carefully planned and executed backup strategy, you can minimize the amount of work that will be lost if you have to restore a file from your archives.

TIP Encourage your users to store their critical files in network directories so you can be sure the files are backed up on a regular basis.

There are many different backup products available on the market. NetWare 5 includes a basic backup solution, called Enhanced SBACKUP, that you can use. If you prefer, you can purchase a third-party product that may provide additional features you need.

Backing up network files involves more than just making a copy of the files. It is important to use a backup product, such as NetWare's Enhanced SBACKUP, that backs up not just the files themselves, but also the NetWare 5 information associated with those files, such as trustee rights, Inherited Rights Filters, and file and directory attributes.

Planning a Backup Strategy

Planning an efficient backup strategy is one of the most beneficial tasks you can do as part of network management. With a good backup strategy, you can limit the time it takes to do backups, ensure that the least amount of working time is lost by your users, and avoid unnecessary headaches from searching for lost files.

Backup strategies can be different for every network. What works for someone else may not work well for you, and vice versa. When planning a backup strategy, you'll need to consider the following questions:

- What type of backup media do you need to use?
- What backup schedule should you follow?
- How frequently should you rotate your backup media?
- Where should the backups be stored?
- How often will you test the restore procedure?

The tips and suggestions in the next few sections can help you decide on your own backup strategy.

Choosing Your Backup Media

Before purchasing a backup device, you must decide what kind of backup media you want to use, such as tapes or optical disks. Many manufacturers' backup products can back up data onto a variety of storage media, but it's a good idea to know what you want before you buy something that limits your choices. The media you choose will probably depend upon the following factors:

- How much you're willing to spend
- How large your network is
- How long you need to retain your backed-up data (Some media deteriorates after a few years; other media may have a 100-year guarantee.)

Tape is probably the most common backup media in use today, especially in small- to medium-sized businesses. Tapes are relatively easy to use, can be used in any size network, and are fairly inexpensive.

TIP

One of the downsides of tape is that backup manufacturers tend to use different, proprietary tape formats that aren't compatible with each other. Two tape standards have been established (one from Novell, and another from Microsoft), so some efforts have been made to standardize on one or the other, but there are still differences between manufacturers. Be sure any backup product you buy will be compatible with any other system with which you may need to share tapes.

Currently, the two most affordable and popular tape formats used in smaller businesses are:

- DAT (Digital Audio Tape)
- QIC (Quarter-Inch Cartridge)

A newer tape format, called *Digital Linear Tape* (DLT), has much higher performance and capacity than DAT or QIC, but it is also much more expensive. Its higher, more expensive performance makes it better suited for large networks. Another tape format, *8mm*, is also faster and has more capacity than DAT and QIC, but isn't quite as expensive as DLT.

Tape, while easy to use and relatively affordable, is not necessarily suited to long-term storage of data. Like any magnetic medium, tape can oxidize or otherwise deteriorate over time; therefore, for long-term storage, you may want to consider some of the different types of optical disks. Some optical disks that are currently available include: CD-R (Compact Disk-Recordable), DVD, magneto-optical, and floptical disks.

These technologies are constantly being improved with innovative features and compatibility with earlier or existing products. Talk to your reseller about your network's specific needs, and choose the media that best suits your network.

NetWare's Enhanced SBACKUP product supports quarter-inch tape, 4mm tape (DDS-certified, computer grade), and 8mm tape formats.

NOTE

Planning a Backup Schedule

A good way to determine how often to back up critical data is to calculate how long you could afford to spend re-creating the information if it was lost. If you can't afford to lose more than a day's worth of work, you should perform daily backups of that information. If losing a week's worth of work is more of a nuisance than a devastating blow, perhaps you don't need to do daily backups and can rely on weekly backups instead.

Most backup products, including NetWare's backup product, will let you determine not only when you back up your network, but also what types of information you back up each time. In many cases, you'll find that there's no point in backing up your entire network every night if only a few of the files change during the day.

With most products, you can choose between doing a full backup and an *incremental* backup. In an incremental backup, only the files that have been changed are detected and backed up. With a little careful planning, you can create a schedule that staggers complete backups with incremental backups, so you still get full coverage without spending more time and money than necessary.

For example, you can do a full backup of the network once a week. Then, once a day, do incremental backups of only those files that have changed (the backup product can usually detect changed files for you). In the event of a total loss of files, you can restore all the files from the weekly backup, and then restore each of the daily tapes to update those files that changed during that week. In this way, you can cover all of your files while minimizing the time each backup session takes during the week. Figure 7.7 illustrates how you can use full and incremental backups during the week to ensure total coverage.

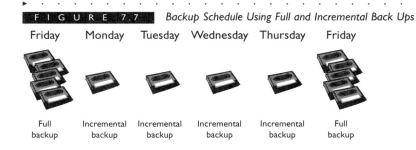

FIGURE 7.7 *Backup Schedule Using Full and Incremental Back Ups*

Friday	Monday	Tuesday	Wednesday	Thursday	Friday
Full backup	Incremental backup	Incremental backup	Incremental backup	Incremental backup	Full backup

TIP

Any good backup product can detect changed files when doing an incremental backup. It does this by looking for a special file attribute called the *Archive Needed* attribute (also called the *Modify bit*). When a file is changed, this attribute is assigned to it. Then, the backup product detects this attribute and knows to back up this file.

In many cases, you can specify whether the backup product should then remove the attribute. (This is done so the file isn't backed up unnecessarily during the next incremental backup.) You can also choose to leave the attribute set so it still appears to be a changed file.

Another tip for minimizing backup time is to organize your directory (folder) structure so that often-changed files are separate from seldom-changed files. For example, there is no point in wasting your time by frequently backing up files such as applications and utilities, which seldom change. If you put applications in one directory and work files in another, you can skip the application directory completely during incremental backups, making the process go faster.

Finally, be sure to document your backup schedule and keep a backup log. A written record of all backups and your backup strategy can help someone else restore the files if you aren't there.

Planning the Media Rotation

It's important to plan a rotation schedule for your backup media. You should decide in advance how long you will retain old files, and how often you will reuse the same tapes or disks.

Assume you're using tapes (although any rewriteable media gives you the same situation). If you have only one backup tape that you use every week, you could unknowingly back up corrupted files onto your single tape each time you replace the previous week's backup with the new one. In short, you're replacing your last good copy with a corrupted one.

To prevent this type of problem, plan to keep older backup tapes or disks on hand at all times. Many network administrators will use four or more tapes or disks for the same set of files — cycling through them one at a time. Each week, the most outdated tape or disk is used for the new backup. This way, three or more versions of backups are available at any given time. How many tape or disk sets you'll need depends on your rotation schedule. If you want to keep four weeks' worth of daily and weekly backups, you'll need at least 20 sets of tapes or disks — five for each week. Figure 7.8 shows a possible media rotation schedule.

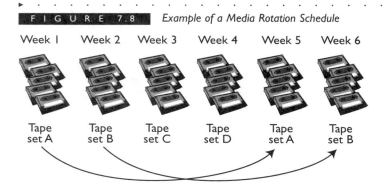

F I G U R E   7 . 8   *Example of a Media Rotation Schedule*

| Week 1 | Week 2 | Week 3 | Week 4 | Week 5 | Week 6 |

| Tape set A | Tape set B | Tape set C | Tape set D | Tape set A | Tape set B |

Some backup products offer preset rotation schedules for you. They will automatically prompt you for the right set of media and keep track of the schedule.

Decide Where to Store the Backups

Another important aspect of your backup strategy is to plan where to store your backups. If you have backups of noncritical data, you may be comfortable keeping them onsite. However, when storing backups onsite, you should at least store them in a room separate from the server's room. If an electrical fire breaks out in the server room, your backup tapes won't do you much good if they burn right beside the server.

For mission-critical data, you may need to keep backups in an offsite location. That way, if there is a physical disaster (such as a fire, flood, or earthquake), they'll be safe. If the data is critical enough to store offsite, but you also want to have immediate access to it, consider making two backups, and storing one offsite and the other onsite.

Test the Restore Process

A final tip: Make sure your backups can be restored! A backup is only useful if the data in it can be restored successfully. Too many people discover a problem with their backups when they're in the middle of an important restoration process. Practice restoring files before you need to do so. By practicing, you may identify problems you didn't realize you had. Don't wait until it is too late.

Preparing to Use Enhanced SBACKUP

Enhanced SBACKUP, the backup utility included in NetWare 5, can be used either from the server console or from a workstation. With this product, you can back up all the different types of files that can be stored on your server: DOS, Macintosh, OS/2, Windows NT, Windows 95 and 98, and UNIX.

Enhanced SBACKUP enables you to select the type of backup you want to perform. There are three choices (all of which can be customized for your particular needs):

► *Full backup* — This option backs up all network files. It removes the Archive Needed file attribute from all files and directories. (This attribute is also called the *modify bit*. It is assigned to a file whenever the file is changed. When the file is backed up, most backup products can remove the attribute so the next time the file is changed, the attribute is once again assigned.)

► *Differential backup* — This option backs up only files that were modified since the last full backup. It does not remove the Archive Needed attribute from these files.

► *Incremental backup* — This option backs up only files that were modified since the last full or incremental backup. It removes the Archive Needed attribute from these files.

To use Enhanced SBACKUP to back up files, you first need to install a backup device and load the device's drivers on a server. Then you need to load some necessary backup NLMs on this server. This server is called the *host server*. Next, you load Target Service Agents (TSAs), which also come in the NetWare 5 product, on any servers or workstations whose files you want to back up. These servers are called *targets*. (TSAs are NetWare Loadable Modules.)

Finally, you need to launch the NetWare backup utility on either the host server or a workstation. The server-based version of the backup utility is called SBCON.NLM. The workstation-based utility is called NWBACK32.EXE. Both utilities accomplish the same tasks, enabling you to back up and restore network files. It doesn't matter which utility you choose, so select the utility most convenient for you.

Before you can use either SBCON.NLM or NWBACK32.EXE, you must prepare the host server and then set up target servers or workstations, as explained in the following sections.

Setting Up the Host Server and Targets

Before you can run the NetWare backup utility, you must first prepare the host server and any targets you want to back up, by completing the following steps:

1. Attach the backup device (tape or disk drive) to the host server.

2. Load the necessary backup device drivers on the host server. Then enter the following command at the console to register the device with the server:

   SCAN FOR NEW DEVICES

   Check the manufacturer's documentation to find out which drivers you need. Place the commands that load the backup device drivers in the server's STARTUP.NCF file if you want them to load automatically when the server is rebooted.

3. At the server console, load SMDR.NLM. This module loads the SMS Data Requester on the server, and automatically creates an SMS SMDR Group object in the server's context. This Group object will contain each server and workstation that will be backed up by this host server. Load SMDR.NLM by typing:

   SMDR

   (If you want to create a new SMDR Group object, type **SMDR NEW** at the console instead, and enter a new name and context for the SMDR Group object.)

4. Load the SMS Device Interface module, which will let the SBACKUP program communicate with the backup device, by typing:

   SMSDI

5. Load the SMS Queue Manager, which will create a job queue for the backup program to use. The backup queue is an object named "*Server*

Backup Queue" (with the server's name substituted for *Server*). To load the Queue Manager on this server, type:

QMAN

(If you want to create a new Queue object, type **QMAN NEW** at the console instead, and enter a new name and context for the job queue.)

6. Load the SBACKUP Communication module on this server by typing:

SBSC

7. (Optional) If you are going to back up the network files that reside on this server (in other words, this server is both the host and the target), load the NetWare 5 TSA on this server by typing:

TSA500

8. (Optional) If you are going to back up Windows 95/98 or Windows NT workstations from this host server, load TSAPROXY.NLM on this server by typing:

TSAPROXY

9. If you are going to back up another server from this host server, go to that server and load the appropriate TSA. Once the TSA is loaded on a server, that server is called a *target server*. You can use the following TSAs, depending on the type of server you want to back up:

   • TSA500 — Load on NetWare 5 servers

   • TSA410 — Load on NetWare 4 servers

   • TSANDS — Load on a server whose NDS tree you want to back up (it's usually best to load this on a server that contains a replica of the tree's Directory partition)

   • TSADOSP — Load on a server if you want to back up its DOS partition

At this point, the host server is prepared, and the target server is ready to be backed up. If you want to back up a Windows 95/98 or Windows NT workstation, you must take extra steps to configure TSAs on those workstations, as explained in the following sections. If you are ready to back up or restore files, skip to "Backing Up Files" or "Restoring Files" later in this chapter.

Preparing to Back Up Workstations

Although most people use Enhanced SBACKUP to back up files from network servers, you can also use it to back up files from the hard disks of Windows 95/98 or Windows NT workstations. To do this, you must load and configure TSA software on the workstations. TSA software is an optional set of software that you can install as part of the Novell client software. During the client installation, be sure you check the Target Service Agent option to install the TSA support.

After the TSA software is installed, you must configure it, as described in the following sections.

Configuring the Windows 95 TSA Before you try for the first time to back up files that reside on a Windows 95/98 workstation, you must configure the TSA. If you have installed the TSA software during the client installation, a small, round, shield-shaped icon will appear in the Windows 95/98 system tray (usually at the bottom right-hand corner of the screen). When you put the cursor over this icon, the words "Novell TSA (Not Registered)" will appear. If the words "Novell TSA (Listening)" appear, this workstation has already been configured, and you can skip this section and go straight to "Backing Up Files."

To configure the TSA and register it with the host server, complete the following steps:

1. Double-click the shield icon in the workstation's system tray. The Properties page for the Novell Target Service Agent for Windows 95 appears, as shown in Figure 7.9.

FIGURE 7.9 *The Properties Page For The Windows 95 TSA*

2. Enter your user name and password.

3. If necessary, choose the protocol you want to use (IPX or IP).

4. Enter the name of the host server that will back up this workstation's files.

5. Under the Resources Available to TSA heading, choose the local drives you want to back up.

6. Check Auto Register, to automatically register this workstation with the host server.

7. Make sure the option to Show TSA Icon on Taskbar is checked.

8. Click OK.

9. Reboot the workstation to make the changes take effect.

After the workstation is rebooted, the TSA's icon in the system tray should display the words "Novell TSA (Listening)." Now the workstation is ready to be backed up. Skip to the section "Backing Up Files" later in this chapter.

Configuring the Windows NT TSA   Before you try for the first time to back up files that reside on a Windows NT workstation, you must configure the TSA. Make sure you installed the TSA software during the client installation.

To configure the TSA and register it with the host server, complete the following steps:

1. Open the Properties page for the Windows NT TSA.

2. Open the Preferences tab.

3. In the Workstation field, enter the name of this workstation.

4. In the Preferred Server field, enter the name of the host server that will back up this workstation's files.

5. In the Protocol field, choose the protocol you want to use (IPX or IP).

6. In the Events to Log field, check the items you want to log.

7. Check Allow Backup User to grant the backup user rights.

8. Check Auto Register to automatically register this workstation with the host server.

9. Open the Registration tab. If all the information shown is correct, click Register. If some of the information is incorrect, click Withdraw and return to the Preferences page to make any necessary changes.

10. Open the Connections tab. If you need to change or add information to these fields, make the changes and click Apply. If all the information is correct, click OK.

11. Reboot the workstation to make the changes take effect.

After the workstation is rebooted, it is ready to be backed up, as explained in the following section.

Backing Up Files

After you've loaded the necessary NLMs on the host server and loaded a TSA on the target server or workstation, you can use the NetWare backup program (Enhanced SBACKUP) to back up the target's files. You can use either the server-based backup program (SBCON.NLM) or the workstation-based backup program (NWBACK32.EXE). Both programs accomplish the same tasks, so choose the program that is most convenient for you to use. The following sections explain how to use these programs.

Using the Server-based Utility (SBCON)

To use the server-based SBCON.NLM to back up files, complete the following steps:

1. At the host server, load SBCON.NLM by typing:

    ```
    SBCON
    ```

2. From the main menu, choose Job Administration, and then choose Backup.

3. At the Target Service field, press Enter.

4. Choose the target server you want to back up. If you're backing up a workstation, choose the workstation's host server.

5. Choose whether you want to back up the server's file system or a workstation attached to the server.

6. Enter a user name and password for the target. (Use the user's full context name, beginning with a period.)

7. Choose What to Back Up.

8. From the Resource List that appears, choose the directories and files you want to back up. If the list is blank, or if you want to make changes, press Ins. Then select whether you want to back up the server, only server-specific information, or a volume. You can also specify directories and files within a volume by choosing the volume

and then pressing Ins again. When you select a directory, press Esc to make it appear in the Resource List box. When finished selecting what you want to back up, press Enter to save the information and return to the Backup Options page.

9. In the Description field, enter a descriptive name for this backup session.

10. Choose the backup device and medium you will use. If only one device is available, the backup program will choose it for you. (The wildcard characters . will select the default device.)

11. At the Advanced Options field, press Enter. From the screen that appears, you can select the backup type (full, differential, or incremental), the subset of directories you want to back up, scan options, the time to execute the backup session, and scheduling options. When finished selecting these Advanced Options, press Esc to save the information and return to the Backup Options menu.

NOTE

The Advanced Options screen lets you use *include* and *exclude* options to customize what you want to back up. Use exclude options when you want to back up most of the file system while omitting only a small part. Everything that you don't specifically exclude is backed up. Use include options when you want to back up only a small portion of the file system. Everything you don't specifically include is excluded.

When specifying subsets to back up, two options enable you to exclude or include Major TSA resources. A *Major TSA resource* is simply a server or volume. You can choose to include or exclude volumes, directories, or files.

12. If your backup device enables you to put multiple sessions on a single tape, and if a session is already on the tape you're using, select Append Session and answer Yes to add the new session to the tape. To overwrite any existing sessions, choose No. When finished, press Esc to save the information and return to the Backup Options menu.

13. Press Esc to return to the main SBCON menu.

14. When asked if you want to submit a job, answer Yes to begin the backup session.

Using the Workstation-based Utility (NWBACK32)

To use the workstation-based NWBACK32.EXE from a Windows 95/98 or Windows NT workstation to back up files, complete the following steps:

1. From the workstation you are using to run the backup program, log in to the host server.

2. Create a shortcut to NWBACK32.EXE, which is located in the SYS volume, under the Public directory.

3. Launch NWBACK32.

4. The first time you run NWBACK32, you will be asked to enter NDS information. Enter the tree name, and then the contexts for the SMDR and the SMDR Group objects. You must enter the context for these objects using the format O=*container* or OU=*container*.O=*container*. The O= and OU= designations are required in this release. If you are using IPX on your network, make sure SAP is checked. Then click OK to save the information. To make sure the changes take effect, exit and then relaunch NWBACK32.

5. Click Backup.

6. Double-click What to Backup.

7. Double-click the item you want to back up: NDS, NetWare servers, workstations, or a DOS partition on a NetWare server. A list of servers appears beneath the item you double-clicked, as shown in Figure 7.10.

8. Double-click a server, and then enter a user name and password for that server.

9. Click the information you want to back up (NetWare server, server-specific information, or volumes), so that an X appears in the box next to the item you want.

10. Double-click Where to Backup.

11. Double-click the context. (If you need to change contexts, click the Change to Context button on the toolbar.)

12. Double-click Queues to open a list of backup queues.

13. Right-click a queue and choose Submit the Job. The screens that appear enable you to choose the backup type (full, differential, or incremental), subsets of directories you want to back up, filtering options, the time to execute the backup session, and other scheduling options. At the last screen, indicate whether you want to append this session to a tape that already contains previous sessions, then enter a

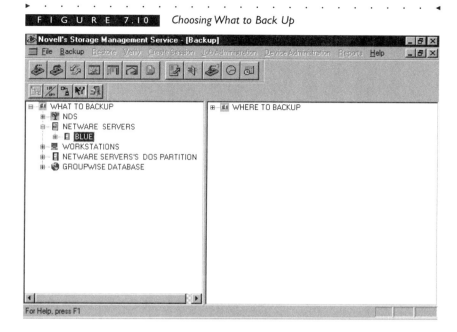

FIGURE 7.10 *Choosing What to Back Up*

description of this session and indicate whether you want to keep this job. Then press Finish.

NOTE

These screens let you use *include* and *exclude* options to customize what you want to back up. Use exclude options when you want to back up most of the file system while omitting only a small part. Everything that you don't specifically exclude is backed up. Use include options when you want to back up only a small portion of the file system. Everything you don't specifically include is excluded.

When specifying subsets to back up, two options enable you to exclude or include Major TSA resources. A *Major TSA resource* is simply a server or volume. You can choose to include or exclude volumes, directories, or files.

14. When asked if you want to submit the job, answer Yes to begin the backup session.

Restoring Files

To restore files from a backup, you need to prepare the host server and targets the same way you did for the backup procedure. (See the section "Setting Up the Host Server and Targets" earlier in this chapter.)

After you've loaded the necessary NLMs on the host server and loaded a TSA on the target server or workstation, you can use the NetWare Enhanced SBACKUP program to restore files to the target. You can use either the server-based backup program (SBCON.NLM) or the workstation-based backup program (NWBACK32.EXE) to restore files. Both programs accomplish the same tasks, so choose the program that is most convenient for you to use. The following sections explain how to use these programs.

Using the Server-based Utility (SBCON)

To use the server-based SBCON.NLM to restore files, complete the following steps:

1. At the host server, load SBCON.NLM by typing:

   SBCON

2. From the main menu, choose Job Administration, and then choose Restore.

3. At the Target Service field, press Enter.

4. Choose the target server to which you want to restore. If you're restoring to a workstation, choose the workstation's host server.

5. Choose whether you want to restore the server's file system or a workstation attached to the server.

6. Enter a user name and password for the target. (Use the user's full context name, beginning with a period.)

7. In the Description field, enter a descriptive name for this restore session.

8. Choose the backup device and medium you will use. If only one device is available, the backup program will choose it for you. (The wildcard characters *.* will select the default device.)

9. In the Session to Restore field, press Enter, and then choose a backup session from the list that appears.

10. At the Advanced Options field, press Enter. From the screen that appears, you can select to rename the data sets (which will send the restored files to a different location that you specify), the subset of

directories you want to restore, and Open Mode options (which let you pick the types of information about files and directories to restore). You can also specify whether you want to overwrite "parents" (which are simply servers, volumes, or directories) if they exist, and whether to overwrite "children" (which are files). Finally, you can specify the time to execute the restore session and other scheduling options. When finished selecting these Advanced Options, press Esc to save the information and return to the Restore Options menu.

11. Press Esc to return to the main SBCON menu.

12. When asked if you want to submit the job, answer Yes to begin the restore session.

Using the Workstation-based Utility (NWBACK32)

To use the workstation-based NWBACK32.EXE from a Windows 95/98 or Windows NT workstation to restore files, complete the following steps:

1. From the workstation you are using to run the backup program, log in to the host server.

2. Launch NWBACK32.

3. Click Restore.

4. Double-click What to Restore.

5. Double-click the context. (If you need to change contexts, click the Change to Context button on the toolbar.)

6. In succession, double-click Queues, then the queue object, then Servers, then the server object, then Devices, and then the backup device you want to restore from.

7. From the list of backup media, choose the one that has the files you want to restore.

8. Double-click Where to Restore.

9. Double-click the item you want to restore: NDS, NetWare servers, workstations, or a DOS partition on a NetWare server. A list of servers appears beneath the item you double-clicked.

8. Double-click a server, and then enter a user name and password for that server.

9. Right-click the server and choose Submit the Job. The screens that appear enable you to choose filtering options and scheduling options. Then press Finish.

10. When asked if you want to submit the job, answer Yes to begin the restore session.

Beyond the Basics

This chapter explained the most common aspects of managing network files on a NetWare 5 network.

The following topics, mentioned in this chapter, are explained more fully in other chapters in this book:

- ▶ For instructions on installing the NetWare Administrator utility on your workstation, see Chapter 4.
- ▶ For information about login scripts, see Chapter 5.
- ▶ For information about file system trustee rights and Inherited Rights Filters, see Chapter 6.
- ▶ For more information about installing Novell's online documentation, see Chapter 10.

There are many advanced NetWare 5 features you can use to further manage network directories and files if your network situation requires it, once you're comfortable with the basics. For more information about the following topics, refer to the Novell online documentation, or to *Novell's NetWare 5 Administrator's Handbook* from Novell Press:

- ▶ File compression (which compresses less frequently used files)
- ▶ Block suballocation (which allows several files to share a single block to avoid wasting space unnecessarily)
- ▶ Data migration (which lets you automatically move less frequently used files to an alternate storage device, such as an optical jukebox system)
- ▶ Additional NetWare 5 utilities, such as RENDIR, NCOPY, NDIR, PURGE, and FILER, that allow you to work with file and directory information
- ▶ Restricting the amount of network disk space that users can access
- ▶ Purging and salvaging files
- ▶ Managing volumes (creating, deleting, and repairing them)

CHAPTER 8

Setting Up Printers

NetWare 5 print services allow your network users to share printers connected to the network. With NetWare 5 print services loaded, you can gain benefits such as:

- ▶ Increasing productivity and saving on hardware expenses by allowing users to share a smaller number of printers instead of buying each user a stand-alone printer. (You may also be able to buy a single, more sophisticated printer instead of multiple lesser-quality printers.)

- ▶ Letting users send their print jobs to different printers for different purposes, all from a single workstation.

- ▶ Prioritizing print jobs so that important print jobs are sent to the printer ahead of less important print jobs.

How NetWare Printing Works

In standalone printing, a printer is connected directly to the serial or parallel port (usually LPT1) on the workstation. When the user prints a file, the print job goes from the application to the print driver, which formats the job for the specific printer. (The print driver is software that converts the print job into a format that the printer can understand.) Next, the print job goes to the parallel port, and then directly to the printer. Often, the application has to wait until the print job is finished before it can resume working. Figure 8.1 illustrates the path a print job takes when a printer is attached directly to a workstation.

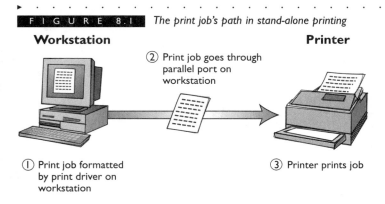

FIGURE 8.1 *The print job's path in stand-alone printing*

Workstation   **Printer**

② Print job goes through parallel port on workstation

① Print job formatted by print driver on workstation

③ Printer prints job

With NetWare 5 print services, the print job goes to the network instead of directly to the printer, though this process is transparent to users. Then the network takes care of sending the print job to the correct printer.

NetWare 5 provides two different ways to set up your printing services: queue-based printing and NDPS (Novell Distributed Print Services).

Queue-based printing is the older system used in all previous versions of NetWare. If you have been using earlier versions of NetWare, you're familiar with queue-based printing. If you would like to continue using queue-based printing, you can. NetWare 5 fully supports queue-based printing, and you can keep using this system if you'd like.

NDPS, the preferred method of setting up your printing services, is a new printing system designed by Novell, Hewlett-Packard, and Xerox, that provides advanced printing features. NDPS is fully compatible with existing queue-based printing. You can install NDPS and have it support existing print queues. Or, if you prefer, you can install only NDPS, so that all of your printing is handled through this newer architecture.

The first half of this chapter explains queue-based printing. The second half of this chapter explains NDPS.

Queue-Based Printing

Queue-based printing is the printing system that has been used in NetWare for years. Although NDPS is the newest printing system created by Novell, queue-based printing is still a strong, reliable printing option. If you have been using queue-based printing in previous versions of NetWare and don't feel the need for the newer features offered by NDPS, rest assured that you can safely retain queue-based printing in NetWare 5.

Understanding Queue-Based Printing

Before planning and installing queue-based printing, let's look at the components and processes that make up NetWare queue-based printing. In queue-based printing, NetWare employs two features, called *print queues* and *print servers*, to move the print job from the workstation to the printer.

- The print queue is a special network directory (folder) that stores print jobs temporarily before they are printed. Multiple network users can have their jobs stored in the same print queue. The print queue receives all incoming print jobs from various users, and stores them in a first-come, first-served order.

▶ The print server is a software program, called PSERVER.NLM, that runs on the NetWare 5 server. The print server controls how the print queues and printers work together. The print server takes the jobs from the print queue one at a time, and forwards them on to the printer when the printer is available.

TIP

You can have more than one print queue on a network. Furthermore, you can set up one print queue so it services several printers (although this can be confusing because you never know which printer will print the job you send). You can also set up a single printer so it services several print queues.

However, it generally simplifies your administration tasks and reduces your users' confusion if you use a one-to-one correspondence between print queues and printers, so that each print queue sends jobs to its own printer.

When you set up NetWare queue-based print services, you assign a printer, a print server, and a print queue to each other so all three work together. Then you tell the workstation's parallel port to point to a network print queue instead of a directly attached printer. (This is called *redirection*.)

To redirect the workstation's LPT port, you can use the NetWare utility called CAPTURE (usually placing the CAPTURE command in a login script so it is executed automatically). You can also use the NetWare User Tools utility (which runs under Windows 3.1) to assign LPT1 to a print queue.

Alternatively, most network-aware applications let you set them up so they redirect print jobs to a print queue themselves. In many cases, you can simply specify a printer in the application, and because the printer, print queue, and print server are all assigned to each other, the job is sent automatically to the correct print queue.

You can attach printers on a NetWare 5 network to any of the following three different places:

▶ Directly to the server

▶ To a workstation on the network

▶ Directly to the network cabling

If you attach printers directly to the NetWare server, the server must run an NLM called NPRINTER.NLM. This NLM is a port driver, which is software that routes jobs out of the print queue, through the correct port on the server, to the printer.

If you attach a printer to a workstation on the network, that workstation must also be running a port driver. (This port driver is called NPRINTER.EXE for DOS and Windows 3.1, and NPTWIN95 for Windows 95/98.) The workstation's version of NPRINTER or NPTWIN95 works the same way as the server's version, sending print jobs through the port on the workstation to the printer.

To attach the printer directly to the network cabling, you must use a network-direct printer (see the sidebar "Using Network-Direct Printers") that contains its own printer port driver (like NPRINTER). Figure 8.2 shows the various places printers can exist on a network.

FIGURE 8.2 *Printers can be attached to servers, workstations, the network cabling, or any combination of the three.*

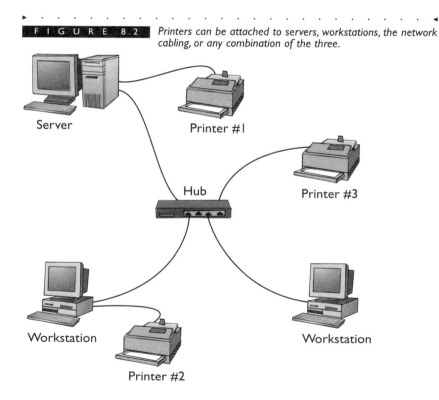

Server

Printer #1

Hub

Printer #3

Workstation

Workstation

Printer #2

Using Network-Direct Printers

Currently, a common type of printing connection is to use printers that connect directly to the network cabling, rather than to a server or a workstation. These types of printers, often called *network-direct printers*, may run in either remote printer mode or queue server mode.

Remote printer mode lets the printer function as if it were running its own NPRINTER port driver. It doesn't need to be connected to a workstation; its internal NPRINTER-like software lets it be controlled by the NetWare print server and allows it to take advantage of NDS functionality.

Queue server mode is bindery-based, and is used when the printer device has not been designed to work with NDS. (As mentioned in Chapter 2, the bindery is a simple form of network database used in NetWare 3.1*x* and earlier forms of NetWare. NDS replaced the bindery in NetWare 4.)

Be sure to read the manufacturer's documentation for more information about installing these types of printers, because there are usually restrictions on how they can be installed.

With NetWare queue-based print services, the journey of a print job follows this path:

- ▶ The application works with the print driver to format the print job, just as it does in standalone mode.

- ▶ Instead of the parallel port pointing directly to a printer, the parallel port is redirected to a print queue. If you specify that one print job goes to one printer and another job goes to a second printer, they will both be redirected from the same parallel port to the correct print queues.

- ▶ When the printer is available, the print server takes the print job from the print queue and sends it to the port driver (such as NPTWIN95.EXE, NPRINTER.EXE, or NPRINTER.NLM) running wherever the printer is connected.

- ▶ The port driver then sends the print job to the printer, and the job is printed.

Even if a workstation has a printer attached to it, it can still be used as a regular workstation. The workstation simply acts as a connection to the network for that printer.

Figure 8.3 illustrates the path a print job takes through the network. In this particular example, the printer is attached to a workstation that is running NPRINTER.EXE.

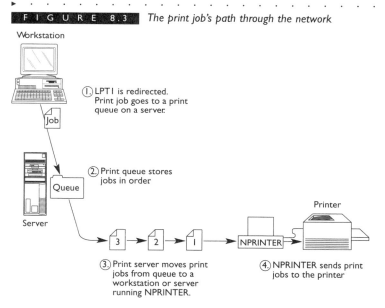

F I G U R E   8 . 3   *The print job's path through the network*

Workstation

①. LPT1 is redirected. Print job goes to a print queue on a server.

②. Print queue stores jobs in order

③. Print server moves print jobs from queue to a workstation or server running NPRINTER.

④. NPRINTER sends print jobs to the printer.

TIP

The workstation attached to the printer should still redirect its own parallel port to the network. This way, the workstation uses network printing services like all the other workstations, instead of printing directly to the printer.

Even if a printer is attached directly to the workstation, it is usually more efficient to send the print job from the workstation to a network print queue, and then back to the printer. This also allows other workstations to use the printer.

Planning Queue-Based Printing

The process of setting up printing services correctly can intimidate a lot of people. However, if your printing needs are straightforward, using Novell's Quick Setup program can greatly simplify the process. (The Quick Setup program is part of the NetWare Administrator utility.) After you install NetWare queue-based print services, the printers, print queues, and print servers will all appear as NDS objects in the Directory tree. You can use the NetWare Administrator utility (which runs on Windows 95/98 or Windows NT) to manage those objects whenever you need to, just as you use it to manage other types of NDS objects.

As you plan your printing setup, decide how many printers you need and where you want to locate them. If you will be attaching printers to workstations, you may want to choose workstations that aren't as heavily used as others. In addition, it will be important for the users of those workstations to remember not to turn off the workstation when other users are using the network. Instead, those users should just log out of the network when they are finished using the workstation.

When you plan how to set up NetWare queue-based print services, you may want to keep the following guidelines and restrictions in mind:

▶ In general, PSERVER.NLM uses about 27K of server RAM for each configured printer.

▶ PSERVER.NLM can service DOS, UNIX, and Apple printers.

▶ A single print server can service up to 255 printers, although performance begins to degrade after about 60 printers or so.

▶ If you need more than one print server in your network, you can load PSERVER.NLM on additional NetWare servers, and those print servers can service more network printers.

▶ When you use the CAPTURE utility to redirect an LPT port to a network print queue, you can also use CAPTURE to specify options such as whether or not to print a banner page, whether to use tabs, and so on.

▶ Instead of using CAPTURE, you may prefer to set up print job configurations. A print job configuration can simplify a user's task of selecting print options by predefining settings such as the designated printer, whether to print a banner page, and the paper form to print on. Print job configurations are stored in databases. Global (or public) print job configuration databases are properties of container objects, and they can be used by multiple users. A private print job configuration database is a property of a user object and can be used only by that user. To create a print job configuration, you can use the NetWare Administrator.

▸ To print a job from outside an application (such as printing an ASCII file or a workstation screen), you can use a command-line utility called NPRINT, which runs in DOS.

Installing NetWare Queue-Based Printing

The Print Services Quick Setup option in the NetWare Administrator utility is the quickest, easiest way to set up print services. If you want to set up each printer to service a single print queue — which greatly simplifies printing administration — this is the installation option to use. This option also assigns printers, print servers, and print queues to each other automatically so there is no chance for you to miss a connection and end up with a broken link somewhere in the print communication chain. After you've set up printing using this quick option, you can modify the setup later if needed.

 The NetWare Administrator utility runs under Windows 3.1, OS/2, Windows 95/98, or Windows NT. For instructions on setting up the NetWare Administrator utility on a workstation, see Chapter 4.
NOTE

To set up print services using the Quick Setup option, complete the following steps:

1. Decide where you want to locate your printer and attach it to the server, workstation, or network cabling. See the printer manufacturer's instructions for installing the printer.

2. Log in to the network from any workstation as user Admin.

3. Launch the NetWare Administrator utility on the workstation.

4. Select the container object that will contain the print server, printer, and print queue. Quick Setup will put them all in the same container.

5. From the NetWare Administrator's Tools menu, select the Print Services Quick Setup (non-NDPS) option. The screen that appears shows the default names and information that NetWare Administrator will assign to the print server, printer, and print queue. See Figure 8.4 for an example of the Quick Setup screen.

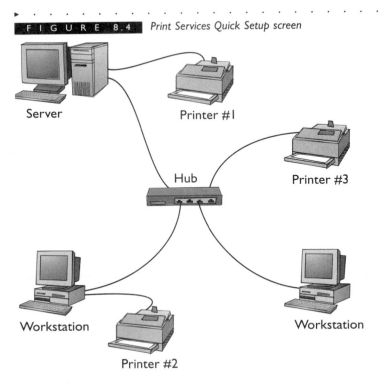

Server   Printer #1

Hub   Printer #3

Workstation   Workstation

Printer #2

6. If necessary, change the name of the print server, printer, or print queue to something you prefer.

7. Choose the printer type you are using (parallel, serial, UNIX, AppleTalk, AIO, and so on) and fill in any necessary information about that printer type. Refer to the printer manufacturer's documentation for specific information about your printer.

8. If necessary, choose a different volume in which to store the print queue. (If you only have one volume, skip this step. If you have more than one volume, you should put the print queues in a volume other than SYS. This will allow you to preserve SYS just for NetWare 5 files, and give the print queues more room on another volume.)

9. Click Create. The Quick Setup program will take just a moment to create the necessary printing objects in NDS. When the NetWare Administrator utility displays the Directory tree's objects now (see

Figure 8.5), you'll see the new printer (P1 in this example), the print server (PS-BlueSky), and the print queue (Q1).

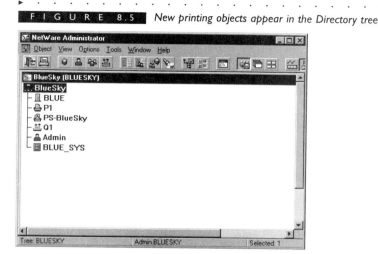

FIGURE 8.5 *New printing objects appear in the Directory tree*

10. Install a print server, if necessary. (If there's already a server on the network running a print server (PSERVER.NLM), skip to Step 11. Because a single print server can service up to 255 printers, you probably need only one print server running on the network.)

If you need to install a print server, go to the network server that will run the print server (or use Remote Console to access that server's console) and load the print server software using the following command:

```
LOAD PSERVER printserver
```

where *printserver* is the name of the newly created print server. For example, you might type:

```
LOAD PSERVER PS-BLUESKY
```

11. If the printer is attached to a network server that is not running PSERVER, load the NPRINTER.NLM on the network server, specifying the print server name and printer number in the NPRINTER command.

To find the printer's number, double-click the print server object's icon in NetWare Administrator, and then click the Assignments page. This page lists all the printers associated with this print server, and indicates each printer's number.

For example, to load NPRINTER for printer P1 (printer number 0), which uses print server PS-BlueSky, use the following command:

```
LOAD NPRINTER PS-BLUESKY 0
```

If you have more than one printer attached to this server, load NPRINTER multiple times, specifying a different printer number (and print server if necessary) for each printer.

12. If the printer is attached to a workstation, run NPRINTER.EXE (for DOS and Windows 3.1) or NPTWIN95.EXE (for Windows 95/98) on that workstation.

a. *For DOS and Windows 3.1,* type **NPRINTER**, followed by the print server name and printer number in the command. (You can include this command in the workstation's AUTOEXEC.BAT file.) For example, to load NPRINTER for printer number 0, which uses print server PS-BlueSky, use the following command:

```
NPRINTER PS-BLUESKY 0
```

b. *For Windows 95/98,* start up the NetWare Client 32 software on the workstation. From the Network Neighborhood, locate the NPTWIN95.EXE file in SYS:PUBLIC\WIN95, and double-click it to launch it. Fill in the Add Network Printer dialog box. (To ensure that NPTWIN95 loads every time the workstation reboots, add this file to the Startup folder. Choose Start, then Settings, then Taskbar, and then select the Start Menu Programs tab. Choose Add, and then Browse to find NPTWIN95.EXE. Choose Next, and then Startup. Enter a name for the icon, such as NPRINTER, and choose Finish.)

13. If you want to modify any information for the printing objects you've created, simply select the object from the NetWare Administrator Browser, choose Details from the Object menu, and edit the fields you want to change.

14. Configure your applications so that they send print jobs to the correct printer. Follow the manufacturer's instructions for setting up the application for network printing. In most cases, applications are network-aware. This means that you can simply supply the application with the printer's name, and the port redirection will be taken care of automatically.

15. If you have applications that may not redirect workstation ports to a print queue automatically, you'll have to tell the workstation to redirect its parallel port to a print queue. To do this, see the section "Redirecting a Parallel Port to a Print Queue" later in this chapter.

Now your NetWare queue-based printing services are ready to use.

TIP

Server commands, such as those you used to load the print server and the server's NPRINTER, can be added to the NetWare 5 server's AUTOEXEC.NCF file. This way, they automatically load whenever the server is rebooted.

To add these commands to this file, go to the server's console and type: LOAD EDIT AUTOEXEC.NCF. This will bring up the file in a simple text editor. When the file appears, type in the server commands you want. (Put the commands to load the print server and NPRINTER, if necessary, toward the end of the AUTOEXEC.NCF file, after the command MOUNT ALL.) When finished, press Esc to save the file and exit the EDIT program.

Print Device Definitions

After you install queue-based printing, you may need to install printer drivers for your printers. *Printer drivers* are software programs that control printer functions, regulating how printers handle print jobs. Many network-aware applications contain printer drivers for a variety of common printers. If your application doesn't recognize your type of printer, you will either have to use a Novell *print device definition* (also called a *printer definition file*, or PDF), or you will have to create your own.

To see if NetWare came with a printer definition file that you can use, look at the files with the .PDF extension in the SYS:PUBLIC directory. If yours is there, you can import that file into the device database.

To import one of Novell's printer definition files so you can use it, use the NetWare Administrator utility. Choose the container object, and then choose Details from the Object menu. Open the Print Devices page, click Import, and select the correct .PDF file from the SYS:PUBLIC directory.

If the driver you need isn't in the SYS:PUBLIC directory, you need to create your own printer definition file. For more information on how to do this, see *Novell's NetWare 5 Administrator's Handbook*.

Redirecting a Parallel Port to a Print Queue

After installing print services on your network, you must ensure that the applications your workstation uses can find the right printers. To do this, you must ensure that the workstation's parallel port is redirected to a print queue.

There are several methods for redirecting the workstation's parallel port, such as the following:

- ▶ Let the application redirect the parallel port.

- ▶ Use the NetWare 5 CAPTURE utility or the NetWare User Tools utility on a Windows 3.1 or DOS workstation.

- ▶ Use the Network Neighborhood on a Windows 95/98 workstation.

The method you choose depends on your needs and on how your workstation is set up, as explained in the following sections.

Letting the Application Redirect the Port

In most cases, you can configure your applications so that they send print jobs to the correct printer. Most network-aware applications let you set them up so they redirect print jobs to a print queue by themselves. In many cases, you can simply specify a printer in the application. Because the printer, print queue, and print server are all assigned to each other, the job is sent to the correct print queue automatically. Follow the application manufacturer's instructions for setting up the application for network printing.

While you're setting up your application, you'll probably be asked for the printer's driver. If the printer uses a print driver that the application already has preinstalled, you can select that driver and continue the printer setup. If the application doesn't have the driver you need, you'll have to supply it (printer manufacturers usually supply the necessary print driver on a diskette).

Redirecting the Port on a DOS or Windows 3.1 Workstation

If you have applications that do not redirect workstation ports to a print queue automatically, you will have to use other methods to redirect the port. On a DOS or Windows 3.1 workstation, you can use the NetWare 5 utility called CAPTURE.

When typing a CAPTURE command, you may need to specify the queue's full name. For example, to redirect users' LPT1 ports to the queue named Q1, with no banner page, no tabs, no form feed, and a five-second timeout interval, type the following command at the workstation's DOS prompt:

```
CAPTURE L=1 Q=.Q1.Sales.Satellite.RedHawk NB NT NFF
TI=5
```

TIP

You can place the CAPTURE command in a login script so that it executes automatically. See the Novell documentation for more information about using login scripts for DOS or Windows 3.1 workstations.

You can also use the NetWare User Tools utility to assign the parallel port to a print queue. See Chapter 5 for more information about using the NetWare User Tools utility. See the Appendix for more information about the options you can use with the CAPTURE utility.

Redirecting the Port on a Windows 95/98 Workstation

On a Windows 95/98 workstation, use the Network Neighborhood to select a printer and redirect its port. Open the Network Neighborhood, then double-click the printer you want to use. Windows 95/98 will then ask you to select the printer you want to use. If the printer uses a print driver that Windows 95/98 already has preinstalled, you can select that driver and continue the printer setup. If Windows 95/98 doesn't have the driver you need, you'll have to supply it (printer manufacturers usually supply the necessary print driver on a diskette).

Answer the remaining setup questions and specify that you want to capture the port.

Verifying Your Printing Setup

After you've set up your queue-based printing services, you can use the NetWare Administrator utility to see a graphical representation of your printing setup. Using this feature, you can see if all your printing objects are assigned to each other correctly.

To see this printing layout diagram, select the print server you're interested in. Double-click the print server's icon (or choose Details from the Object menu), and then open the Print Layout page. Figure 8.6 shows an example print layout diagram.

If all you see is a list of print servers, click a print server to expand the view to show its assigned printers and queues. Lines connecting the printing objects indicate that the objects are assigned to each other correctly. A dashed line connecting them indicates that the connection is only good for this session. When the server is rebooted, the connections will be removed.

If any printing object has an icon with an exclamation mark (!) beside it, there's a problem with that object. (Notice the print server object in Figure 8.6

FIGURE 8.6 *Print Layout Page in NetWare Administrator*

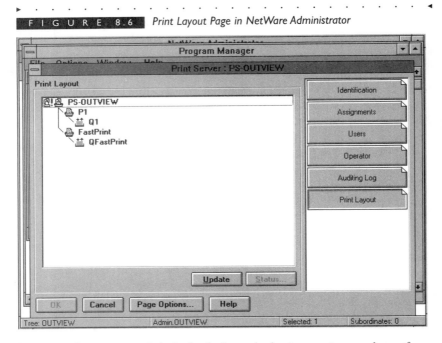

has an exclamation mark.) Go back through the instructions and see if you missed any steps when assigning print queues, print servers, and printers to each other.

You can also right-click any of the objects to see more information about that particular object. In addition, you can see the print jobs in a queue by double-clicking the queue object. However, you cannot modify the print jobs from this screen. To modify the print jobs, you have to go back to the NetWare Administrator Browser, select a print queue, and open its Print Jobs page.

Handling Print Jobs

After NetWare queue-based print services are set up on the network, users can send their jobs to network print queues as long as they have access to those printers.

A user has access to a queue if he or she is assigned as a *print queue user*. By default, the container in which a print queue resides is assigned as a user, so all objects within the container are also users of the queue. A print queue user can do the following:

- ▶ Add jobs to a print queue
- ▶ See the status of all jobs in the queue
- ▶ Delete his or her job from the queue

A queue user cannot delete other users' print jobs from the queue.

A *print queue operator* is a special type of print queue user who has the capability to manage the print queue. A queue operator can delete other users' print jobs, put them on hold, and so on. The user Admin is the default queue operator.

You can add or remove users and operators from the list of print queue users by using the NetWare Administrator utility. You can also use the same utility to look at the current print jobs in the print queue.

To use the NetWare Administrator utility to change users and operators, double-click the Print Queue object (or choose Details from the Object menu), and then open the Users or Operator page.

To see the current print jobs in the queue, open the print queue's Job List page. Here, users can delete their own print jobs or put them on hold. Queue operators can put on hold or delete any users' print jobs. Press the F1 key to read help on each of the available fields in the Job List screen. Figure 8.7 shows the Print Jobs page.

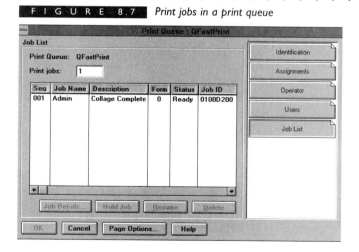

FIGURE 8.7 *Print jobs in a print queue*

Unloading PSERVER.NLM is easy. From the NetWare Administrator utility, select the print server object. Then, from the Object menu, choose Details and click Unload.

To reload PSERVER, type the following command at the network server's console:

```
LOAD PSERVER printserver
```

where *printserver* is the name of the newly created print server.

NDPS Printing

Novell Distributed Print Services (NDPS) is the newest printing system that Novell has developed in conjunction with Hewlett-Packard and Xerox. In addition to providing normal network printing capabilities, NDPS also includes the following new features that weren't available in queue-based printing:

- Bi-directional communication so you can communicate with the printer and the printer can communicate with you

- Event notification, so the printer can notify appropriate personnel when something occurs (such as the printer running out of toner)

- Automatic downloading of printer drivers and other printing resources (such as fonts, banners, or printer definition files) to workstations that need them

In addition, NDPS software can be embedded directly into a printer by the printer manufacturer. That way, future printers can be smarter, providing more customized features to communicate with users effectively. These printers will be called "NDPS-aware" in this chapter, to distinguish them from existing printers that do not have NDPS software embedded.

NDPS is fully compatible with older queue-based network printing, so you can easily support existing queues and printers if you're installing NetWare 5 into an existing network.

Understanding NDPS Printing

Before installing NDPS printing, it's important to have a good understanding of the components that make up NDPS. The following sections explain the NDPS components, how to use those components with the types of printers you have, and the difference between public access and controlled access printers.

In a NetWare network, you can have multiple printers all working at the same time, and users from all over the network may be sending print jobs to those printers simultaneously. To take care of all that traffic and potential conflicts, NDPS uses the following software components, which are explained in the following sections:

- Printer agents
- Gateways
- NDPS Manager
- NDPS Broker

NDPS Printer Agents

A *printer agent* is a software entity that manages a printer. Every printer must have its own unique printer agent. An NDPS-aware printer contains a printer agent embedded in the printer itself. All other printers must have a printer agent created on the server.

The printer agent for a printer performs the following tasks:

- It manages the printer's print jobs.
- It answers client queries about print jobs or printer attributes (such as whether the printer supports color printing).
- It receives notification from the printer when something goes wrong, or when a requested event occurs.
- It services existing queues from queue-based printing setups, so the NDPS printer can print jobs from those queues.

Gateways

If a printer requires that a printer agent be installed on the server (in other words, if the printer is not NDPS-aware), the printer also must have a gateway installed. The gateway is software that translates NDPS commands into language the printer can interpret. Gateways aren't necessary for NDPS-aware printers (those that have their own printer agents embedded).

NDPS Manager

The NDPS Manager is the software program that controls all the printer agents on a server. (If you're familiar with queue-based printing, the NDPS Manager is similar to the print server.)

You load the NDPS Manager by loading an NLM on the server. Then you create an NDS object for it so you can manage it from the NetWare Administrator utility.

If all of your printers are NDPS-aware and have embedded printer agents, you will not need this NDPS Manager. It's only required for printer agents that reside on the server.

NDPS Broker

The NDPS Broker is an NLM loaded on the server. The Broker NLM is loaded and a corresponding NDS object is created during the NetWare server's installation. The Broker manages centralized printing services for all the printers on the network.

NDPS Brokers are created automatically by the regular NetWare server installation. However, because a Broker doesn't need to exist on every single server in the network, the installation program analyzes each server to determine whether the Broker needs to be installed.

If an existing Broker is within three hops of the server you're currently installing, the installation program will not install a Broker automatically on this server. If the nearest existing Broker is four or more hops away, the installation program will install a Broker on this server. (A *hop* is simply the connection between two servers.) Figure 8.8 illustrates this concept.

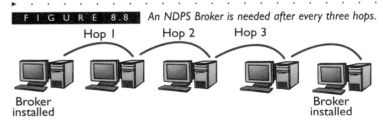

FIGURE 8.8 *An NDPS Broker is needed after every three hops.*

Hop 1   Hop 2   Hop 3

Broker installed   Broker installed

In addition to the "three-hop" guideline, there may be other situations where you want to have the installation program create a Broker. For example, you may want to have two Brokers on a network for reliability — if one server goes down, the Broker will still exist on the other server.

If your network is spread across a large geographical area and is connected by phone lines, you should plan to have a Broker at each site. This lets the Broker handle local network traffic more efficiently.

Which NDPS Components Do You Need?

If all the printers on your network are NDPS-aware, meaning they have NDPS printer agents embedded in them, the only NPDS software component you need on your network is an NDPS Broker. (You may need more than one Broker, depending on the size of your network.) If at least some of your printers are non-NDPS printers, you must create:

- ► A printer agent for each non-NDPS printer
- ► A gateway so the non-NDPS printer can communicate with NDPS
- ► An NDPS Manager to manage the printer agents on the server
- ► An NDSP Broker

Public Access Printers versus Controlled Access Printers

When you install a printer with NDPS, you can choose to make the printer available to users in one of two ways. You can make the printer a public access printer, or you can make it a controlled access printer.

A *public access printer* doesn't have an object in the NDS tree. It only has a printer agent. As soon as the printer agent is created for this printer, the printer is immediately available to anyone on the network. Because there is no printer NDS object for this printer, it isn't subject to the same security measures and other controls as NDS objects. This public access printer advertises itself to users through the Broker, and users can locate it by using the Novell Printer Manager utility from their workstations.

You create a public access printer by using the NDPS Manager object in NetWare Administrator to create a printer agent for the printer.

Because they are installed so simply and don't exist in the NDS tree, public access printers are also limited in the NDPS features they support. For example, they are only capable of job notification, rather than the full gamut of event notifications.

If you want a printer to support all the features of NDPS, you can create it as a *controlled access printer*. To do this, you create an NDPS Printer object for the printer in the NDS tree. When you create this printer object, the printer agent is created automatically. Once the printer has its own object, it can be controlled by NDS trustee rights and then managed through NetWare Administrator's Browser like any other object. (See Chapter 6 for more information on trustees.) It can also take advantage of all NDPS features. A controlled access printer can also be configured to service existing print queues.

You can easily convert a public access printer to a controlled access printer at any time, just by creating an NDPS Printer object for the printer.

Planning NDPS Printing

If you consider each of the following suggestions before beginning the installation process, your NDPS installation may go more smoothly:

- If you're upgrading a network from a previous version of NetWare, you may find it easiest to install NDPS, and then make sure that all the existing queues are assigned to new NDPS printer agents. That way, all your users can continue to print normally using their existing client software on their workstations. Then you can upgrade those workstations to the new NDPS-aware client software at your leisure.

- Although NDPS doesn't use print queues, you may still want to configure each printer agent so it has space on a volume to store files that are waiting to be printed. (This is called *job spooling*.)

- Decide which printers you want to make public access printers, and which ones you want to make controlled access printers.

- Decide which printers you want to be "installed" on users' workstations automatically (which basically consists of automatically downloading the appropriate printer driver to the workstations). You will need to make sure those printers' drivers are added to the Broker's Resource Management database. (If a user needs a printer driver that isn't in the database, he or she can install the driver from a diskette or other site, just as users have done in the past.)

- Plan which servers need to have an NDPS Broker installed. Plan for at least one Broker per geographic site (two Brokers per site is better, in case one server goes down). Also, any server should be no more than three hops away from a Broker.

- Create an NDPS Manager object on each server that will control NDPS printers. (One NDPS Manager can support an unlimited number of printer agents.) You may want to assign printer agents on one server to multiple NDPS Manager objects (on other servers) to make sure that if one server goes down, network users can still print. Assigning printer agents to multiple NDPS Managers also helps balance the load of printing traffic. (However, you should keep printer agents assigned to NDPS Managers within the same geographical site, so that printing traffic isn't going across phone lines unnecessarily.)

- After NDPS has been fully implemented and you no longer need to support print queues on your network, remove all CAPTURE commands from batch files, login scripts, AUTOEXEC.BAT files, or other locations. (Do not remove CAPTURE commands until all of the workstation's dependencies on queues have been removed, however.)

- Decide which roles you want your users to fulfill. Users can be assigned three separate roles for working with NDPS printers: Manager, Operator, and User. A Manager has full control over printing, and can change or delete Printer objects, assign other Managers, Operators, or Users, configure event notification, and so on. An Operator can control assigned printers, but can't modify NDS objects. A User can send print jobs to a printer, and can modify or delete his or her own print jobs only.

The following sections explain how to install and manage NDPS printing on your network.

NDPS Printing Setup Planning

As you plan your NDPS printing setup, keep in mind the following information about NDPS:

- NDPS supports IP, IPX, and mixed networks. If both protocols are available, NDPS will default to using IP. (See Chapter 1 for more information about network protocols.)

- NDPS is fully compatible with queue-based printing. If you already have queues created from an existing system, you can assign a printer agent to accept jobs from one or more of those queues.

- To take advantage of NDPS printing, workstations must use the version of NetWare Client software included in your NetWare 5 package (or download the new client software from Novell's Web site). See Chapter 3 for more information about installing updated NetWare client software.

- Only Windows 3.1, Windows 95/98, and Windows NT clients have been updated to support NDPS features at this time. Macintosh, OS/2, and DOS workstations must continue to send jobs to queues. (Of course, since NDPS printing supports queues, you can still install NDPS on your network — you'll just need to keep the queue-based printing system in place simultaneously).

- You can perform some NDPS activities from more than one tool. For example, you can create a printer agent from the server console (using NDPSM.NLM), from an NDPS gateway, or from the NetWare Administrator utility. In general, this chapter explains how to accomplish tasks from the NetWare Administrator utility, because that is usually the most common and easiest way.

Installing NDPS Printing

Several steps are involved with installing NDPS printing on your NetWare 5 network. The following sections explain how to:

- ▶ Set up the NDPS Broker on a server, and add printer drivers to it if necessary.

- ▶ Create the NDPS Manager.

- ▶ Create a public access printer or a controlled access printer (controlled access printers can also be configured to service print queues).

- ▶ Install printer support on workstations.

Setting Up the NDPS Broker

The easiest way to set up the NDPS Broker on a server is to do it while you're installing the server itself. At the end of the server installation program, you are given the option to install "additional products." One of the products listed is NDPS.

If you choose to install NDPS, the installation program will copy all the necessary NDPS files to the server and, by default, create an NDPS Broker object in the NDS tree.

During installation, a command to load the Broker NLM is automatically added to the server's AUTOEXEC.NCF file so it will be loaded every time the server is rebooted.

If you did not install NDPS when you first installed the server, you can install it at any time. Load the NWCONFIG.NLM on the server by typing the following command at the server's console:

```
NWCONFIG
```

Then, from the list of options that appears, select Product Options. Then select Choose an Item or Product Listed Above. Next, select Install Other Novell Products. You will need to insert the *NetWare 5 Operating System* CD-ROM and specify the path to the CD-ROM to install NDPS. The screen will then display a list of available products you can install. Select NDPS, click Next, and follow the prompts to install it.

NetWare 5 ships with many printer drivers for common printers. However, this is not a complete set of all available printer drivers that exist in the market, so you should make sure that the printer drivers you need for your printers are included. If they are not in the Broker's database, you can add them from the manufacturer's diskette (or some other source).

To see the list of existing printer drivers (or other resources), and to add a driver to the list, complete the following steps:

1. From any workstation, log in to the network as user Admin, and launch the NetWare Administrator utility.

2. From the NetWare Administrator's Browser window, double-click the Broker object (or select the Broker object and choose Details from the Option menu).

3. Open the Resource Management (RMS) page, shown in Figure 8.9.

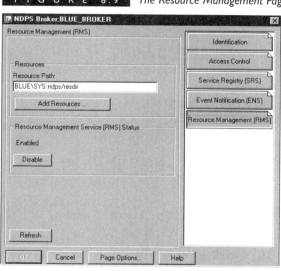

FIGURE 8.9 *The Resource Management Page*

4. Click the Add Resources button.

5. Choose the icon for the type of resource (such as Windows 95/98 Printer Drivers) you want to see (or add). A list appears, showing all resources of that type that are currently loaded.

6. If the driver you need does not appear, click Add. You can click the Browse button to search for the location of the driver you want to add.

7. Enter the appropriate information about the printer driver, and follow prompts as they appear. You need to supply the driver on a diskette or from some other location.

8. Click OK.

Now the new printer driver will appear in the list of available printer drivers in the Resource Management database.

Creating the NDPS Manager on a Server

To create an NDPS Manager on your server, you have to create an NDPS Manager object in the NDS tree, and then load NDPSM.NLM on the server. To do this, complete the following steps:

1. From any workstation, log in to the network as user Admin, and launch the NetWare Administrator utility.

2. To create the NDPS Manager object in the NDS tree, open the NetWare Administrator's Browser screen and select the container object that will contain the NDPS Manager.

3. From the Object menu, choose Create.

4. Select NDPS Manager from the list of class objects that appears.

5. In the Create NDPS Manager Object screen, enter the name you want to give this NDPS Manager object. (If you have a queue-based print server running on the network, be sure you don't give the NDPS Manager object the same name as the print server, or both will be advertising the same name, creating a conflict.) See Figure 8.10.

6. In the Resident Server field, enter the server where this NDPS Manager and its database of information will be located. (Click the Browse button to search for the server in the tree.)

7. In the Database Volume field, enter the name of the volume that will hold the NDPS Manager's database. (This volume must be located on the Resident Server you selected in Step 6.) The volume you select should have at least 5MB of disk space available for this database.

8. Click Create. The NDPS Manager object has now been created, and will appear in the Browser window the next time you open it.

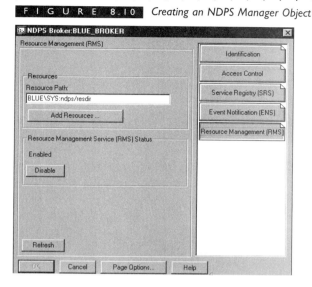

F I G U R E 8.10 *Creating an NDPS Manager Object*

9. Go to the server and load NDPSM.NLM on the server by typing the following command, substituting the new NDPS Manager object's full name for *name*:

   LOAD NDPSM name

   (If the NDPS Manager's object name contains spaces, use underscores instead of the spaces in the name.)

10. To make sure NDPSM.NLM loads every time the server is rebooted, add the same LOAD command to the server's AUTOEXEC.NCF file.

NOTE

When you load the NDPSM module on the server, a console screen will appear, showing any created printer agents. You can manage the NDPS Manager from this screen if you like. However, you can also manage the NDPS Manager from the NetWare Administrator utility, which is often easier to use. For consistency, this chapter discusses only the NetWare Administrator approach to managing NDPS printing.

Creating Network Printers

When you are ready to create network printers, you must first decide whether to create public access printers or controlled access printers. (You can convert a public access printer to a controlled access printer at any time.)

Creating a Public Access Printer   To create a public access printer, you will use the NDPS Manager object to create a printer agent and select a gateway for the printer. Use the NetWare Administrator utility, as explained in the following steps:

1. From any workstation, log in to the network as user Admin, and launch the NetWare Administrator utility.

2. From the NetWare Administrator's Browser window, double-click the NDPS Manager object (or select the NDPS Manager object and choose Details from the Option menu).

3. Open the Printer Agent List page. (If asked to choose a printer agent list, select the one you need to use.) A list of any current printer agents is displayed.

4. Click New.

5. In the Printer Agent (PA) Name field, enter a name for the new printer agent you are creating.

6. Choose the Gateway Type you want to use. Hewlett-Packard and Xerox have provided gateways in NetWare 5 for use with some of their printers. The generic Novell printer gateway is provided for all other printers. See the Novell online documentation for more information about the HP and Xerox gateways if you have one of their printers.

7. Click OK.

8. Choose the printer type and port type for your printer, and select any other information necessary for your printer (such as the connection type). This information varies depending on the gateway you selected. (If you are installing a printer that attached directly to the network, such as a JetDirect printer, and you have to choose between installing it in queue server mode or in remote printer mode, choose remote printer mode.)

9. Choose the printer drivers necessary for each workstation operating system that your users may be using (Windows 3.1, Windows 95/98, or Windows NT). You can choose more than one driver if necessary. If

you select None, users will have to provide the printer driver on a diskette the first time they install this printer on their workstation. (If the printer driver you want is not in the driver list, you can add it to the Broker's Resource Management Service, as explained earlier in this chapter.)

10. Click Continue. A new printer agent has now been created for this printer, and the printer is now available to anyone on the network.

NOTE You can also create a public access printer by using a gateway provided by a printer manufacturer, or by using NDPSM.NLM at the server console. See the Novell online documentation or the manufacturer's documentation for more information about these methods.

To manage a public access printer, use the Tools menu from the NetWare Administrator utility.

Creating a Controlled Access Printer   To create a controlled access printer, you need to create an NDPS Printer object in the NDS tree. (You must have already created an NDPS Manager object.) You can configure an NDPS Printer object so that it services existing print queues.

Use the NetWare Administrator utility to create a controlled access printer, as explained in the following steps:

1. From any workstation, log in to the network as user Admin, and launch the NetWare Administrator utility.

2. Open the NetWare Administrator's Browser screen and select the container object that will contain the NDPS Printer object.

3. From the Object menu, select Create.

4. Choose NDPS Printer from the list that appears and click OK.

5. In the NDPS Printer Name field, enter a name for this Printer object.

6. Under Printer Agent Source, click Create a New Printer Agent, and then click Create.

7. Choose the name you want to use for the new printer agent. The default name is the same as the new Printer object you're creating. See Figure 8.11.

F I G U R E   8.11   *Specifying information for an NDPS Printer object*

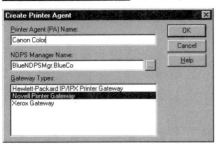

8. Assign the printer agent to an NDPS Manager object. (Click the Browse button to search the tree for the NDPS Manager you want to use.)

9. Choose the gateway you want to use. Hewlett-Packard and Xerox have provided gateways in NetWare 5 for use with some of their printers. The generic Novell printer gateway is provided for all other printers. See the Novell online documentation for more information about the HP and Xerox gateways if you have one of their printers.

10. Click OK.

11. Choose the printer type and the port type for your printer. (The Novell port handler may be adequate for most printers.)

12. Select any other information necessary for your printer. This information varies depending on the gateway you selected. If asked to select the connection type, choose Local Printer only if the printer is attached directly to the server where the NDPS Manager is loaded. Choose Manual only if you want to manually build the port handler string. Choose Queue-based to support printers and print systems that require print jobs to be sent to queues. If you are installing a printer that is attached directly to the network, such as a JetDirect printer, and you have to choose between installing it in Queue Server mode or in Remote Printer mode, choose Remote Printer mode (and specify whether you're using IPX or TCP/IP). When finished making selections, click Finish.

13. Choose the printer drivers necessary for each workstation operating system that your users may be using (Windows 3.1, Windows 95/98, or Windows NT). You can choose more than one driver, if necessary.

If you select None, users will have to provide the printer driver on a diskette the first time they install this printer on their workstation.

14. Click Continue. The new controlled access printer is now available on the network for anyone with the appropriate NDS trustee rights to access it. (See Chapter 6 for more information about trustee rights.)

15. Make sure the new printer's job spooling area on the server's volume is set up the way you want it to be. Double-click the new NDPS Printer object in the Browser window. Click Jobs, and select Spooling Configuration. You can change the location of the spooling area (the default is the same volume as the NDPS Manager information), the maximum size of the spooling area's disk space, and the schedule that determines the order in which jobs are printed.

16. If you want this printer to service print queues, go to the same Spooling Configuration screen (described in Step 15). Under Service Jobs from NetWare Queues, click Add. Then choose the print queues you want this printer to service. Click OK. Now this printer can service those existing print queues.

Converting a Public Access Printer to a Controlled Access Printer   You can convert a public access printer to a controlled access printer at any time. To do this, you create an NDPS Printer object in the NDS tree, and assign it to the printer agent that was created when you first installed this public access printer. Use the NetWare Administrator utility, as explained in the following steps:

1. From any workstation, log in to the network as user Admin, and launch the NetWare Administrator utility.

2. Open the NetWare Administrator's Browser screen and select the container object that will contain the NDPS Printer object you are about to create for this printer.

3. From the Object menu, select Create.

4. Choose NDPS Printer from the list that appears, and then click OK.

5. In the NDPS Printer Name field, enter a name for this Printer object.

6. In the Printer Agent Source field, click Public Access Printer, and then click Create. (You'll receive a message warning you that you will have to reinstall this printer support on every workstation that has used it. Click OK to continue.)

7. From the list of public access printers that appears, choose the public access printer you want to convert, and click OK. The new controlled access printer is now available on the network for anyone with the appropriate NDS trustee rights to access it.

8. Make sure the new printer's job spooling area on the server's volume is set up the way you want it to be. Double-click the new NDPS Printer object in the Browser window. Click Jobs, and select Spooling Configuration. You can change the location of the spooling area (the default is the same volume as the NDPS Manager information), the maximum size of the spooling area's disk space, and the schedule that determines the order in which jobs are printed.

9. If you want this printer to service print queues, go to the same Spooling Configuration screen (described in Step 8). Under Service Jobs from NetWare Queues, click Add. Then choose the print queues you want this printer to service. Click OK. Now this printer can service those existing print queues.

Installing Printer Support on Workstations

With NDPS, you can designate specific printer drivers to be automatically downloaded and installed on users' workstations, so the users don't have to worry about installing their own printer support. The printers you specify will appear automatically on the user's installed printers list. The feature that lets you designate the printers that should be installed automatically on workstations is called Remote Printer Management. You can also use Remote Printer Management to designate which printer should be a user's default printer, and to remove printers from workstations.

You aren't required to designate printers to download and install automatically. Users can also install printer support manually. However, you will probably find that it saves time to designate automatic downloads instead.

With Remote Printer Management, you configure printer drivers and other information you want to be installed. When a user logs in, the workstation software checks the user's container object for any new printer information. If new printer information (such as a new driver to be downloaded) exists, the workstation is automatically updated.

Automatically Installing Printer Support   You can access Remote Printer Management in one of three ways, depending on how many printers you want to manage for a given task:

▸ To manage all the printers in a single container, select the container object in NetWare Administrator, and choose Details from the Object menu. Then open the NDPS Remote Printer Management page.

▸ To manage a single controlled access printer, select the NDPS Printer object in NetWare Administrator, and choose Details from the Object menu. Then open the NDPS Remote Printer Management page.

▸ To manage a single public access printer, use the Tools menu in NetWare Administrator and select NDPS Public Access Printers. Select the printer, and choose Details from the Object menu. Next, open the NDPS Remote Printer Management page.

After you access the Remote Printer Management feature for the container or printer you selected, you can designate the printers you want to automatically download and install on workstations. You can also specify default printers for the users.

Manually Installing Printer Support   If a required printer driver isn't automatically downloaded, users can still install the printer support on their workstations manually. They can either install a printer driver from a diskette, or they can install a public access or controlled access printer that resides on the network (the drivers for these printers will be in the NDPS Broker's database).

There are two ways to install printer support manually on a workstation:

▸ Using the Add Printers feature in Windows 95/98 and Windows NT (Windows 3.1 workstations can't use this option.)

▸ Using a Novell utility called Novell Printer Manager

To use the Windows Add Printers feature, press Start, then Settings, and then Printers. Then click the Add Printers icon and follow the instructions to load the printer driver on the workstation.

To use the Novell Printer Manager utility to manually install printer support on the workstation, complete the following steps:

I. Launch the Printer Manager utility by using the Windows Run command. For a Windows 3.1 workstation, run the file called NWPMW16.EXE, located in the PUBLIC folder on volume SYS. For Windows 95/98 and Windows NT workstations, run the file called

NWPMW32.EXE, located in the WIN32 folder, which is in the PUBLIC folder on volume SYS.

2. From the Printer menu, select New. A list appears, showing any printers that are already installed on this workstation. It also shows this workstation's default printer.

3. Click Add. A list appears, showing all available public access printers and all the controlled access printers in your context. To see controlled access printers in other parts of the NDS tree, click the Browse button.

4. Choose the printer you want to install on your workstation, and click Install.

5. If you wish, change the printer name and choose a printer configuration that matches your needs.

6. Click OK. The printer driver for the printer should download automatically. If the printer driver is not available, you will need to provide a diskette or alternate location for the driver.

7. Click Close to finish.

Managing NDPS Printers

After NDPS printers have been installed, managing them is relatively easy.

To manage controlled access printers, use the NetWare Administrator utility and double-click the NDPS Printer object. When the Details page for the printer opens, you can add or modify information about it, such as assigning operators or users, filling in a description of the printer, and so on. You can also configure the printer so that print job owners are notified of events that occur with their print jobs. In addition, you can use the Access Control Notification feature to enable notification to be sent to "interested parties," such as the printer's Manager or Operator.

To manage a public access printer, you also use the NetWare Administrator utility. However, instead of opening a printer object (because there's no printer object for a public access printer), you pull down the Tools menu, and select NDPS Public Access Printers. Select the printer you want to manage, and then choose Details from the Object menu.

Users who want to see information about network printers can use the Novell Printer Manager utility. Users can launch the Printer Manager utility by using the Windows Run command. (Windows 95/98 and NT users may want to create a shortcut to the Printer Manager utility.) The executable file a user must run depends on the workstation's operating system:

- For a Windows 3.1 workstation, run the file called NWPMW16.EXE, located in the PUBLIC folder on volume SYS.

- For Windows 95/98 and Windows NT workstations, run the file called NWPMW32.EXE, located in the WIN32 folder, which is in the PUBLIC folder on volume SYS.

The main Printer Manager window displays all the NDPS printers currently installed on the workstation. From here, users can add more printers to their workstation, if necessary.

In addition, the Printer Manager utility displays information about the printer, such as its status, its attributes (such as whether it prints in color), any problems with the printer (such as a paper jam or low toner), and so on. Users can also use the Printer Manager utility to see and change the status of their print jobs, as explained in the next section.

Managing NDPS Print Jobs

Users can use either the NetWare Administrator utility or the Printer Manager utility to see the status of their print jobs. They can also change certain aspects of their own print jobs, such as canceling them or putting them on hold. Printer users can only change their own jobs. Printer Operators can change print jobs for any users on a printer.

From either the NetWare Administrator or the Printer Manager, select the printer whose jobs you want to see and select Details from the Object menu to open the main Printer Control page. Then click Jobs and select Job List.

After displaying a list of all active jobs, you can perform any of the following tasks:

- To see information about the print job, highlight the job and click Information. This displays the job's status, details, owner, submission date and time, and size.

- To see which print jobs have been processed but retained (put on hold), click Show Retained Jobs.

- To copy or move a job to another location, select the job and click Job Options. Then choose Copy (or Move) and specify the new location.

- To see or change the properties of a job, select the job, click Job Options, and then click Configuration. Click each tab to see the different properties of this job.

- To delete a job, select the job and click Job Options. Then choose Cancel Printing.

► To change the order of print jobs waiting to be printed, select Job Options, and then select Reorder. Select the job you want to move and specify the position to which you want to move it (you can only move jobs down the list).

Beyond the Basics

This chapter explored the foundations of NetWare 5 printing, and it also explained how to set up a quick and easy system of network printing.

Although the majority of network users can (and should) use the basic printing setup without making any customized changes, NetWare 5 printing has numerous features built in that make it tremendously flexible. In fact, once you begin dabbling in customized printing setups, printing can become one of the more complex aspects of a network.

You can find more information about the following topics in Novell's online documentation (which came with your NetWare 5 package), and in *Novell's NetWare 5 Administrator's Handbook* and *Novell's Guide to NetWare Printing* (both from Novell Press):

► Using the CAPTURE utility to redirect an LPT port to a network print queue. (You can also use CAPTURE to specify options such as whether or not to print a banner page, whether to use tabs, and so on.)

► Using print job configurations to predefine settings such as the designated printer, whether or not to print a banner page, and the type of paper form to print on (such as invoice forms, paychecks, legal-sized paper, and so on).

► Using the NPRINT utility to print a job from outside an application (such as printing an ASCII file or a workstation screen).

► Using printer definition files if your applications don't have a printer driver for your type of printer.

► Customizing your printing environment, such as designating multiple queues that will be serviced by a single printer or multiple printers that will service a single queue

► Creating login scripts (for DOS and Windows 3.1 workstations) that let you specify certain files and programs that should load whenever the user logs in.

CHAPTER 9

Netscape FastTrack Server for NetWare

The Netscape FastTrack Server for NetWare is a robust, high-performance, industry-leading Web server included in NetWare 5. It was made available to Novell through a partnership between Netscape and Novell called Novonyx, a research and development division of Novell.

The FastTrack server is based on open standards. It supports many leading Internet application development languages, and enables NetWare 5 to be a powerful Web development platform. The FastTrack Server is very different from the Novell Web Server, which you may currently be using. It has many features that were not available with the Novell Web Server.

The FastTrack Server is easy to install and use. Tight integration with NDS and the use of LDAP makes the FastTrack Server excellent for use with intranets or the Internet. (See Chapter 4 for more information about LDAP Services for NDS.)

The FastTrack Server includes an Administration Server that allows browser-based management of FastTrack and other Netscape servers. The Netscape Administration Server (also called the Admin Server) enables you to manage the Netscape FastTrack Server and any other Netscape servers you may be using. The Admin Server is a Web server of its own and operates on a port separate from the FastTrack Web server. This enables you to change, load, and unload other Netscape servers remotely. Because the Admin Server is always up, you always have control of your Web servers.

You access the Admin Server through a Netscape browser (version 3.01 or higher). Older versions of Netscape's browser, Microsoft Internet Explorer 4.0, and other browsers do not support all of the JavaScript functions that are required for administration.

This chapter discusses the Netscape FastTrack Server's installation procedure, features, and functionality.

Installing the FastTrack Server for NetWare

The installation of the FastTrack Server is one of its best features. You run the installation program from a workstation, and the installation program sets up the entire configuration for you. Before you can install FastTrack Server, however, be sure that your workstation and server meet the minimum hardware and software requirements for installation.

Client requirements include:

- ▶ Windows 95/98 or Windows NT
- ▶ Novell's Client software

- A CD-ROM drive, if you are installing the FastTrack server from the CD-ROM

- A minimum of 100MB of free space on the workstation's hard disk

- Administration rights to the SYS volume

Server requirements include:

- A minimum of 100MB free on the SYS volume

- 64MB of memory

Complete the following steps to install the FastTrack Server on a NetWare 5 server:

1. From a Windows 95/98 or NT workstation, open the Start menu and choose Run. Browse the NetWare 5 Operating System CD-ROM to the \PRODUCTS\WEBSERV folder, and then select the SETUP.EXE file.

2. When an information screen appears, click the Finish button to continue (see Figure 9.1).

FIGURE 9.1 *FastTrack Server Installation Welcome screen*

This unpacks the necessary installation files onto your workstation. If you do not have sufficient disk space, the installation will fail. (These files will be automatically deleted after the installation completes.)

3. At the Welcome screen, click Next to continue.

4. Read the Software License Agreement and click Yes to continue.

5. Select the server and SYS volume where you want to install the FastTrack Server. (You must select the root of the SYS volume.) When finished, click OK and then click Next to continue.

6. The installation procedure will now verify long filename support and will verify that you have IP properly configured. Enter the IP address of the server you selected in Step 5. Then enter the hostname for your server. If there is no DNS entry for the IP address you are using, enter the IP address of the server in the hostname field. When finished, click Next to continue.

7. Enter the port for the Web server. By default, this will be 80. Then click Next to continue.

8. Enter an admin port number and click Next to continue. (It is very important that you remember the port number. This is the number you will use to access the Admin Server. If you forget the port number, it is located in the NS-ADMIN.CONF file located in the SYS:\NOVONYX\SUITESPOT\ADMIN-SERV\CONFIG\ directory. This number should only be known to network administrators.)

9. An information screen appears. Click OK to continue.

10. When prompted, enter a user name for the SuperUser, and then enter a password and confirm the password. (Remember the SuperUser name and password.) Click Next to continue.

11. When the installation program displays LDAP (Lightweight Directory Access Protocol) information, click Next to continue. (As explained in Chapter 4, LDAP is a protocol for accessing network information directories.)

12. Select whether to add the NSWEB.NCF command to your NetWare server's AUTOEXEC.NCF file. If you choose not to add this command, you will be required to manually start the FastTrack Web server anytime you restart your NetWare server.

13. When the summary of the server's configuration appears, check the information to make sure it is correct, and click Next to continue.

14. After all files have been copied, you have the option of automatically launching the FastTrack Web Server and viewing the ReadMe file. If you elect not to launch the Web server now, you can type **NSWEB** at the server console later to launch the FastTrack Server.

15. Click Finish to complete the installation.

The FastTrack Web Server is now installed.

Connecting to the Administration Server

Once you have FastTrack up and running, you can connect to the Admin Server by opening your Netscape browser and entering your server's Uniform Resource Locator (URL) and administration port number. If you launched NSWEB when you finished the install, the browser will automatically load and the login prompt will appear.

A login box appears and requires that you enter the name and password of the SuperUser that you entered during the installation process. After you enter this information, the Netscape Server Administration page appears.

There are two different sections of the Server Administration page, as shown in Figure 9.2: General Administration and Servers Supporting General Administration.

FIGURE 9.2 *Server Administration page*

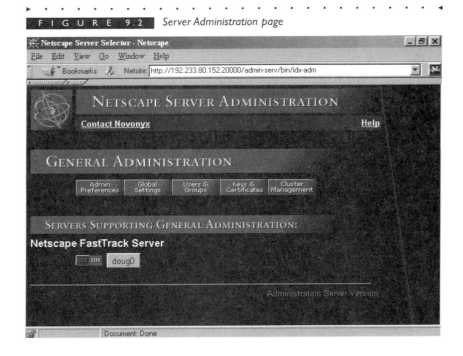

General Administration Options

The General Administration section contains buttons for configuring the Admin Server and general configurations for all installed Netscape servers. Any changes you make in this section will affect the Netscape FastTrack Server and any other Netscape servers that have been installed on your NetWare server.

The following options are available under the General Administration section of the Server Administration page:

- ▶ Admin Preferences
- ▶ Global Settings
- ▶ Users and Groups
- ▶ Keys and Certificates
- ▶ Cluster Management

Admin Preferences

This button enables you to configure the Admin Server itself. You may select from the following options:

- ▶ *Shutdown* — To shut down the Admin Server.

- ▶ *Network Settings* — To configure the Admin Server port chosen during installation.

- ▶ *SuperUser Access Control* — To configure SuperUser access for the Admin Server.

- ▶ *Turn On/Off SSL* — To turn on or off Secure Sockets Layer (SSL), which is a communications privacy feature. (See the "Keys and Certificates" section later in this chapter for more information on SSL.)

- ▶ *Security Preferences* — To make choices about SSL connections.

- ▶ *Logging Options* — To specify the location of Admin Server log files.

- ▶ *View Access Log* — To view the Admin Server log files.

- ▶ *View Error Log* — To view the Admin Server error log file.

Global Settings

This page specifies which directory service you want to use with your FastTrack Server. This directory service stores all of your user and group information. It also handles all authentication and access control for the FastTrack Server. You can choose from three directory services:

- ▶ Local Database
- ▶ LDAP Directory Server
- ▶ Novell Directory Services (NDS)

Figure 9.3 shows the NDS Configuration page.

FIGURE 9.3 *Novell Directory Services Configuration page*

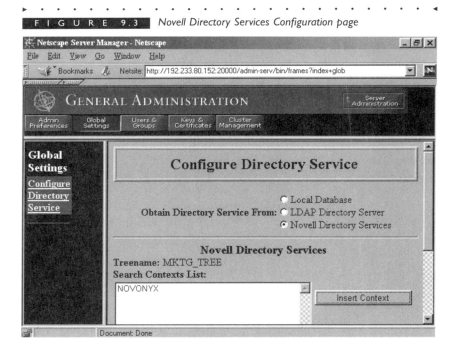

Users and Groups

This page enables you to add new users, groups, or Organizational Units. You can also edit existing users, groups, or Organizational Units, and import or export directory information. (See Chapter 4 for more information about Organizational Units in NDS.) You can choose from several options:

▶ *New User*, *Group*, or *Organizational Unit* — These options enable you to enter all information about your new object. When you select Create, the object information you have entered will be added into the directory. (Figure 9.4 shows the New User screen.)

F I G U R E   9 . 4   *New User entry page*

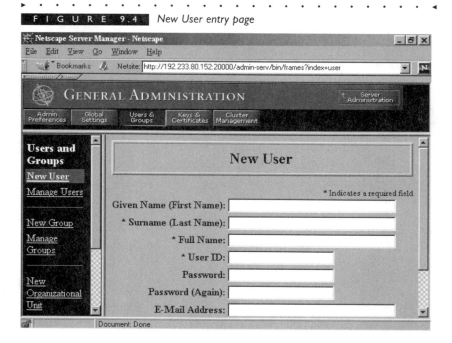

▶ *Manage Users, Groups*, or *Organizational Units* — These options give you simple query options for finding specific objects in the directory. Once you find the object you are looking for, you can make changes and update the information.

▶ *Import/Export* — These options let you import or export LDIF files. LDIF files can be very helpful in moving large amounts of directory information from one location to another.

NOTE

If you decided to use Native NDS for your directory, the Users and Groups page will be disabled and you will need to use the NetWare Administrator utility for user and group administration.

Keys and Certificates

The Secure Sockets Layer (SSL) supported by the FastTrack Server is the protocol that keeps your data safe. SSL preserves data security on three levels: confidentiality (through encryption), integrity (also through encryption), and authentication (through digital certificates purchased from third-party companies). Before using SSL on your FastTrack server, you should consult the security manager for your company, because creating a secure environment requires significant planning. Before configuring the Keys and Certificates sections of the administration server, read the online documentation included with the FastTrack Server and create a careful plan for implementing a secure environment.

Cluster Management

In the Netscape world, a *cluster* is a group of similar Netscape servers that can be administered from a single Netscape Admin Server. This feature enables you to manage multiple FastTrack Servers from a single location.

Servers Supporting General Administration Options

Every Netscape server has individual configuration options that affect only that specific server. In the previous section, you learned about General Administration, which controls all Netscape servers on a single machine. On the main Administration Server page, there is another section called Servers Supporting General Administration. Under that section, you see Netscape FastTrack Server, and beneath that is a button with the name of your NetWare server. Click this button to go to the pages that are specific to the FastTrack Server.

When the FastTrack Server Administration page appears, the Server Preferences button is selected by default, as shown in Figure 9.5.

On the left side of the screen, you will see all the options available under Server Preferences. Near the top right of the screen you will see two buttons: Apply and Admin.

When you click the Apply button, it saves any changes you have made, and stops and restarts the server to make them take effect. Remember that if you are making many changes, you may not want to click Apply after every change. Instead, wait to click Apply until after you have made all your changes.

Server Preferences page

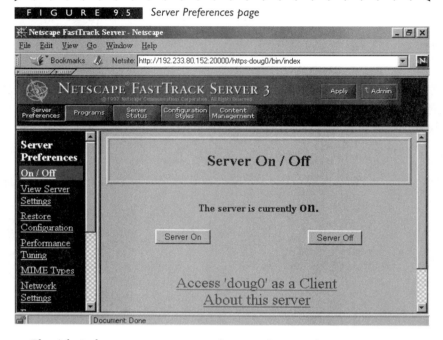

The Admin button returns you to the main Server Administration page.

On the FastTrack Server Administration page, you will see five buttons near the top. These are links to the FastTrack configuration pages, which enable you to make modifications to the FastTrack Server configuration. The five available buttons are:

▸ Server Preferences

▸ Programs

▸ Server Status

▸ Configuration Styles

▸ Content Management

Each of these pages is described in the following sections, beginning with Server Preferences.

Server Preferences

The Server Preferences page enables you to manage a specific FastTrack Server's configuration. To open the options under Server Preferences, click the Server Preferences button. The options under Server Preferences are as follows:

- *On/Off* — This page lets you start and stop the FastTrack Server. If you click the Off button, the Admin Server will unload all FastTrack files on the NetWare server. It will not, however, unload the Admin Server itself. The Admin Server stays up so you can click the On button to restart the server. This page also contains a link to the server's home page and an About This Server link. Remember that you can also start and stop the server from the Servers Supporting General Administration page by clicking the On/Off buttons located just left of the server's name.

- *View Server Settings* — Netscape server products use configuration files to store information about the servers. These files are virtually identical across all supported platforms. The main configuration files for the FastTrack Server are MAGNUS.CONF and OBJ.CONF. These files are contained in the /NOVONYX/SUITESPOT/HTTPS*servername*/ CONFIG/ directory. (Replace *servername* with the name of your server.) The View Server Settings page displays an abbreviated look at MAGNUS.CONF, showing information about your server. Just below the MAGNUS.CONF file is a partial listing of information contained in the OBJ.CONF. Click any of the links to display a page that enables you to edit the information in these files. Make any necessary changes, click OK, and then click Save to apply the changes. Because changes made to either of these files can have serious consequences, consult the online help before making changes.

- *Restore Configuration* — If you have made changes to your server that have caused unwanted results, the Restore Configuration page can help you get back on track. Down the left side of the page, you will see a list of dates and times. These are backups of every configuration that your server has had. FastTrack makes a backup copy of MAGNUS.CONF, OBJ.CONF, and all other configuration files each time you make a change. By clicking the button for a particular date and time, you can restore your server to the exact configuration it had at that specific time. Along with restoring a complete configuration, you can select specific configuration files you would like to restore. The View button enables you to look at a file before you restore it.

▶ *Performance Tuning* — The Performance Tuning page enables you to make some performance adjustments to the server. However, the changes made through this page are minor in comparison to the performance enhancements that can be made by editing the OBJ.CONF by hand. Consult performance-tuning documents available through Netscape's and Novell's Web sites for complete performance-tuning information.

▶ *MIME Types* — MIME (Multi-purpose Internet Mail Extensions) types control which file types the FastTrack server recognizes and supports. The configuration file MIME.TYPES (located in the SYS:/NOVONYX/ SUITESPOT/HTTPS-*servername*/CONF/ directory) also specifies which applications support different file extensions. For example, if you want to put MP3 files on your server, you must add the MP3 extension to your MIME types. If this is not added, the server will transfer the file to the user as text, instead of as a sound file. The Global Mime Types page makes it easy to add new types. From this page, you can also delete or modify existing types.

NOTE

For information on adding new MIME types to your server, see *Novell's NetWare 5 Administrator's Handbook.*

▶ *Network Settings* — The Network Settings page enables you to view or change configuration information contained in the MAGNUS.CONF file. (You are automatically brought to this Network Settings page when you click any of the MAGNUS.CONF change links in the View Server Settings page.) Any changes you make to MAGNUS.CONF should be made with care.

▶ *Error Responses* — The error messages sent to a client are fairly generic and do not give much information, so you can use the Error Responses page to create custom error messages. When a server cannot complete a request, it can send one of the following four different error messages to the client: *Unauthorized* (occurs when a user tries unsuccessfully to access a file in a secure area of the Web server), *Forbidden* (occurs when the server does not have file system rights sufficient to read the requested data), *Not Found* (occurs when a user tries to access data that does not exist), and *Server* (occurs when the server is improperly configured or when a fatal error occurs, such as the system running out of memory).

TIP

There are many situations in which you may want to use custom messages. For example, if users are denied access, instead of receiving a message that simply says "Unauthorized," they could receive a custom error message that explains the reason they were denied access and points them to the help desk to have an account created. For information on changing error responses on your server, see *Novell's NetWare 5 Administrator's Handbook*.

▶ *Restrict Access* — Restrict Access is one of the pages you will use most often when working with the FastTrack Server. This is where LDAP access control is configured. From this page, you can use many options for restricting access to the server. You can limit access by specific user or group. You can give access to every user in the authentication database. If you are using the LDAP Directory Server option on the Global Settings page, you can restrict access based on IP address or hostname. (This option is not available if you chose to use Native NDS for your directory type.) Restricting access by IP address or hostname enables you to require users to be on a specific network (or even using a certain IP address) if they are going to access information on the Web server. Using the Restrict Access page also gives you the capability to assign different levels of security to the FastTrack server. These levels include:

- *Read access* — Lets a user access data, including HTTP methods GET, HEAD, POST, and INDEX.

- *Write access* — Lets a user change, delete, or modify data, including HTTP methods PUT, DELETE, MKDIR, RMDIR, and MOVE.

- *Execute access* — Applies to server-side applications (such as CGI programs, Java applets, and agents).

- *Delete access* — Allows a user to delete data.

- *List access* — Allows the user to access directory information (for example, the user can get a list of files in that specific directory).

- *Info access* — Allows the user access to header information, including the HTTP HEAD method.

NOTE

For information on setting access levels for your server, see *Novell's NetWare 5 Administrator's Handbook*.

Programs

FastTrack Server offers many options for Web application development, such as PERL, Java, JavaScript, CGI, and Netbasic. The Programs section of the Admin Server helps you manage the locations and configurations for your Web applications. To open the Programs section, click the Programs button at the top of the Admin Server screen. The available options under Programs are as follows:

▶ *CGI Directory* — There are two ways to store Common Gateway Interface (CGI) programs on your FastTrack server. The first way is to select a directory that contains only CGI programs. (The second way is described in the bullet item.) Every file located in this directory will be run as a program. You can modify or remove any CGI directory using this page.

For information on specifying a CGI directory in which to store CGI programs, see *Novell's NetWare 5 Administrator's Handbook.*

NOTE

▶ *Server Side JavaScript* — JavaScript is one of the most widely used languages on the Internet today. Most JavaScript is client-based, meaning the JavaScript code is downloaded by the browser and executed on the workstation. Server-side JavaScript, however, is code that has been compiled to form a Web file, which is executed on a Web server. The information processed on the server is then passed to the client to be viewed. The JavaScript compiler included with the Netscape FastTrack Server is located in SYS:/NOVONYX/SUITESPOT/BIN/HTTPS. You need two files in this directory: JSAC.EXE and LIBESNSPR20.DLL. It is important to note that you can write and compile your JavaScript applications on any platform, but they will only run on Windows NT or Windows NT Server. See Netscape's developer Web site (`developer.netscape.com`) for more information on developing JavaScript applications.

Because server-side JavaScript requires some server resources, it has been disabled by default. You should leave it disabled if it is not being used, so it doesn't use server resources unnecessarily. For information about turning on server-side JavaScript, see *Novell's NetWare 5 Administrator's Handbook.*

TIP

▶ *Application Manager* — After you have activated server-side JavaScript, you will see a link to the Application Manager located on the Server

Side JavaScript page. When you click the link, it will launch a new browser window for the JavaScript Application Manager, as shown in Figure 9.6. The JavaScript Application Manager (which looks similar to the Admin Server, but does not run on its own port) is a server-side JavaScript application that runs on the FastTrack server. You use it to manage all the server-side JavaScript applications running on your server. You can also access it through the URL `http://server.com/appmgr`. (Replace *server* with the name of your server.) On the Application Manager page, you will see a box listing all the applications currently running on the FastTrack Server. When you click one of the applications, an information page appears, showing information about that JavaScript application.

F I G U R E   9.6   *Javascript Application Manager*

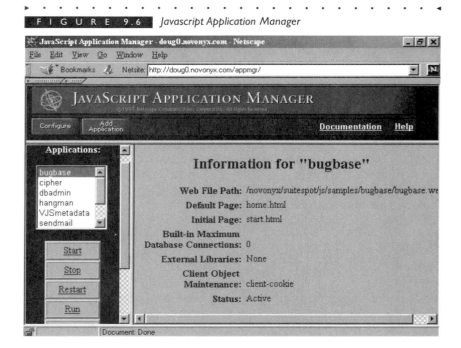

TIP

If you click the Configure button at the top of the JavaScript Application Manager screen, you will see a page that enables you to enter default values that will be inserted each time you add a new application. This can be helpful if you are adding many applications that share the same files. There is also a list of preference changes you can make.

Server Status

The FastTrack Server gives you two ways to monitor your server's activity. The first method enables you to monitor the server's status in real time (showing what is happening at the current moment compared to past performance). The second method is to monitor your server by recording, archiving, and viewing log files.

To open the Server Status page, click the Server Status button at the top of the Admin Server screen.

FastTrack also offers a log analyzer that lets you generate statistical reports such as a summary of activity, the most accessed URLs, highest utilization time frames, and which hosts are frequently accessing your server. The log analyzer can be run from the Server Manager or command line.

Configuration Styles

Configuration styles give you an easy way to apply logging options to specific files or directories you want to monitor. To set configuration styles, click the Configuration Styles button at the top of the Admin Server screen.

Content Management

The Netscape FastTrack server supports a variety of methods for organizing the information on your server. This information is managed through the Content Management page of the Admin Server. To open the Content Management page, click the Content Management button at the top of the Admin Server screen.

Document directories are the most common way to manage your content. These directories enable you to keep all Web documents in a single location. This allows for easier management and provides a better structure for implementing access control.

The Content Management section of the Admin Server also manages the use of hardware virtual servers, software virtual servers, forwarding URLs, default pages, and other document preferences. All these available options allow flexibility and structure in the organization of Web documents. The following options are available in the Content Management page:

▶ *Primary Document Directory* — The primary document directory is the default location for all Web files. By default, this document directory is /NOVONYX/SUITESPOT/DOCS. You may change this to any location on your NetWare server by opening the Primary Document Directory screen, and then entering the complete path to the new directory.

▶ *Additional Document Directories* — In addition to your primary document directory, you can create additional document directories. This can be helpful if you would like to separately manage a group of documents. Using additional document directories enables you to use an additional URL prefix for your documents. When you specify a new URL prefix, any client that requests that URL will be served a file from your additional document directory. Figure 9.7 shows the Additional Document Directories screen.

FIGURE 9.7 *Additional Document Directories Page*

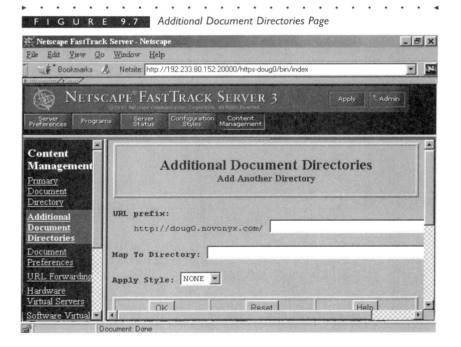

For information on creating an additional document directory, see
Novell's NetWare 5 Administrator's Handbook.

NOTE

▶ *Document Preferences* — The Document Preferences section of Content
Management enables you to set default values for your Web site.
Figure 9.8 shows the Document Preferences screen. You can configure
the following document preferences from this screen:

FIGURE 9.8 *Document Preferences Configuration Page*

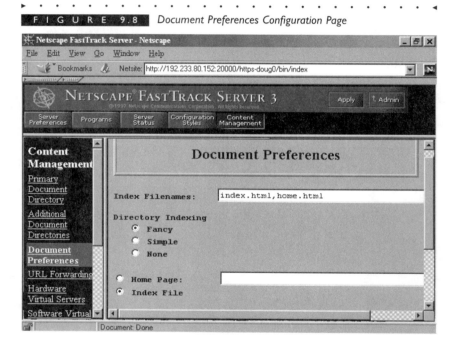

- *Index Filenames* — When a user connects to a URL and does not
specify a document name, the server automatically displays the
index file for that directory. By default, the FastTrack server will first
display index.html. If that file cannot be found, it will then display
home.html. Through the Document Preferences link, you can
change the default index files or add to the current list.

- *Directory Indexing* — You will most likely have subdirectories off the root of your main document directory. You may want to access this directory structure through a browser interface. If you access a URL without specifying a file, the server will first look for your index files. If there is no index file present, the server will then generate an index file that lists all files located in that directory. This listing is similar to looking at a directory in File Manager or Windows Explorer. It will list filenames, sizes, and other information. From this option, you can choose one of the following ways to show directory listings: either *Fancy* (to show a graphic representation of the file, including file type, the date the file was last modified, and the file size) or *Simple* (to show only the filename).

- *No directory listing* — Use this option if you want the contents of your directory to be hidden.

- *Server Homepage* — To access your Web server, most users will probably type www.server.com. By default, the server will display the index file for that directory. With the Server Homepage option, you can specify another file to be the server's homepage.

- *Default MIME Type* — MIME types give information to the client about each file that is requested. This information helps the client know in what format the file should be displayed. With file types that are not currently located in the MIME.TYPES file, the server does not know how the file should be displayed. When a default MIME type is set, any file that has not been defined will be set as the default type. In most situations, this will be set to a text format, but any file type can be used.

▶ *URL Forwarding* — Forwarding URLs is a common task on the Internet, because Web sites move to new locations for various reasons. URL forwarding enables you to specify a forwarding address for any URL on your server. That way, if you move your Web site, a user can still type the old URL, but his or her browser will automatically connect to the new location.

▶ *Hardware Virtual Servers* — Hardware virtual servers have become an important feature for all Web servers that host multiple domains or have high traffic volumes. Hardware virtual servers allow a single Web server to serve pages on multiple IP addresses by mapping a document directory to each of these IP addresses. With NetWare 5, these additional addresses can all be bound to a single network board in your server, or you can add more network boards to handle the extra IP addresses. Using multiple network boards and hardware virtual servers will enable you to achieve the highest performance from your Web server. The FastTrack Server enables you to map a document directory to each virtual server you are using. You can map a different document directory to each virtual server to host multiple sites, increase security, or more easily manage your Web site. Hardware virtual servers also enable you to map the same document directory to each virtual server for increased performance (see Figure 9.9).

FIGURE 9.9 *Hardware Virtual Server Configuration Page*

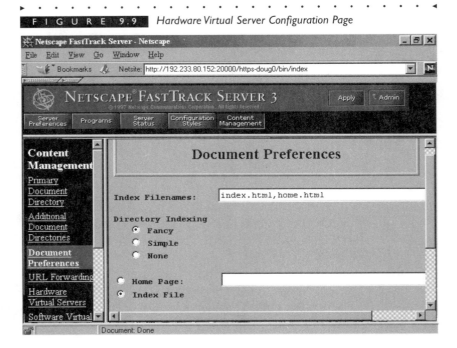

For information on setting up a hardware virtual server, see *Novell's NetWare 5 Administrator's Handbook.*

NOTE

▸ *Software Virtual Servers* — Software virtual servers enable you to use the same IP address to host multiple Web sites. This is accomplished by first assigning multiple DNS names to the IP address on your server. After these names have been assigned, both names will resolve to the same IP address.

TIP For example, suppose www.server1.com and www.server2.com both resolve to the address 100.100.100.112. After you set the software virtual server, a client requesting www.server1.com will receive a different page than a client requesting www.server2.com. Be aware that some older browsers will not support software virtual servers and will receive the page from the original DNS entry. Remember, for software virtual servers to work correctly, DNS information must be configured correctly for your IP address. For more information about DNS and setting up a software virtual server, see *Novell's NetWare 5 Administrator's Handbook.*

▸ *International Characters* — The FastTrack Server follows the character set specified in RFC 1700 (a document that defines Internet character set standards). You can override a browser's default character set setting for a document, a set of documents, or a directory by selecting a resource and entering a character set for that resource.

▸ *Document Footer* — The document footer allows you to include the last-modified time in the footer of all the documents in a specific area on the server, without using server-parsed HTML. The default footer displays the modification date.

▸ *Parse HTML* — When a client requests HTML data, the server normally reads the data and sends it "as is." However, with this option set, it is possible for the server to search the HTML files for special commands, modify the data (according to specific instructions), and then send it off to the requesting client. HTML parsing is disabled by default.

▸ *Cache-Control Directives* — Cache-control directives are a way for the FastTrack Server to control what type of information is cached by proxy servers, and how it is cached. Cache-control directives allow you to override the default caching of the proxy to protect sensitive files or directories from being cached and retrieved.

Beyond the Basics

This chapter introduced you to a new NetWare 5 feature called the Netscape FastTrack Server for NetWare. The discussion provided an overview of the installation of the FastTrack Server, and a description of the features and functionality of this high-performance Web server.

The following topics, mentioned in this chapter, are explained more fully in other chapters in this book:

▶ For an overview of network protocols (such as IP), see Chapter 2.

▶ For a description of LDAP Services for NDS, see Chapter 4.

▶ For information about Organizational Units in NDS, see Chapter 4.

▶ For more information about installing Novell's online documentation, see Chapter 10.

You can find more information about the following topics in Novell's online documentation (which came with your NetWare 5 package) and in *Novell's NetWare 5 Administrator's Handbook* (from Novell Press):

▶ Adding new MIME types to your server

▶ Changing error responses on your server

▶ Setting access levels for your server

▶ Specifying a CGI directory in which to store CGI programs

▶ Turning on server-side JavaScript

▶ Setting up a hardware or software virtual server

CHAPTER 10

Installing and Using
Online Documentation

NetWare 5's online documentation has been improved, and also takes advantage of current technology. NetWare 5's online documentation uses Hypertext Markup Language (HTML) based documents and works with either the Netscape Navigator browser or Microsoft Internet Explorer browser. (A *browser* is a utility that enables users to view pages formatted with HTML for transmission on the Internet.) The Novell documentation CD-ROM also has the Autorun feature enabled, and no longer uses the DynaText of the past versions of NetWare.

Novell's Online Documentation

In an effort to save trees, bookshelf space, and the administrator's time, most of the documentation for NetWare 5 is online—located on a CD-ROM. The only printed documentation included in the NetWare package is the documentation you'll need to get your server up and running. The rest of the documentation is located on the CD-ROM.

Having the documentation online allows you to access the documentation from anywhere on the network. Obviously, this is more handy than having to tote two dozen manuals with you to another user's office, and much cheaper than buying multiple sets of printed documentation for multiple users. In addition, the online documentation's search features can help you locate the information you need quickly.

To allow network users to access the online documentation, you can store the documentation on the server in a network directory, or you can read the online documentation directly from the CD-ROM. You can also install the documentation files directly onto a workstation. However, other network users won't be able to access the documentation if it's only on one workstation, so most administrators put the documentation into a network directory.

The Novell online documentation is in HTML format, which means it can be read using any browser. However, to use the searching and printing features of the online documentation, you will need to use Netscape 4.*x* (or higher) or Microsoft Internet Explorer 4.*x* (or higher). The *Novell Documentation* CD-ROM comes with the correct version of Netscape Navigator on it, so if you choose to read the documentation directly from the CD-ROM, the Navigator browser will open automatically for you.

To read the online documentation directly from the CD-ROM, insert the CD-ROM in your workstation's drive, open the CD-ROM, and select View Documentation from the main Product Documentation window that appears.

The online documentation will automatically open, and you can select topics from the table of contents.

To install the documentation on a network so additional users can view it, you first use the installation program on the CD-ROM to install the documentation files into a network directory. Then you run the Workstation Install program from the CD-ROM on each workstation to set up the browser to point to the documentation files.

The following sections describe how to install the online documentation files onto the server and how to set up the workstation browsers.

NOTE   A full set of printed documentation, which you can purchase separately, is also available. To order the printed documentation, you can send in the order form that came in your NetWare 5 box or call 800-336-3892 (in the United States) or 512-834-6905.

Installing the Online Documentation Files

Use the following steps to install the online documentation files into a network directory, or onto a workstation's hard disk. (If you install the files into a network directory, users can access the files from anywhere on the network, as long as they have trustee rights to do so. See Chapter 6 for more information about trustee rights.)

NOTE   While installing the documentation, you will also be required to install a browser on the workstation you're using for the installation, if one doesn't already exist. The following instructions include steps for installing both the documentation and the Netscape browser, because Novell has integrated the two procedures into a single, convenient program. If you install the documentation into a network directory, you need to install only the browser on additional workstations. Instructions for installing the Netscape browser alone are in the section "Setting Up a Browser on a Workstation," later in this chapter.

1. From a workstation, log in as a user who has sufficient rights to copy files into the network directory that will contain the online documentation.

2. Close all programs that are running on the workstation, so the installation program won't encounter any file conflicts.

3. Insert the *Novell Online Documentation* CD-ROM for NetWare 5 into the workstation's drive, and open the CD-ROM. (It may open automatically, displaying the main Product Documentation window.)

4. Choose Install Documentation. The Product Documentation Setup program begins running.

5. At the Welcome screen, click Next to continue.

6. Choose the destination where you want to install the documentation. (The default may be a location on the hard disk. If you want to install the files into a network directory, click Browse to locate and select the appropriate directory.) When finished selecting the destination, click Next to continue.

7. Select the language you want to install. (This screen also enables you to select which "services" you want to install. Click Services if you want to install only some of the documentation — you can specify which portions of the documentation you want to ignore.) When finished selecting the language and, if necessary, the services you want to install, click Next to continue.

8. At the confirmation screen that displays your choices, click Next to continue (or click Back to make changes). The installation program begins copying files to the destination you specified.

9. A message appears, indicating that the Novell Search Engine installation will now begin. Click OK.

10. At the Search Engine Welcome screen, click Next.

11. The installation program now checks this workstation for Netscape 4.*x*. If you have already installed the Netscape 4.*x* browser on this workstation, a message appears telling you that bookmarks to the Novell documentation are being added to your browser. A *bookmark* allows you to mark a location in an online document so you can return to the location quickly. Skip to Step 12. If you do not have Netscape 4.*x* on this workstation, the installation program will install it now.

   a. When asked if you want to install Netscape, click Yes.

   b. A message appears, telling you not to reboot the computer automatically if prompted. Click OK. The Netscape browser installation begins. (If the Search Engine Welcome screen still appears on your screen, ignore it.)

c. At the Netscape Communicator Welcome screen, click Next.

d. At the license agreement screen, click Yes.

e. Select whether you want to do a Typical installation or a Custom installation. A Typical installation installs Netscape's Communicator (which includes the Navigator browser), Conference, Netcaster, and Multimedia support. If you choose the Custom installation, you can choose not to install one or more of these components.

f. From the same screen, also select the destination for the Netscape software on this workstation. If the folder you select doesn't yet exist, you will be asked if you want to create it. Choose Yes.

g. Select the program folder for the Netscape software, and then click Next.

h. At the confirmation screen, confirm your selections and click Install to continue (or click Back to make changes).

i. When asked if you want to view the README file for Netscape Communicator, choose either Yes or No.

j. A message appears, indicating the setup is complete. Click OK.

k. When asked if you want to restart the computer now, choose No.

12. If you want to install Adobe Acrobat, click Yes when prompted. (If Adobe Acrobat is already installed on this workstation, skip to Step 13.) Follow the prompts on the screen as Adobe Acrobat is installed. At the end of this installation, click Finish.

13. When prompted to select the HTML Browser's location, make sure you select the location of the Netscape browser on this workstation, and then click Next.

14. Select the location of the NetWare 5 documentation you installed earlier (such as SYS:\PUBLIC\NOVDOCS), and then click Next.

15. At the confirmation screen, verify your selections, and then click Next. The installation program copies files and makes system modifications.

16. A message appears telling you to reboot your server. Click OK.

17. Another message appears, telling you that bookmarks for the NetWare documentation are being added to your Netscape browser. Click OK.

18. When the installation is complete, decide if you want to read the README file. If you do, click Finish; if you don't, unmark the box beside the option to view the README before clicking Finish.

19. At the main Product Documentation screen, choose Exit.

20. Reboot the workstation to make all the new settings take effect.

Now you need to make sure that every workstation that needs to access the online documentation has a browser available to read the documentation. The next section explains how you can use the NetWare documentation CD-ROM to set up the Netscape Communicator on any workstation and automatically add bookmarks to the documentation you installed.

Setting Up the Browser on a Workstation

As mentioned previously, you can use any browser to read the NetWare 5 online documentation. However, to use the search and print features of the documentation, you must use the Netscape 4.x browser or the Microsoft Internet Explorer 4.x browser. Version 4.x of Netscape is included on the NetWare 5 documentation CD-ROM, so you can easily install it on your workstations. The installation program for the Netscape browser also installs Adobe Acrobat, which you use to read some portions of the documentation.

If you've chosen to install the online documentation into a network directory, you must install the browser on each workstation that will access the documentation.

To install Netscape 4.x on a workstation, complete the following steps:

1. Close all programs that are running on the workstation, so the installation program won't encounter any file conflicts.

2. Insert the *Novell Online Documentation* CD-ROM for NetWare 5 into the workstation's drive, and open the CD-ROM. (It may open automatically, displaying the main Product Documentation window.)

3. Choose Workstation Install. The Novell Search Engine Setup program begins running.

4. At the Search Engine Welcome screen, click Next.

5. The installation program now checks this workstation for Netscape 4.x. If you have already installed the Netscape 4.x browser on this workstation, a message appears telling you that bookmarks to the Novell documentation are being added to your browser. Skip to Step 6. If you do not have Netscape 4.x on this workstation, the installation program will install it now.

a. When asked if you want to install Netscape, click Yes.

b. A message appears, telling you not to reboot the computer automatically if prompted. Click OK. The Netscape browser installation begins. (If the Search Engine's Welcome screen still appears on your screen, ignore it.)

c. At the Netscape Communicator Welcome screen, click Next.

d. At the license agreement screen, click Yes.

e. Select whether you want to do a Typical installation or a Custom installation. A Typical installation installs Netscape's Communicator (which includes the Navigator browser), Conference, Netcaster, and Multimedia support. If you choose the Custom installation, you can choose not to install one or more of these components.

f. From the same screen, also select the destination for the Netscape software on this workstation. If the folder you select doesn't yet exist, you will be asked if you want to create it. Choose Yes.

g. Select the program folder for the Netscape software, and then click Next.

h. At the confirmation screen, confirm your selections and click Install to continue (or click Back to make changes).

i. When asked if you want to view the README file for Netscape Communicator, choose either Yes or No.

j. A message appears, indicating the setup is complete. Click OK.

k. When asked if you want to restart the computer now, choose No.

6. If you want to install Adobe Acrobat, click Yes when prompted. (If Adobe Acrobat is already installed on this workstation, skip to Step 7.) Follow the prompts on the screen as Adobe Acrobat is installed. At the end of this installation, click Finish.

7. When prompted to select the HTML Browser's location, make sure you select the location of the Netscape browser on this workstation, and then click Next.

8. Select the location of the NetWare 5 documentation you installed earlier (such as SYS:\PUBLIC\NOVDOCS), and then click Next.

9. At the confirmation screen, verify your selections, and then click Next. The installation program copies files and makes system modifications.

10. A message appears, telling you to reboot your server. Click OK.

11. Another message appears, telling you that bookmarks for the NetWare documentation are being added to your Netscape browser. Click OK.

12. When the installation is complete, decide if you want to read the README file. If you do, click Finish; if you don't, unmark the box beside the option to view the README before clicking Finish..

13. At the main Product Documentation screen, choose Exit.

14. Reboot the workstation to make all the new settings take effect.

Now the workstation's browser is set up and ready to access the NetWare 5 documentation.

Launching the Netscape Communicator

The first time you launch the Netscape Communicator from a workstation, you will need to create a new *profile* for yourself, to store your personal settings and files that Netscape will use. If several people use this workstation, each user should have his or her own profile to make logging in to the browser easier. Complete the following steps to set up a profile:

1. Launch the Netscape Communicator by double-clicking its icon.

2. A message appears, telling you to create a new profile for yourself. Click Next.

3. Enter your name and e-mail address, and then click Next.

4. Enter a name for this profile and a location in which to store the settings. Then click Next.

5. A screen appears, asking for information relating to your outgoing mail. This information is optional, and is used if you are connected to the Internet and expect to send and receive mail through the Internet. You can add it now or later. To add it now, verify your name and e-mail address, and then specify the name of your outgoing mail server. Then click Next.

6. Now a screen appears asking for incoming mail information. Again, this information is optional. If you wish, enter your user name, the name of your incoming mail server, and the type of mail server. Then click Next.

7. A screen appears, asking for information relating to discussion groups. This information is also optional at this time. If you wish, enter the name of the news server and port you will use. Then click Finish.

Your Netscape profile is now stored, and the browser opens. From Netscape's Bookmarks menu, select the Novell documentation to open the NetWare 5 information.

Viewing the Novell Online Documentation

After the browser is installed on the workstation and the documentation is installed on the network, you can access the online documentation. To do this, double-click the browser icon from your workstation to start up the browser, and then open the Novell documentation from the Netscape list of bookmarks.

NOTE

You can also read the Novell documentation directly from the CD-ROM without having to install either the documentation or a browser on the workstation. The only difference between running the documentation from a CD-ROM and running it from the network or a local hard disk is that the CD-ROM tends to be a little slower.

The NetWare 5 documentation's home page appears. The left-hand panel indicates the types of information included in the documentation. Click one of the related buttons to see a Table of Contents for that information. Click a heading in the Table of Contents to go to that piece of documentation.

Throughout the documentation, the left-hand panel usually displays the table of contents for the section of documentation you're in currently. The right-hand panel shows the actual documentation.

As you read through the manual's text, you will see references to related information. These references appear in a different color and are underlined. If you click those references, they take you instantly to the location of the related information.

To search for a particular word or phrase in the documentation, click the magnifying glass icon at the bottom of the browser screen. The Netscape Search Console appears, enabling you to type in the word or phrase for which you want to search.

To print a page from the online documentation, click the printer icon at the bottom of the Netscape screen. Clicking the home icon will return you to the initial screen of the NetWare 5 documentation.

Beyond the Basics

You can find more information in Novell's online documentation after you've installed it.

Disaster Planning and Troubleshooting

Disasters come in many guises. A disaster that affects your network could be anything from a crashed hard disk on your server, to a security breach, to a fire that destroys your building. When it comes to computers, a malfunctioning water sprinkler system can cause as much damage as a hurricane.

If your company depends on your network to do business daily, every day — or even hour — that the network is out of commission means lost revenue. Therefore, getting the network back up and functioning is a priority for most businesses after a disaster.

The best way to recover from a disaster, regardless of the type of disaster, is to have planned for it ahead of time. Armed with a disaster plan, good backups, and accurate records of your network, the task of re-establishing your network will not seem nearly as daunting.

Planning Ahead

If you haven't already created a disaster plan — do it today. It doesn't need to be a difficult task, and it could save you a tremendous amount of wasted time, frustrated users, lost revenue, and sleepless nights. An earthquake or electrical fire isn't going to wait for a convenient time in your schedule to occur, so the sooner you plan for it, the better.

Be sure to document the plan. Write it down, get it approved by your organization's upper management, and then make copies and store them in several locations so you'll be able to find at least one copy if disaster strikes.

It's important to have a documented plan, because having the plan in your head only works if you happen to be around, of course. In some cases, though, it's even more important to have the plan approved by management. If you've had the CEO approve your plan to restore the production department's network before the administration department's, you won't have to deal with politics and egos while you're trying to restring cables.

What should be included in a disaster plan? Everyone's disaster plan will be different, but there are a few key points to consider when planning yours:

- ► Decide where you will store your emergency plan. It needs to be in a location where you or others can get to it easily. Ideally, there should be multiple copies of the plan, perhaps assigned to different individuals. Just storing the emergency plan in your office will not be adequate if the building burns down, so you may want to consider storing a copy offsite, such as in a safety deposit box or even at your home.

▸ List people to call in case of an emergency and include their names, home phone numbers, pager numbers, and cellular phone numbers in your emergency plan. Remember to list key network personnel, such as any network administrators for various branches of the NDS tree, personnel who perform the weekly and daily backups, and so on. You may want to include names of security personnel who should be notified in case of a potential security breach.

▸ Plan the order in which you will restore service to your company. Who needs to be back online first? Is there a critical department that should be restored before any other? Are there key individuals who need to be reconnected first?

▸ Once you've identified the key people who need to be reconnected, determine if there is an order to the files or services they'll need. Which servers need to be restored first? What applications must those users have immediately? Which files will they need to access?

▸ Document the location of your network records. Where do you keep your hardware inventory, purchase requisitions, backup logs, and so forth?

▸ Document the location of your network backup tapes or disks. Don't forget to document instructions for restoring files — or indicate the location of the backup system's documentation — in case the backup operator is unavailable. Record your backup rotation schedule so other people can figure out how to restore the network files efficiently.

▸ Include a drawing of the network layout, showing the exact location of cables, servers, workstations, and other computers. Highlight the critical components, so anyone else reading your plan will know at a glance where to find the priority servers.

Keeping Good Records of Your Network

Another line in your defense against disaster is to maintain up-to-date records about your network. When something goes wrong with your network, it is much easier to spot the problem if you have accurate documentation.

Good network documentation isn't just helpful in an emergency, it more than likely will play a critical part in a successful recovery of your system. Doing paperwork is always a distasteful task, but you'll be thankful you did it the next time you have to add new hardware to the network, resolve an interrupt conflict, justify your hardware budget to management, get a work-station repaired under warranty, call for technical support, or train a new assistant.

How you track your network information is up to you. You may want to keep a three-ring binder with printed information about the network, or you may prefer to keep the information online in databases or spreadsheets.

However you document your network, be sure you keep the information in more than one location. If a disaster occurs, you don't want to lose your only copy of the information that can help you restore the network quickly. Try to keep copies of your network information in separate buildings, if possible, so you won't lose everything if you can't access one building.

What types of network information should you record? Again, networks vary, so your documentation needs will vary, too. However, the following types of information are recommended:

▶ *An inventory of hardware and software purchases* — Record the product's version number, serial number, vendor, purchase date, length of warranty, and so on. This can help you when management asks for current capital assets or budget-planning information. It can also help you with insurance reports and replacements if a loss occurs.

▶ *A record of configuration settings for servers, workstations, printers, and other hardware* — This information can save you hours that you would otherwise spend locating and resolving interrupt conflicts.

▶ *A history of hardware repairs* — You may want to file all paperwork associated with repairs along with the paperwork that documents your original purchase of the item.

▶ *A drawing of the network layout* — If you store this with your disaster plan, you (and others) will be able to locate critical components quickly. On the drawing, show how all the workstations, servers, printers, and other equipment are connected. The drawing doesn't have to be to scale, but it should show each machine in its approximate location. Label each workstation with its make and model, its location, and its user. Show the cables (and indicate the types of cable) that connect the hardware.

▶ *Batch files and workstation boot files* — Use a text editor or other program to print out these files and keep them with the worksheets that document the workstation. You may also want to store copies of the files on diskette. If you need to reinstall the workstation, you can re-create the user's environment quickly if you have archived these files.

▶ *Backup information* — It is important to record your backup rotation schedule, the location of backup tapes or disks, the names of any backup operators, the labeling system you use on your backup tapes or disks, and any other information someone may need if you're not around to restore the system.

Troubleshooting Tips

Unfortunately, despite the best possible planning, something may go wrong with your network. The majority of network problems are related to hardware issues — interrupt conflicts, faulty components, incompatible hardware, and so on. However, software creates its own set of problems, such as application incompatibility, operating system bugs and incompatibility, and installation errors.

There are endless combinations of servers, workstations, cabling, networking hardware, operating systems, and applications. This makes it impossible to predict and document every possible problem. The best anyone can do is to use a methodical system for isolating the problem and then fixing it.

The following troubleshooting guidelines can help you isolate the problem and find solutions.

Narrow Down the List of Suspects

First, of course, you need to try to narrow your search to suspicious areas by answering the following types of questions:

▶ Were there any error messages? If so, look up their explanations in the documentation that came with your NetWare 5 package. See Chapter 10 for more information about installing and using the online documentation.

▶ How many machines did the problem affect? If multiple machines were affected, the problem is affecting the network and could be related to the network cabling or network software. If the problem is isolated to one workstation, the problem is most likely contained within the workstation's own hardware or software configuration.

▶ Can you identify a particular cabling segment or branch of the Directory tree that has the problem? This will help you isolate likely problem candidates.

▸ Does the problem occur only when a user accesses a particular application, or does it occur only when the user executes applications in a particular order? This could indicate an application problem that has nothing to do with the network. It could be related to the workstation's memory, to a conflict between two applications or devices that both expect to use the same port or address, or the like.

▸ If the problem occurred when you installed new workstations or servers on the network, have you checked their network addresses, IP addresses (IP and/or IPX, if used), and hardware settings for conflicts with other boards or with machines that already exist on the network? Also double-check the installation documentation to make sure you didn't misspell a command or accidentally skip a step.

▸ If a user is having trouble working with files or applications, have you checked the security features? Does the user have appropriate rights in the necessary directories? Are the files already opened by someone else? Have the files or directories been assigned attributes that restrict the user from some actions? See Chapter 6 for more information about network security.

▸ Is a user missing some of his or her DOS path commands? Look in the login scripts for search drive mappings that were mapped without using the INS keyword (which inserts the mapping into the DOS path instead of overwriting existing paths). See Chapter 5 for more information about login scripts and search drives.

▸ For printing problems with queue-based printing, have you checked that the printer, print server, and print queue are all correctly assigned to each other? You can use the NetWare Administrator utility to check your printing setup. Select the print server from the Browser, choose Details from the object menu, and then open the Print Layout page to see whether the print server, printer, and queue are all assigned together correctly. See Chapter 8 for more information about printing.

▸ If a user can't see an NDPS printer, did you configure the printer so that its drivers will be installed automatically on users' workstations? See Chapter 8 for more information about NDPS printing.

▸ If NDPS printers aren't available, make sure NDPSM.NLM is loaded on the server. See Chapter 8 for more information about NDPS printing.

▸ Have you verified that applications are using the correct print drivers for your printers? See Chapter 8 for more information about network printing.

- Do you have a volume that won't mount? If it is an NSS volume, you may need to run the REBUILD utility to fix it. If it is a traditional NetWare volume, you may need to run VREPAIR.NLM to fix it. (However, VREPAIR will usually run automatically if NetWare detects a problem with a volume.) See the Novell documentation for more information about running REBUILD and VREPAIR.

- Are all the servers in the Directory tree running the same version of DS.NLM? If all servers are not running the same version, some conflicts could occur. See Chapter 4 for more information about NDS and DS.NLM.

Check the Hardware

Hardware problems can be relatively common in networks. Network cables are notorious for developing problems, partly because of the abuse they get from being coiled up, walked on, bent around corners, and so on. A network analyzer, such as NetWare LANalyzer, can be a useful tool for diagnosing cable problems. As you diagnose hardware problems, keep the following tips in mind:

- Cables have an annoying tendency to work loose from their connectors — seemingly all by themselves — so check all connections between cables and boards first.

- Test suspicious cables by replacing them with cables you know are working, and then see if the problem persists.

- Ensure that cables are terminated correctly and don't exceed length limits. Also ensure that the cables are not connected into endless loops (unless you're using a topology that permits loops).

- If the problem is with a computer or printer, try disconnecting the problematic machinery from the network and running it in standalone mode. If the problem still shows up in standalone mode, it's probably not a problem with the network connection. You can then eliminate the network components and concentrate on the configuration of the machine itself.

- Isolate sections of the network segment until the problem disappears. Add each section back to the network one at a time until you have identified the problem cable, board, connector, terminator, or other component.

▶ If the problem occurred when you installed a new workstation or server, or added a board to an existing computer, check hardware settings for conflicts with other boards or with machines that already exist on the network.

Refer to the Documentation

Forget the jokes about only reading the manual as a last resort. The NetWare online documentation contains explanations of the error messages that may occur. In addition, the documentation includes troubleshooting tips, configuration instructions, and so on.

Be sure to check the manufacturer's documentation for any network hardware or applications you're using. Some applications have special instructions for installing them on a network.

Look for Patches or Workarounds

Despite rigorous testing, every software product on the market is subject to bugs or unexpected problems. Novell's NetWare 5 is no exception. When Novell engineers find a problem with NetWare, they usually solve the problem with either a *patch* (a piece of software that loads as an NLM on your server and repairs it) or a recommended workaround.

Novell distributes these patches and workarounds on its Internet Web site (www.novell.com) and in the *Novell Support Connection* (a set of update CD-ROMs available by subscription). It's a good idea to periodically check this Web site to see if there are any new downloadable files that can help solve your problems.

Try Each Solution by Itself

After you've isolated the problem, try implementing the solutions you've found one at a time. Start with the easiest, cheapest solution, and work up from there.

Most of us give in to the tendency to try several possible fixes simultaneously to save time. Trying solutions simultaneously may save time in the short run, but it could cost you extra money for unnecessary repairs or replacements. For example, if you change the cable, the network board, and reinstall the NetWare Client software all at the same time, you will have no way of knowing which one was the real solution. You may have just wasted money on a new network board unnecessarily.

In addition, if you try several fixes at once, you won't know for sure what fixed the problem, so you'll have to start from scratch again if the problem reappears on another machine or at another time.

Document the Solution

When you find a solution, write it down and store it with your network documentation. This may prevent you or someone else from going through the same troubleshooting process to fix a similar problem later.

Beyond the Basics

There is a wide variety of places you can go to get help, advice, tips, and fixes for your NetWare problems or questions. These resources range from Novell technical support, to Internet user groups, to classes, to publications that deal with NetWare support issues. If you're looking for help or information, try some of these ideas:

- You can often find the technical help you need online, through the Internet Usenet groups that focus on NetWare or through the Novell Web site on the Internet, www.novell.com.

- Try calling your reseller or consultant for help.

- Novell's technical support is available by calling 800-NETWARE. However, Novell's technical support is not free. You'll be charged a fee for each incident, so have your credit card handy. (An incident may involve more than one phone call, if necessary.) Before you call technical support, be sure you've tried your other resources first — especially the documentation. It's embarrassing and expensive to have technical support tell you that the answer to your question is on page 25 of the installation manual.

- The main Novell information number, 800-NETWARE, is also your inroad to all types of information about Novell or its products. By calling this number, you can obtain information about Novell products, the locations of your nearest resellers, pricing information, and so on.

- To order the printed manuals for NetWare, you can use the order form that came in your NetWare box, or call 800-336-3892 (in the United States) or 512-834-6905.

▸ The *Novell AppNotes* is a useful resource for network management information. This is a monthly publication put out by the Novell Research Department, and each issue contains research reports and articles on a wide range of advanced topics. To order a subscription, call 800-377-4136 in the U.S.A., or 303-297-2725 worldwide.

▸ NetWare classes are taught at more than 1,000 Novell Authorized Education Centers (NAECs) throughout the world. These classes typically offer the best way to get some direct, hands-on training in just a few days. Some of the classes are also available in Computer-Based Training (CBT) form, in case you'd rather work through the material at your own pace, on your own workstation, than attend a class. For more information about Novell Education classes or to find the nearest NAEC near you, call 800-233-3382. To purchase a CBT version of a class, contact your nearest NAEC.

▸ There are also numerous organizations that provide classes and seminars on NetWare. Some of these unauthorized classes are quite good. Others are probably of lower quality, because Novell does not have any control over their course content or instructor qualifications. If you choose an unauthorized provider for your NetWare classes, try to talk to others who have taken a class from the provider before, so you'll have a better idea of how good the class is.

▸ NetWare Users International (NUI) is a nonprofit association for networking professionals. They sponsor more than 250 Novell user groups worldwide. NUI user groups provide a forum for networking professionals to meet face to face, to learn from each other, to trade recommendations, or just to share war stories. There's usually no fee — or a very low fee — for joining an NUI user group. Membership also gives you a free subscription to *NetWare Connection*, described in the next bulleted point. For more information or to join an NUI user group, call 800-228-4NUI or send a fax to 801-228-4577.

▸ *NetWare Connection* is a bimonthly magazine that provides feature articles on new technologies, network management tips, product reviews, NUI news, and other helpful information. Membership in NUI gives you a free subscription. However, you can also get a free subscription by applying on its Web site, at `www.novell.com/nwc/sub.html`.

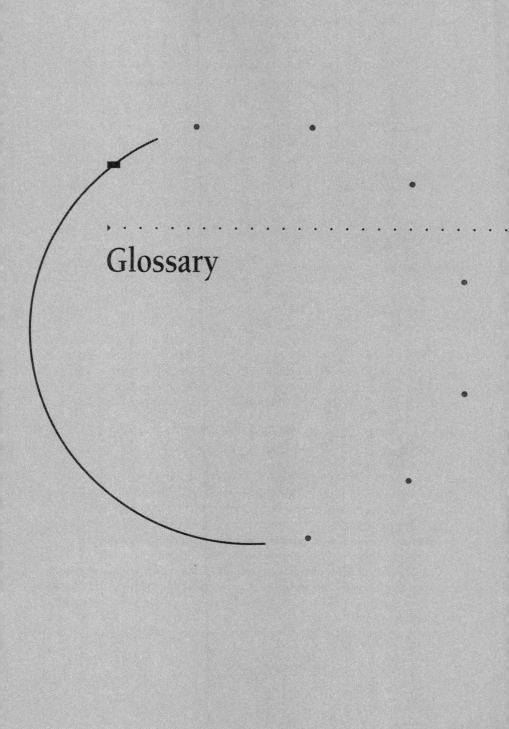

Glossary

Abend (Abnormal End): An unexpected, serious error that causes the server to quit running.

Account restrictions: Properties of a User object that control when the user logs in, how often the user must change passwords, and so on.

Accounting: A NetWare 5 feature that lets you keep track of how people are using your network and lets you charge them for that usage. With accounting turned on, you can charge for the time those users are logged in, the types of resources they use, and so on.

AppleTalk: A networking protocol suite built into every Macintosh. AppleTalk networks can run on several different flavors of network architectures: LocalTalk, EtherTalk, and TokenTalk. AppleTalk provides peer-to-peer networking (serverless networking) between all Macintoshes and Apple hardware.

Application Launcher: An application in NetWare 5 that lets you set up an icon on users' desktops that points directly to network applications. Then the users can simply launch the application from their desktops without having to know where the application is, which drives to map, and so on.

Architecture: *See* Network architecture.

Attribute, file and directory: A property of a file or directory that controls what can happen to that file or directory. Attributes, which are also called flags, can be used to restrict users from deleting files, renaming files, changing files, or the like. Attributes can also be used to identify files and directories that have been changed since their last backup, that should be purged immediately if deleted, and so on.

Attribute, NDS object: *See* Property.

Auditing: A NetWare 5 feature that tracks how your network is being used. An independent auditor can access this information and evaluate it, much like a financial auditor might audit your financial books. With auditing, only the auditor has rights to read the auditing information — even the Admin user cannot access this information.

AUTOEXEC.BAT file: A DOS batch file on a computer, which runs when the computer is booted and executes necessary commands to make the computer boot up correctly, load necessary programs, and so on.

AUTOEXEC.NCF file: A startup file on the server that executes every time the server is rebooted. This file loads the server's LAN drivers, specifies the server name and internal network number, mounts volumes, loads any NLMs you want automatically loaded, and executes additional server parameters. This file is created during the server installation, and contains commands that reflect the choices you made during the installation.

Backup: A copy of a file or set of files that you archive and keep as a precaution, in case the original files are lost or corrupted. A *full backup* backs up all network files, and removes the Archive Needed file attribute from all files and directories. A *differential backup* backs up only files that were modified since the last full backup, and does not remove the Archive Needed attribute from these files. An *incremental backup* backs up only files that were modified since the last full or incremental backup, and removes the Archive Needed attribute. A *custom backup* lets you specify particular directories to back up or restore, and lets you specify whether or not to remove the Archive Needed attribute.

Bindery: The database of network information that was used in previous versions of NetWare (version 3.12 and earlier). The bindery is a flat database, which means it cannot recognize container objects that help organize other network entities. In addition, the bindery is specific to a server. Each server has its own unique bindery, and cannot recognize objects in another server's bindery. The bindery was replaced by the NDS database in NetWare 4.*x*, intraNetWare, and NetWare 5.

Bindery context: A portion of the NDS database assigned to look like a flat bindery database to specific applications that require network objects to be in a bindery format. This feature is provided so that older bindery-based applications can still function in an NDS environment.

Board: *See* Network board.

Bookmark: A feature that allows a user to mark a location in an online document so the user can return to the location quickly.

Bridge: The connection between two networks where data can flow from one network to the other. A bridge can join two networks that are using different network architectures. *See also* Router.

Browser, Internet: An application that runs on a workstation, allowing the user to search, access, and view information stored on the Internet or an intranet. Netscape Navigator and Microsoft Internet Explorer are two popular brands of Internet browsers.

Browser, NetWare Administrator: The view of the NDS tree and its objects, as displayed by the NetWare Administrator utility. You can see information about NDS objects by opening objects from within the Browser.

Cable: Used to connect all the hardware components (workstations, servers, printers, and so on) of a network together. Network cabling comes in a wide variety of forms, such as coaxial cable (like your TV cable), twisted pair and shielded twisted pair cable, and fiber optic cable.

Capture: To redirect a workstation's parallel port so that print jobs sent to that port are directed to a print queue instead of an actual printer.

Client: Often used to refer to a workstation, *client* indicates a computer or application that requests services from a network resource (such as a server). For example, the NetWare 5 Client software is a set of programs installed on a workstation so the workstation can communicate with and request services from the rest of the network.

Command-line utility: A utility that is executed by typing a command at the DOS prompt.

Concentrator: A piece of network equipment into which workstation cables must feed before being connected to the main network cable. Concentrators boost the signals before sending them on their way. Concentrators are sometimes called active hubs.

Connectors: Hardware that joins cables together or connect them to other pieces of hardware.

Console utility: A command you type at the server's console (keyboard and monitor) to change some aspect of the server or view information about it. Console utilities are built into the operating system, just as internal DOS commands are built into DOS.

Container Login script: *See* Login script.

Container object: An NDS object that contains other NDS objects. Organization objects and Organizational Unit objects are both container objects. *See also* Leaf object.

Context: *See* Name context.

Controlled access printer: A printer that supports all the features of NDPS. A controlled access printer is identified by an NDPS Printer object in the NDS tree. Because it has its own object, the printer can be controlled and managed through the NetWare Administrator browser like any other object.

Controller board: A circuit board on a storage device, such as a hard disk, that plugs into the computer. Each hard disk or other type of storage device installed in your server has its own controller board. The computer and the disk communicate through this controller board.

Device driver: *See* Driver.

DHCP (Dynamic Host Configuration Protocol): A protocol that dynamically assigns Internet Protocol (IP) addresses to workstations in a local-area network and that allows the network administrator to assign a set of IP addresses.

Differential backup: *See* Backup.

Directory attribute: *See* Attribute, file and directory.

Directory context: *See* Name context.

Directory Services: *See* NDS.

Directory Tree: *See* NDS tree.

Disk controller board: *See* Controller board.

Disk driver: Software that allows a disk drive (such as a hard disk drive or a CD-ROM drive) to communicate with the computer (via the disk's controller board). Each brand of disk controller board has a unique disk driver associated with it.

Disk mirroring: Setting up a server's hard disks so that they are "mirrored" to each other. (Actually, the disks' partitions are mirrored.) This means that all network data is copied to both hard disks, so that they are identical. That way, if one hard disk fails, the other disk takes over seamlessly, so the network data is still available.

Disk partition: *See* Partition, disk.

Dismount: To bring down a volume so users cannot see or access it on the network.

DNS: *See* Domain name service (DNS).

Domain name service (DNS): An Internet protocol that allows administrators to associate Internet addresses with names that people can remember. A DNS server stores the names and their corresponding IP addresses, and responds to clients that need name services.

DOS partition: *See* Partition, disk.

Drive mapping: The assignment of a drive letter (such as G or H) to a specific network directory. Mapping a drive letter to a network directory works the same way as making drive C point to your hard disk, or drive E point to a CD-ROM. *See also* Search drive.

Driver: A software program that lets a piece of hardware communicate with other parts of a computer or with the network. For example, a mouse driver is the software that controls how a mouse works with the computer, a LAN driver controls how the network board communicates with the computer, and a disk driver controls how the disk drive communicates with the computer. Sometimes called a device driver.

Effective rights: The combination of trustee rights that the user can ultimately execute. A user can have effective rights to NDS objects, as well as effective rights to files and directories. A user's effective rights to an object, directory, or file are determined in one of two ways: the user's inherited rights minus any rights blocked by the IRF, or the sum of all the user's direct trustee assignments and security equivalences to other objects. *See also* Trustee rights; Inherited Rights Filter (IRF).

Ethernet: Currently the most common network architecture. It provides good performance at a reasonable cost, and is relatively easy to install.

Fake root: A special type of drive mapping to an application's directory. A fake root makes the application's directory appear to be a root directory, even though the directory may be located under other directories. *See also* Drive mapping.

File attribute: *See* Attribute, file and directory.

Full distinguished name: An object's full name, which also indicates its position in the tree. An object's full distinguished name (or full name) consists of the object's name, followed by the names of each of the container objects above it in the tree. Each name is separated by a period, such as Eric. Sales.BlueSky.

Gateway: Connects one network to a completely different type of network or computer system, through a single point. The gateway takes a request from a network client and transfers it to the other system, reversing the process when the other system replies back to the network client. For example, the IPX/IP Gateway in NetWare 5 lets all workstations on the NetWare 5 network connect to the Internet through the gateway, eliminating the need for each workstation to have its own IP address.

Group object: An NDS object that contains a list of users who belong to the Group object. Groups allow you to manage security, printer assignments, and other issues that may affect many or all of the users in the same way.

Hexadecimal number: A number that uses the numerals 0 through 9 and the letters A through F. Hexadecimal numbers are often used to specify addresses or locations in computer programs.

Home directory: A directory (folder) on the network created especially for a specific user. All users can have their own home directories, in which they can store their applications, work files, or personal files. Users generally have full trustee rights to their own home directories.

Host server: When using Enhanced SBACKUP to back up network files, a host server is the server that is running Enhanced SBACKUP, and which is attached to the backup device (such as a tape drive or optical disk drive).

HTML (Hypertext Markup Language): The type of formatting used in preparing documents to be published on the Web or on intranets. HTML documents can be read by browsers running on workstations.

HTTP (Hypertext Transfer Protocol): A protocol that allows a Web server to communicate with browsers.

Hub: A piece of network equipment into which workstation cables must feed before being connected to the main network cable. Passive hubs simply gather the signals and relay them. Active hubs actually boost the signals before sending them on their way. Active hubs are also sometimes called concentrators.

Incremental backup: *See* Backup.

Inheritance: The gaining of trustee rights at a lower level of the NDS tree or file system, because you were granted those rights at a higher level. NDS trustee rights can be inherited, as well as file system trustee rights. If you are granted a new trustee assignment at a lower level, you no longer inherit rights from a higher level.

Inherited Rights Filter (IRF): A way to restrict the rights that a user can inherit from a higher level in the NDS tree or file system. If you remove a right from an object's or directory's IRF, users can no longer inherit and use that right at this level.

Internet: A global network, originally started as a way to link various research, defense, and education systems together. Since then, it has expanded greatly, as thousands of other networks have connected into it. Universities, corporations, individual users, small businesses, nonprofit organizations, and others can all access the Internet to research libraries of information stored all over the world, or to communicate with other users via e-mail.

Intranet: A private network that provides information to its users in the same formats available on the Internet. Users can use normal Internet browsers to view the information posted on an Intranet — the only difference is that outside users are not permitted to access the Intranet.

Intruder detection: A feature of NetWare 5 that lets you limit the number of times a user can attempt to log in without succeeding. This prevents users from guessing passwords or from using a password generator to try to break into the network.

IP (Internet Protocol): The suite of network protocols used by the Internet. NetWare 5 supports the IP protocol by default, but can support the IPX protocol if you prefer.

IP address: A unique number that identifies a computer on the Internet.

IPX/SPX: A network protocol supported by NetWare.

IRF: *See* Inherited Rights Filter (IRF).

LAN driver: Software that allows a network board to communicate with its computer. Each brand of network board has a unique LAN driver associated with it. Sometimes called a network driver.

Leaf object: An NDS object that can't have any other objects beneath it in the NDS tree. Users, groups, printers, and print queues are all examples of leaf objects. *See also* Container object.

Login script: A set of commands that execute when the user logs in. Login scripts automatically set up the users' workstation environments with necessary drive mappings and other types of useful environmental settings. Container login scripts execute for all objects within a container. User login scripts execute for specific users. Profile login scripts can be created to execute for a group of users.

Major TSA resource: A volume or server. (This term is used in the Enhanced SBACKUP program, which is used to back up network files.)

Mapping: *See* Drive mapping.

Menu utility: A utility that runs in DOS, that lets a user select a task to perform by choosing an option from a menu.

Migration: Transferring data from one machine or storage device to another. Specifically in NetWare 5, server migration means transferring all network information off an old server machine, across the network, and onto a new machine. This process lets you upgrade to NetWare 5 from an older version of NetWare, while at the same time using a brand new server machine.

Mirroring: *See* Disk mirroring.

Mount: To bring up a volume so users can see and access it on the network.

NAL: *See* Application Launcher.

Name context: An NDS object's location in the NDS tree. For example, if user Eric is located in an Organizational Unit object called Sales, under the Organization object called BlueSky, Eric's name context is Sales.BlueSky. The names of the container objects in a name context are separated by periods.

Name space module: A software program (loaded on the server) that allows a server's volumes to store files created in non-DOS operating systems. These non-DOS files may have different file formats (as with Macintosh files) or may support longer filenames than DOS (as with Windows 95/98).

NDPS (Novell Distributed Print Services): The NetWare 5 printing system that not only provides normal network printing capabilities, but also bi-directional communications, even notification, and automatic downloading of printer drivers and other printing resources to workstations.

NDPS Printer Agent: A software entity that manages a printer. Every printer on the network must have its own unique printer agent.

NDS: A database that contains information about every object in the NetWare 5 network. Using this database, NetWare 5 can identify each object, know where it's supposed to be in the network, know who's allowed to use it, know what it's supposed to be connected to, and so on.

NDS object: An entity defined in the NDS database that represents a physical network resource (such as a server, workstation, or printer), a software network resource (such as a printer server, print queue, or volume), or a human or organizational resource (such as a user, group, or department). An NDS object contains properties that define the object, specifying such characteristics as the object's name, security rights, and so on.

NDS object class: A particular type of object that has been defined, such as Server object, User object, Print Queue object, or Volume object.

NDS schema: The overall plan that defines and describes the allowable NDS object classes, their properties, and the rules that govern their creation and existence. The schema determines how objects can inherit properties and trustee rights of other container objects above it. In addition, the schema defines how the Directory tree is structured and how objects in it are named.

NDS tree: The figurative representation of the NDS database's hierarchical structure, showing the Root object at the top, and container objects forming branches beneath the root.

Netscape FastTrack Server for NetWare: A high-performance Web server available in NetWare 5 that includes features for browser-based management of FastTrack and other Netscape servers.

NetWare Administrator: A NetWare 5 utility that allows you to work with NDS objects on the network. This is one of the primary utilities used in NetWare 5 for management tasks, and can be run on workstations using Windows 3.1, Windows 95, or Windows NT.

NetWare Loadable Module (NLM): A software module that you load into the server's operating system to add or change functionality. Many NLMs are automatically installed with the NetWare 5 operating system. Others are optional, which you can load if your particular situation requires them. Other manufacturers also produce NLMs for products such as backup software.

NetWare partition: *See* Partition, disk.

NetWare User Tools: A NetWare 5 utility that runs only on Windows 3.1. It is used primarily by network users, to help them manage their network drive mappings, print capture assignments, and so on.

Network architecture: The cabling scheme that specifies the types of cabling, connectors, and network boards used in a network. Ethernet, Token Ring, and AppleTalk are all examples of network architectures.

Network board: A special type of circuit board installed in a computer. A network board is connected to the network cable, and allows the computer to send data onto the network and receive data from the network. Also called network interface board, network card, and network adapter.

Network Neighborhood: The Windows 95/98 program that allows users to see the NetWare 5 network, log in to it, locate network directories, and so on.

Network operating system: The NetWare 5 software that runs on the server. The network operating system replaces the regular operating system (such as DOS or Windows 95/98) on the computer, and manages the communication that takes place over the entire network. NetWare 5 controls data transfer, file storage, security (to make sure only authorized users access the right files), communication between multiple networks, and other network activities.

NFS: The protocol used to support UNIX files on a network.

NLM: *See* NetWare Loadable Module (NLM).

Novell Directory Services: *See* NDS.

NSS (Novell Storage System): A new file system in NetWare 5 that is ideally suited for networks that require extremely large volumes, extremely large files, or huge numbers of files. NSS volumes can handle up to 8 trillion files, or a single file up to 8TB in size.

NWAdmin: *See* NetWare Administrator.

Object: *See* NDS object.

Organization object: An NDS container object, located immediately beneath the Root object in the NDS tree, which generally represents the company or organization to which the network belongs. The Organization object contains all other container objects, as well as all the leaf objects (such as servers, users, and printers) that reside within that organization.

Organizational Unit object: An NDS container object that is located beneath an Organization object or another Organizational Unit object. The Organizational Unit object often represents a department, division, or project team within a larger organization. The Organizational Unit object can contain leaf objects (such as users or printers), as well as other Organizational Unit objects.

Packet: The unit in which data is packaged to be sent across the network. Each packet includes a small amount of data, plus addressing information to make sure the data gets to the right destination. In addition, packets may include information that will help the receiving station know that the data arrived safely without corruption, and other types of helpful tidbits. A protocol dictates exactly how these packets should be formed, so that all devices on the network can understand the packets they receive.

Partial name: *See* Relative distinguished name.

Partition, Directory: Portions of the NDS database that can be replicated on different servers. A Directory partition is a branch of the Directory tree, beginning with any container object you choose. Partitions can also hold sub-partitions beneath them (called child partitions). If you have a smaller NDS database, the whole database can reside in a single partition. Using partitions can improve network performance, especially if the network spans across a WAN (wide area network). Partitions also can make it easier to manage portions of the tree separately.

Partition, disk: A portion of the hard disk (in most cases, the entire disk belongs to the partition) that is formatted in such a way that it can store and handle files. The NetWare 5 server's hard disk contains a DOS partition (which contains the DOS operating system and DOS-formatted files) and at least one NetWare partition (which contains the NetWare 5 network operating system, NetWare 5 files, and all network files and applications).

Peripherals: Equipment (such as printers, plotters, scanners, or modems) that can be attached to a network or to a computer.

Port driver: Software that routes print jobs out of the print queue, through the correct port on the server, to the printer.

Print driver: Software that converts the print job into a format that the printer can understand.

Print job configuration: Instructions that tell the printer a unique way to print different jobs. Print job configurations can specify printing characteristics, such as the print queue to use and the type of paper to use.

Print queue: A special network directory (folder) that stores print jobs temporarily before they are printed. Multiple network users can have their jobs stored in the same print queue. The print queue receives all incoming print jobs from various users, and stores them in a first-come, first-served order.

Print queue operator: A user that has been granted additional rights to manage a print queue. A print queue operator can delete other users' print jobs, put them on hold, and so on.

Print queue user: A user that has been granted rights to use a print queue.

Print server: A software program running on the NetWare 5 server that manages how print jobs are handled by the network and its printers. The print server takes print jobs from print queues and sends them to network printers when those printers are ready. It controls print traffic, manages the order and priority of print jobs, verifies that users are allowed to use the printers they select, and so on.

Profile login script: *See* Login script.

Property: A piece of information associated with an NDS object, that helps to define that object. For example, a User object's properties could include the user's last name, trustee assignments, login script, and e-mail address. Properties are sometimes called attributes.

Protocol: A set of defined rules that control how processes or machines communicate. Different protocols control different levels of communication on the network. For example, some protocols regulate how two computers establish a connection so they can communicate and how they terminate the connection when they're finished. Other protocols control how data is transferred across network cabling, and still others control how applications communicate.

Public access printer: A network printer that does not have an object in the NDS tree and that is immediately available to anyone on the network.

Purge: Permanently removing a deleted file from the network. Deleted files are normally stored in a salvageable but hidden state, until the files are either purged or salvaged (restored).

Relative distinguished name: A shortened version of an NDS object's full name, showing the name context only partway up the NDS tree. Also called partial name.

Remote Console: A feature of NetWare 5 that lets you temporarily transform your workstation into a server console (monitor and keyboard) for the server, so you can control the server from your workstation.

Replica: A copy of the NDS database stored on a server. You can have several replicas of the NDS database so that if one server goes down, all the other servers can still access the NDS database from another replica on another server.

Restore: To retrieve a backup file from its archived location, and place it back onto the network so it can be accessed.

Rights: *See* Trustee rights; Effective rights.

Root object: The highest-level object in the NDS tree.

Router: A software program (sometimes housed in its own hardware device, sometimes running inside a network server) that allows network communication to travel across mixed networks. Routers take packets of data from one network, reformat the packets if necessary to conform to the next network's protocol requirements, and then send those packets along to their destination. Routers also manage routes between servers or networks, tracking the shortest routes between two servers so network communication isn't slowed. The router software controls the actual routing of packets from one network to the other. The router hardware forms the necessary physical connection by linking the cabling systems together.

Salvage: To retrieve and restore a deleted network file. Deleted files are normally stored in a salvageable but hidden state, until the files are either purged (permanently erased) or salvaged.

Schema: *See* NDS schema.

Search drive: A special type of drive mapping, that acts like a DOS path command. Search drives are used to indicate directories that contain applications or utilities. They let users execute an application without having to know where the application is; the network searches through the designated search drives for the application's executable file when the user types the program's execution command. *See also* Drive mapping.

Security, file system: A set of NetWare 5 security features that control how users work with files and directories. File system security includes trustee rights (which grant users rights to work with files) and file and directory attributes (which restrict any users from performing specified activities on files). *See also* Trustee rights.

Security, login: A set of NetWare 5 security features that control whether or not users can log in to the network (and, optionally, when they can log in, what kind of passwords they use, and so on).

Security, NDS: NetWare 5 access rights that regulate how NDS objects can use other objects (for example, whether or not one user can change another user's allowable login times, or whether one user can delete or change a print server). *See also* Trustee rights.

Security equivalence: An assignment that grants you the same trustee rights as another user. Your trustee rights become "equivalent" to the other user's rights.

Server: A software product, installed in a computer, that provides services to clients. The network server is the most common type of server. Other types of servers include Web servers, fax servers, and e-mail servers; often these specialty types of servers run inside the NetWare 5 network server.

Server, network: A computer with the NetWare 5 network operating system installed on it. The server controls the network, managing data transfer over the network, network file storage, network security, communication between networks, and so on.

SET parameter: A server option you can change to optimize your server's performance. SET parameters control things such as how buffers are allocated and used, how memory is used, and so on. You can change these parameters by loading MONITOR.NLM and selecting the SET parameters you want from menus. SET parameters are also called server parameters.

Stand-alone: Not attached to a network.

STARTUP.NCF: A startup file on the server that executes whenever the server is booted. STARTUP.NCF automates the initialization of the NetWare 5 operating system. It loads disk drivers, loads name space modules to support different file formats, and executes some additional parameters that modify default initialization values. This file is created during the server installation, and contains commands that reflect the choices you made during the installation.

Storage device: The hardware into which storage media is inserted in order to be formatted and used. For example, CD-ROM drives, tape drives, and disk drives are considered storage devices.

Storage media: Tapes, disks, CD-ROMs, or other types of products that can be used to store data.

Surge suppressor: A device that helps protect computer equipment from damage caused by surges in electrical power.

System login script: A type of login script used in previous versions of NetWare. This was replaced in NetWare 5 by container login scripts. *See also* Login script.

Target server: When using SBACKUP to back up network files, a target server is the server whose files you intend to back up.

Target Service Agent (TSA): An NLM that runs on a server (called the target server) whose files you want to back up. The TSA allows the target server to communicate with the host server.

TCP/IP: A type of protocol that can run on NetWare 5 workstations and servers, allowing them to communicate with the Internet's IP protocol suite.

Terminator: A special type of cable connector that should be attached to the open end of certain types of network cable. It keeps electrical signals from reflecting back across the network, corrupting information or communications.

Token Ring: A network architecture with the reliability to work well in situations involving heavy data traffic. It is fairly easy to install, but it is more expensive than Ethernet networks.

Transaction Tracking System (TTS): A NetWare 5 feature that monitors updates to database files, and keeps track of the updates. This way, if the server fails during a database transaction, any unfinished updates can be safely backed out (undone). This prevents the database from being corrupted by unfinished updates.

Tree: *See* NDS tree.

Trustee: A user (or other object) who has been given trustee rights to an object, file, or directory.

Trustee rights: Permissions that allow users or objects to perform specified tasks. NDS trustee rights control whether users can work with other NDS objects and their properties, such as viewing other objects, changing their properties, deleting them, and so on. File system trustee rights control how users can work with files and directories, specifying whether a user can delete a file, change it, open it, and so on. *See also* Effective rights.

TTS: *See* Transaction Tracking System (TTS).

Uninterruptible power supply (UPS): A device that provides the server with a backup battery that takes over in case of a power outage. This backup battery allows enough time for the UPS to shut down the server cleanly, leaving no open files exposed to corruption. A good UPS also protects against spikes, surges, brownouts, and line noise (interference on the wire).

User account: The information about a user that allows the user to log in to the network. When a User object is created in the NDS tree, the user's account is automatically created.

User login script: *See* Login script.

Utility: An application or command used to configure or manage some aspect of NetWare 5 or other operating system.

Volume: A root directory on the NetWare 5 server's hard disk — the highest level of directory in the file system. The SYS volume is created automatically by the Simple Installation. If the server has more than one hard disk attached, each additional disk will have its own separate volume, named VOL1, VOL2, and so on. (If you use the Custom Installation of NetWare 5, you can specify different sizes or names of volumes.)

WAN: *See* Wide Area Network (WAN).

Web authoring: The act of creating Web pages, including writing the text, formatting the pages, creating links to other pages, and so on.

Wide Area Network (WAN): A network that covers a territory so large that it requires some of the network connections to be made over telephone lines.

Workstation: A computer (attached to a network) that users must use to complete their normal work. A workstation contains a network board, which is connected to the network cabling, and runs NetWare 5 client software on it, which communicates with the server. A NetWare 5 workstation still uses its own operating system, and can be running DOS, Windows 3.1, Windows 95, Windows NT, OS/2, Mac OS, or UNIX.

Z.E.N.works: An enhancement to NetWare 5 that includes advanced workstation management features. The Z.E.N.works Starter Pack, included with the NetWare 5 package, contains the Application Launcher (included with NetWare 4.11, but enhanced in NetWare 5). *See also* Application Launcher.

Index

O

T

U